Leslie Mitchell Reporting...

by the same author

March of the Movies
(with Harry Alan Towers)

Leslie Mitchell Reporting...

Hutchinson
London Melbourne Sydney Auckland Johannesburg

Hutchinson & Co. (Publishers) Ltd
An imprint of the Hutchinson Publishing Group
3 Fitzroy Square, London W 1 P 6 J D

Hutchinson Group (Australia) Pty Ltd
30-32 Cremorne Street, Richmond South, Victoria 3121
PO Box 151, Broadway, New South Wales 2007

Hutchinson Group (NZ) Ltd
32-34 View Road, PO Box 40-086, Glenfield, Auckland 10

Hutchinson Group (SA) Pty Ltd
PO Box 337, Bergvlei 2012, South Africa

First published 1981

Set in Linoterm Baskerville by Book Economy Services,
Cuckfield, Sussex

Printed in Great Britain by The Anchor Press Ltd
and bound by Wm Brendon & Son Ltd
both of Tiptree, Essex

British Library Cataloguing in Publication Data
Mitchell, Leslie
  Leslie Mitchell reporting . . .
  1. Mitchell, Leslie
  2. Broadcasters – Great Britain – Biography
  791.44′028′0924   PN1990.72.M/

ISBN   0 09 143920 5

To darling Inge
and to all who sustained me
with love and affection
through the years

Contents

Prologue

For four years I had been a struggling young actor – the inevitable understudy. Now at the age of twenty-two I had 'arrived'. I had been personally congratulated by the great Edgar Wallace himself, and he had undertaken to extend the character I was to perform in his play so that it would become considerably more important. Leslie Banks, the leading actor and producer, had become further interested in my career. I'd signed a contract for £12 a week. After an eight-week tour we were to open in London at the Lyceum Theatre. The play was Edgar Wallace's *Flying Squad*, starring Peggy O'Neill, produced by Leslie Banks, with a large cast of well-known actors.

I managed to raise £15 and bought a second-hand Levis two-stroke motorcycle. No longer would I have to pad the streets of London. From now on I could revisit sylvan glades far from the smoke and grime of the metropolis. Fresh air and all the pastoral delights of summer were open to me again.

I was mentioned in most of the notices. At Oxford, Giles Playfair (Nigel's undergraduate son) presented me with a book inscribed: 'In memory of a superb performance!' Members of the cast were kind, helpful and encouraging. So the tour progressed happily, and we came to the last date at Lewisham. The following week would see our big first night at the Lyceum!

On Saturday night at Lewisham Hippodrome, sharing a dressing-room with several other actors, I started to whistle. Now, one of the hallowed superstitions of the stage pronounces that whistling in a dressing-room can only bring diabolical luck. I was forced to apologize, turn round three times outside, and knock to regain admittance. Ignorant superstition! What utter nonsense!

The show over, I strapped my suitcase on the rack of the motorbike and pushed off from the pavement.

Three days later I recovered consciousness in Lewisham Hospital. I had been knocked down and dragged for more than a hundred yards, caught on the back-axle of a car, before coming out under the rear wheels.

To tot up the damage: severe concussion, left eye dislocated, right side of face deeply lacerated, jaw broken in three places, right shoulder dislocated, right collarbone broken, severe back injuries and four compound fractures of the right leg. For long months I was destined to appear in the wrong theatres.

The year was 1928.

1. Family Album

My first public appearance was not a success. Leaning forward expectantly my mother opened her eyes to look at her first-born. When she saw me hanging upside down with limbs outstretched, she clutched her bosom and fell back on the pillows in horror. 'My God!' she cried, ' – it's a frog!' and fainted dead away.

This drama took place on 4 October 1905 at Number 7, India Street in Edinburgh. The occasion became an oft-repeated family joke, which is why I remember it. And there *is* a slightly *sour* note to it, as my mother had apparently been determined to have a *girl*-child! For several years she drew compensation from dressing me as a girl and letting my curly hair grow long. To double the confusion, she christened me Leslie – the same Christian name as her own and spelt the same way. Finally my father publicly determined my sex by calling me after a lively character who appeared on hoardings advertising a brand-new breakfast cereal – 'Sunny Jim'. Due to him, and to my doggedly cheerful disposition, I became known to all and sundry as Sonny. I have always believed that laughter is a natural defence-mechanism against uncertainty.

Both my parents were young and good to look at. My mother in fact had already earned the title of 'raving beauty', a truly Edwardian sign of appreciation. She was also a brilliant pianist, though she never became a professional performer. Of course, this was long before the days of radio and television – home entertainment was based around the piano. I still recall the muted sounds of music and song which so often lulled me to sleep in the nursery upstairs.

Our relationship to Patersons of Edinburgh, the leading Scottish music publishers and agents in those days, led to a stimulating succession of At Homes and receptions for visiting artists. The Patersons could claim distinction in the arts as painters, composers and musicians; also my aunt 'Rica' Paterson produced a son, Roy Bucher, who became Commander-in-Chief, India, under Lord Louis Mountbatten. I last visited Roy just before the appalling murder of Mountbatten in Ireland. A few months later, he himself died. But at the time of which I am writing he was a small boy, and I was still a baby.

Only one ghostly blemish to the general impression of my early childhood – a rather toothy Nannie with bulging eyes, who, until she was discovered in the act, gave me a nightly injection to ensure herself a good night's sleep. She may well account for my lifelong aversion to hypodermic needles.

My mother taught me to read at a particularly early age. As I grew older she also taught me to sing the popular songs of the period. One of them, which dates me pretty clearly, was made famous by Margaret Cooper in her 'Songs at the Piano'. It went like this:

> Isn't it heavenly, Uncle,
> Up in an aeroplane,
> The speed is terrific,
> And there's the Pacific,
> And there in the distance
> Is Spain.
> Hip, hip, hip –
> Let her rip, Uncle,
> We'll show them what we are worth.
> I feel so merry-oh,
> Let's challenge Blériot
> When we get back to the earth.

Later, when I was being taken for walks, I remember with affection a large, live bear on a chain attached to a diminutive little man with a dripping nose. For a mere bawbee he would dance a heavy-footed jig – the bear, not his keeper – as long as he sensed an appreciative audience. As soon as he'd had enough, he would sink back into a deep brown melancholy from which only his friend – or another bawbee – could arouse him.

Apropos of this, I had learned another popular song of the time – 'The Teddy-Bears' Picnic'. I often imagined taking my bear-friend to a picnic, just to give the other children a surprise. In fact I did feel for many years that bears and I had something special in common, until in my twenties I attempted to stroke one through the bars of his cage at Dublin Zoo. I got away with a bruised arm and the feeling I had been pretty badly let down. Later, when I became a BBC announcer, I found 'The Teddy-Bears' Picnic' was played to me every day of the week. It had become the engineers' test record.

I never saw much of my father in those early days. He was kept pretty busy. He had inherited a very successful catering business, M. Mitchell & Co. Ltd, established by his mother and known to everyone as M.M. & Co. It catered for civic banquets and parties for all

occasions, from royal visits at Holyrood House to big business confer-
ences at the newly built Caledonian Hotel.

Naturally, memories of my father are few and far between, but I do
recall being carried down from the nursery to the dining-room to be
shown off to some of his cronies. Unfortunately, as he heaved me onto
the sideboard to perform unwillingly a little jig, my foot caught the
edge of the carving-knife, and my indignant yells brought the
occasion to a bloody finale. On another occasion he had given me a
toy butcher's shop for Christmas, and after a presumably all-too-
merry luncheon, joined me in the nursery and attempted to grill the
painted carcasses in the fireplace. The smell of burning paint and the
sound of my anguished protests brought my mother to the rescue. She
was not amused.

At home my mother was never without friends and admirers,
though there appeared to be a growing preponderance of the latter.
Owing to my precocious reading ability, I was regularly given the
latest boys' books by Henty, Marryat and the rest. Not, I fear, so
much a sign of my own attraction as proof of my mother's. I was far
less liable to interrupt the grown-ups when there was a new story to
read.

Often when alone in the evenings, she would play the piano for
hours on end, with tears streaming down her face. Try as I might, I
could never stem her misery. At six years old, life is not that easy to
understand. I shared those unhappy hours long enough to find many
of the works she played almost unbearably sad to this very day.

I was too young to grasp the events which ultimately led to the
separation of my parents, so it bothered me not at all that my mother
and I began to spend much of our time visiting friends. But as the gap
between my parents widened, so friends of the family were beginning
to worry about our future.

On the advice of the Patersons a sort of summer tour was arranged.
My mother was to visit a number of her close friends, staying a week
or two at a time, thereby achieving an inexpensive holiday for us both
and also providing a much-needed change of scene.

One of our first visits was to Tweed House at Berwick-on-Tweed
where the Harrison family lived. Mary Harrison, the eldest of five
daughters, was my mother's closest friend. With her sisters she ran
the house for their widowed father.

All the girls were in their twenties and very good-looking so there
was no lack of admirers. Mary's particular beau was a handsome
young doctor, Douglas Whitehead Reid, on holiday from Canterbury
where he was building up a successful practice. They were obviously

very much in love, and shortly after our arrival became officially engaged. This was the occasion for great rejoicing and a splendid celebratory lunch.

As the baby of the party, I was given far more than my proper share of attention, and quickly became over-excited and out of control. In an attempt to calm me down my mother warned me that if I did not behave myself, a birdman would come down from the sky and gobble me up. Idle threats of that kind could usually be taken with a pinch of salt. But, lo and behold, soon after lunch there was a menacing clatter from the clouds above, and in due course a flying-machine made its appearance, spiralling down to an open field just beyond the gardens of the house. Reluctantly I was hurried to the scene with the rest of the party, inwardly terrified that I was to be eaten alive on the spot. The machine ran bumpily to a halt, the pilot jumped from the cockpit and walked towards us. On noticing me, he promptly offered me a sweet from a crumpled paper bag he was holding. The relief was overwhelming. Later he hoisted me into the cockpit to show me the instrument-panel and controls. This was none other than Gustav Hamel – one of the great early pioneers of aviation.

Two years afterwards he disappeared without trace over the North Sea, just before the outbreak of the 1914–18 war. Rumour had it that he was really a German spy who had flown to Berlin with dispatch cases full of secret plans, but I am loath to believe it. To me he remains the original Superman, and certainly from that encounter stems my lifelong interest in flying.

I am reminded of a story I read in an early book about flying. Apparently an ace pilot had been commanded to carry out a display of aerial acrobatics over Windsor Castle. In due course he gave a magnificent show of stunting, climbing, stalling, diving, spiralling and low flying. Eventually, overwhelmed by his own ability, he climbed steeply in order to demonstrate looping the loop. Unfortunately he had omitted to strap himself into the cockpit, so when his biplane hung upside down at the height of the loop, he was thrown out onto the underside of the top wing, and the machine went into an uncontrolled 'maple-leaf' descent.

A lucky gust of wind not only righted the plane, but threw him back into the cockpit. Collecting his wits, he managed to guide the machine toward an open field. Touching down successfully, he found he was about to run into a large hedge. Nothing daunted, he leapt out and hung onto the tailplane, thereby avoiding a crash landing. Flying must have been much more fun in those days.

Shortly after our visit to Berwick, Mary Harrison was married to her doctor. It wasn't long before the new Mrs Whitehead Reid invited us both to stay with them. Their home was a comfortable Georgian house in Canterbury, with stables and a good garden to play in. For playmates Paul and Joan Pitt-Chatham, who were about my own age, lived nearby so we could visit each other regularly.

Their father, Robert, or Bobby, as he was known to everybody, was making an international name for himself as a singer in France and Germany and had recently appeared at the Court of the Tsar in St Petersburg. He was a concert singer with a charm which had a devastating effect on women. The story went that he had run away with his wife, Maria, while she was still married to a leading piano manufacturer, taking with him, for good measure, the unfortunate man's fur-lined coat and his umbrella. After the inevitable divorce case, he and Maria remained happily married to the day of his death.

I saw more of Maria and the children than of Bobby, since he was often touring abroad giving concerts with various orchestras. But Paul and I became close friends and accepted Joan, being a girl, as a pleasant ancillary. As the Reids never had any children, our friendship grew through the years in Canterbury and became for me a sort of family relationship.

Another visit we made was to Corner Hall at Hemel Hempstead, where we had been invited to spend Christmas with William J. Locke, the distinguished novelist, and his wife Aimée. Locke, who had originally been a schoolmaster, was devoted to young people. He had just followed up the enormous success of his novel *The Beloved Vagabond* – the book that made him famous – with another best-seller, *The Joyous Adventures of Aristide Pujol*.

Both Locke and his wife were obviously disturbed at my mother's situation. It seemed that her marriage was in imminent danger of breaking up, and she had no income on which to sustain herself or me. Eventually they offered to take me in *pro tem* as companion to their recently adopted daughter, Sheila, who was about my own age. This generous offer was gladly accepted.

Christmas with the Lockes was an almost Dickensian occasion. A giant, decorated Christmas tree. Multi-coloured mounds of presents for all and sundry – servants, children, visitors and family all included. There was a children's fancy-dress dance and a party with a conjuror. And on Christmas Day a huge turkey with all the trimmings, mince pies, a Christmas pudding blazing with brandy, and giant crackers full of toys and trinkets. A breath-taking orgy for young and old alike.

We sat down some thirty guests in all. There were local children and their parents as well as personal friends.

How far away it all seems now! How little chance there is nowadays to emulate those warm, secure days of mutual affection.

My mother was the heart and soul of the party, and everybody remarked on her vivacity. Seemingly she had returned to her normal health and spirits. But the time came for her to leave and return to Edinburgh without me. As she left, she pressed me firmly to her bosom. 'You do like it here, Sonny, don't you? You do like it?' Happily I assured her that I was having an absolutely ripping time, and thought the Lockes were 'spiffing' – I couldn't have expressed my feelings more adequately. And so we parted.

Back in Edinburgh my mother, in desperation and to the horror of her friends, took a job as pianist in a cinema. The tragedy of the beautiful Mrs Mitchell became a ten-day wonder of Edinburgh gossip. Day after day my mother pounded away unhappily at an upright piano, accompanying the action of the silent films on the screen. This courageous effort broke all the shibboleths of the time. Nicely brought-up young ladies *did not* go out to work, least of all in a dingy kinema.

Some weeks passed, until one morning Mrs Locke, who had slept badly, collected the first post as it was delivered. She noticed a letter in my mother's handwriting and opened it at once. It turned out to be a farewell letter asking the Lockes to look after me as best they could. Since there seemed no way out of her difficulties, she had decided to commit suicide.

Following frantic telephone calls, Aimée Locke finally got through to friends in Edinburgh who managed to break into the flat where they discovered my mother lying unconscious. She was raced to hospital and brought round with considerable difficulty, but remained paralysed from the waist down for some months.

This unhappy drama led to a further council of war between the Lockes and the Whitehead Reids. It was finally decided to send me to King's School at Canterbury of which Douglas Reid was the school doctor. The fees would be paid, as I learned much later, by one of my mother's admirers. The Reids would look after me during school terms and the Lockes would take me during holidays. This generous arrangement agreed, I was sent back to Edinburgh to collect my few belongings, and remember being escorted on the train journey to Canterbury by my Aunt Rica.

I was not to see my father or Edinburgh again for a long time to come.

2. Junior School

Early school days are always a test of morale, and mine at the Junior King's School, Canterbury, were no exception. Nothing is more calculated to arouse the worst in the average small boy than a new arrival who tries to be different. And here was a new boy who had arrived with an Edinburgh accent and wearing the kilt.

I was quickly surrounded by a not-altogether-friendly reception committee. 'You're Mitchell, are you?' 'Why are you dressed like a girl?' 'What do you wear under that thing, knickers?' (Gales of laughter.) After the application of a few school boots to my vulnerable posterior, I started to cultivate an acceptable English accent and fight my way back to normality. The regulation flannel trousers arrived in the nick of time.

It was not long before I started to settle down and make friends. One of them, Bowker Andrews, a budding rugby player, came racing round a corner one day with his head down, not looking where he was going. I was tying up my shoelace at the time and he butted me right in the face. I fell over with my nose bleeding prodigiously and a large swelling rapidly mounting round my eye. The young blockbuster was appalled when he saw what he had done and insisted on taking me to see the matron. After she had stopped the bleeding and bathed the bruise, he took me along to the tuck-shop and bought me a chocolate bar. From then on he established himself as my protector.

Years later when he had indeed become a notable rugby player, we were discussing that first meeting. 'I was so damn scared when I saw what I'd done to you,' he said. 'It wouldn't have been so bad, but you never said a word. You didn't even blub!' God forbid I should have to make more friends so painfully.

Another very different friend I made was the young Carol Reed, who thirty years later was to direct *The Way Ahead* and *The Third Man* – two shining examples of imaginative film-making.

Carol was noticeably unmuscular and much more interested in discussion than athletics. We had a common interest in books – not school books so much as what we regarded as 'literature', though some history turned out to be equally interesting. We both thought cricket a bit of a bore, but were careful not to say so. (Canterbury, after all, is at the heart of the game, and many a wasted summer hour had to be spent watching it.)

There were unaccustomed rigours we all had to learn, of course. Cold baths every morning for instance. We lined up in the main bathroom which contained two baths half-full of what I estimated to be ice-water drawn direct from the North Pole. Each member of two shivering queues had to dive headlong over the sloping end and, artfully avoiding the taps at the far end, jump out and seize a minute towel on which to dry himself.

The junior school buildings had originally been the kitchens of St Thomas à Becket. Most of us, when we left, felt that we had shared at least part of his martyrdom. Fortunately there was very little bullying, though practical jokes and teasing were popular. I say fortunately, being undersized at the time, though years later I grew to a dizzy six foot three.

I did earn a prize or two for literature, but I was never a good scholar. My mind tended to wander. The day came when it was brought to a sharper focus by Mr Latter, our headmaster. 'Algy' Latter was well over six feet tall with a black undulating moustache similar to that which adorned Lord Kitchener on the 1914 enlistment posters. Like the poster, his hand pointing in your direction meant trouble.

He sent for me one day. 'You're not paying attention to your maths, Mitchell,' he said. 'You're not trying. Here are six simple mathematical problems. I will sit at my desk to do my work. Each time you finish a problem, bring the result to me. If it is correct, – all well and good. If it is not, you get three of the best!' My eye caught a glimpse of two whangy-looking canes leaning negligently against his desk. Staring at the questions helped not at all. By sheer concentration I was able to work out that three strokes of the cane and six wrong results would add up to eighteen strokes. He couldn't have meant that? Most boys only got six strokes for something really bad and I had not done *anything* yet.

Ten minutes later I got up and approached him fearfully with the fruits of my labour.

'Now, you could see *this* was wrong, Mitchell, couldn't you? Bend over! One – (ouch) *two* – (that burned a bit) *three* (Cripey!) You'll try harder next time, won't you, Mitchell?'

'Yes, sir. . . . '

The rest of the afternoon I spent trying to sit down between errors.

It seemed a long session. Fortunately he too became exhausted. For my part mathematics in general remained unsolved for life.

Poor Carol Reed had an unfortunate encounter with Mr Latter too. We all had lockers for our private tuck – cakes and jam, sweets and things. These were kept locked as a rule, and left open only by mistake or from sheer negligence. One day a boy reported that he'd lost a whole tin of chocolate biscuits. After investigation suspicion fell on Carol, who indignantly denied stealing them.

The mystery accelerated into a school inquiry, and eventually the headmaster threatened that unless the culprit owned up, all the boys would be kept in school on Saturday. On the Friday a miserable eight-year-old Carol Reed went to the headmaster's study.

'Aha,' said Algy Latter, 'I *knew* it was you all along. I won't punish you, but I *will* let the other boys know you did it. That should prevent you ever doing anything like this again!'

We were both in our fifties when we met after a film première and Carol recounted the story. 'Do you remember it, Leslie?' he asked. 'Do you remember it?' I had in fact completely forgotten it; but not Carol. He explained that he had only gone to the headmaster so that the other boys wouldn't blame *him* for stopping their Saturday half-holiday. But the awful stigma of that accusation remained with him, and more than forty years on, here he was begging me to believe he'd never stolen the damn chocolate biscuits. Of course he hadn't – I never thought he had.

Years later I phoned him to discuss a television programme. To my surprise, Carol once again brought up the story of the chocolate biscuits. Once again I assured him that none of us had ever believed him to be the culprit. It was our last conversation. Ten days later he died.

Back to 1914. My second term was nearly over. Then came news that my mother's health was so improved that she was coming to recuperate with the Whitehead Reids. Not having been told the reason for her illness, there was no undertone of tragedy in my young mind. I was only pleased and happy at her recovery. Her paralysis had almost gone, though at first she walked with the aid of two sticks. Soon she had regained her old health and vigour and I could join her on half-holidays for picnics with the Whitehead Reids in the Kent countryside.

Douglas's practice extended over a wide area so there were opportunities to mix business with pleasure, and we would be dropped in some woodland spot, while he motored to nearby patients. I remember being awed and impressed by meeting Joseph Conrad, the famous novelist, and Lord Kitchener of Khartoum – so soon to meet a tragic death in the destroyer *Hampshire* when it was sunk by a U-boat. But all that was yet to come. England was still incredibly unprepared for what threatened.

I was on my summer holiday with the Lockes when the 1914–18 war was declared. Sheila and I were in the stables with the ponies when we were called back to the house. We were both about eight years old. Locke gave us a brief history of the events leading up to the war and impressed on us the necessity of saying our prayers every night to ensure that right should triumph and Kaiser Bill with his son, Little Willie, should be punished for their unsporting behaviour. We should also pray for poor little Belgium which once again had been invaded by the fearful Hun.

All grown-ups seemed to be much affected by the news. There was, of course, as yet no BBC – so they seized upon every edition of the newspapers with increasing concern. To us youngsters there was an alien feeling of fear in the air. Even the rain clouds seemed to portend some inexplicable disaster.

On our way back to the stables I stopped at the gate of the gardener's cottage to talk to the Lockes' favourite dog, King, a Great Dane, which was lying stretched out on the grass. As I bent over the gate to talk to him I noticed a trickle of blood from his mouth, and there were flies gathering in his ears and eyes. The gardener appeared carrying a piece of sacking which he laid over the dog. 'You shouldn't have come 'ere, Master Leslie. Poor old King. He turned nasty, so we had to put him down.' I wasn't quite sure what 'putting 'im down' meant, but I well understood I'd lost a playmate to whom I had become much attached. That night I cried myself to sleep – not about the outbreak of war, which I couldn't understand, but about the first permanent loss of a close friend.

Back at school, I found a new headmaster, the Rev. Bernard Tower, a young clergyman with a pretty wife and baby daughter. A great contrast to the fearsome presence of Algy Latter.

Bernard Tower rarely relied on the cane for results. He was sufficiently sensitive to understand the foibles of his juniors and sensible enough to play up to their admiration for a good 'sport' and someone who could beat them at their own game. A disciplinarian, he could also descend from the heights and join in youthful pranks on a holiday visit to Whitstable or a bicycle-ride to Folkestone.

Stella Tower was an unusually popular headmaster's wife. She always showed sympathy for those upset by bad news from home and encouragement for the shy and inarticulate. It was inevitable that I was among those who fell for her charm. At the age of nine I came to regard her as a near-permanent friend in my transient existence, and would have done literally anything for her. In general, life at school had become more pleasant, and I was no longer so miserably aware of my deficiencies. Even my school reports were improving.

The realities of war were gradually being brought home to us. Red Cross ambulances were to be seen daily in the streets, carrying recently wounded French or Belgian *poilus* to the local hospitals. The Buffs, stationed nearby, were to be seen training on the local playing-fields or undergoing route-marches carrying full equipment followed by all the panoply of war, including horse-drawn gun carriages, field-kitchens and ambulances. Many of them were actually on their way to active service in France. Meanwhile local recruiting-stations were busily dealing with the long queues of young men anxiously waiting to join up.

Dr Reid was being kept desperately busy at Canterbury Hospital, and my mother volunteered her services as a probationer nurse. Following her education in France and Belgium, she was bi-lingual, and her offer was gladly accepted. She had now completely recovered from her paralysis and started working daily with other VADs.

Feelings ran high throughout the country. Dachshunds were kicked and beaten in the streets because of their German origin. Men in civilian suits were presented with white feathers as tokens of cowardice. Spies were discovered everywhere. Women with big hands were suspected of being *Herrenvolk* in disguise; men with small feet were suspected of being disguised German Mata Haris. Foreigners of *any* nationality, even our allies, became suspect.

Soon Dr Reid was swept up in the growing demand for medical men to join the Services. He joined the RFC and ended up, four years later, a captain in Mesopotamia.

In December 1914 my mother received a letter from an American friend, deploring the wartime news she had received and begging her to come to New York for a holiday, all expenses paid – at this time few people believed the war would last more than a few weeks. In a typically impulsive decision my mother accepted the invitation. I was not to see her again for nearly five years. With the sinking of the *Lusitania* in 1915 civilians were prevented from making the trans-Atlantic crossing in either direction.

In all the hubbub and confusion following the declaration of war I can only suppose my mother's departure affected me no more than all the other changes in my young life. I do however remember a serious talk she gave me in the drawing-room of the Reids' house, about a favourite 'uncle' who had just been killed in Belgium.

Apparently, riding at the head of his troop of cavalry – in full uniform, with shakos, breast-plates, flying pennants and other unsuitable impedimenta of a peacetime army – he turned into a nearby farmyard. As they dismounted, a haystack in the yard opened up with a murderous burst of machine-gun fire. Before they could even reply, the detachment had been decimated. The Germans, emerging from their ambush, took the remaining casualties prisoner. I remember to this day my boyish outrage at her story of this encounter. 'But they *couldn't* have started the battle without a challenge, could they? What a beastly unfair thing to do!'

My mother also told me that my father had enlisted and was now on active service. This gave a sudden added lustre to memories of my father, and I felt a pride that he too was doing his bit. At first, after my mother had left for the USA, I frequently asked about him, until finally they told me that he had died bravely in battle. From then on I gravely saluted the war memorials. There were already many bereaved youngsters who had lost relatives so there seemed no need to question the story. And I didn't.

As the casualty list grew, so did public hatred of the enemy, and I was caught up early in this hysteria. On holiday with the Lockes, my uncle had given me 2s. 6d. as pocket-money. I quickly made my way to a small toyshop in nearby Boxmoor, where I had spotted a cardboard shooting gallery, with a pistol firing rubber-tipped bullets. The targets were six Indian braves, mounted on spring clips, which could be knocked over by a direct hit.

Back in the playroom I assembled my purchase with pride. As I lay on the floor, aiming the pistol, Mrs Locke entered.

'What have you got there, Sonny,' she asked. 'Let me see it.' As she turned it over in her hands, I heard her gasp, 'Do you know where this beastly toy was made?'

Noting the rising tide of anger in her voice, I said, 'No, Auntie, I don't.'

'You should have looked! MADE IN GERMANY is stamped in large letters on the base. You will come to the shop with me tomorrow, and we will return it. I will see that everyone is informed of these unpatriotic shopkeepers.'

Aimée Locke could be very frightening. I reluctantly went back with her to the shop, where she loudly condemned their lack of patriotism. I was given my money back, but it was a super toy, and I never found a replacement.

On another occasion, while I was playing in the garden, there was a loud noise overhead and no less than seven aeroplanes flew over the house. This was very unusual indeed. At that time few people outside the RFC had the chance to see aeroplanes flying in formation. I ran excitedly into the house to tell the Lockes. 'Auntie,' I shouted, 'did you see? – did you hear?' I was almost incoherent. 'Auntie, thousands of aeroplanes just flew right over the house.'

Aimée was not impressed. 'Now, that is a *lie*, Sonny,' she said firmly. 'It's an absolute lie, isn't it?' Finally, having admitted that what I had meant was that there were more aeroplanes than I had ever seen before, I was dismissed to the nursery without my tea.

Will Locke came to visit me in my solitude. 'Don't worry, old chap, I have just heard about your aeroplanes. There were an awful lot, weren't there. That's all you meant.' He gave me a chocolate biscuit, but his understanding meant much more than that.

My imagination obviously did need controlling. Some weeks later I was listening to a grown-up conversation and a visitor introduced an idea quite new to me. 'Well, it is true,' he said. 'You can achieve anything in the world if only you want *it* badly enough.' The speaker was Oswald Watt, the Australian air ace, who became one of the founders of the Royal Australian Air Force.

In bed that night I kept on turning over this statement. One thing that I had most wanted to do was to fly. I had watched birds take off from trees and come effortlessly to the ground. And some people could do it in gliders. Like all children I had made paper gliders which travelled quite long distances. Perhaps if I *believed* enough, *I* could fly.

The following day I sneaked out quietly into the garden. Out of sight of the house was a high wall behind which lay the kitchen gardens and the greenhouse. Cautiously I climbed onto the wall and walked along the top. From a tree nearby a blackbird suddenly swooped in a graceful curve to the far side of the greenhouse below me. It was now, or never. Shutting my eyes and taking a deep breath, I threw myself with arms outstretched into space. The noise as I hit the greenhouse was loud enough to attract the entire household.

First on the scene was the gardener, then the cook, the governess, and finally Mrs Locke. Like all people frightened by an accident to their wards, her first instinct (when she realized I was alive) was to smack me. I was sent back to bed in disgrace.

Luckily, I hit the wooden struts of the greenhouse, displacing the panes of glass and thereby avoiding cutting myself badly. I ended up on the wooden staging inside, still in one piece and very disappointed. Maybe I didn't believe hard enough. Dear Will was once again cautiously sympathetic – he so often found himself having to invent excuses for my dramatics.

At about this time the Lockes travelled to King's School to see Mr and Mrs Tower about my future. The Towers had become worried about me, and between them they all agreed that the best solution would be for the Lockes to adopt me. Will Locke wrote to my mother suggesting this but her indignant refusal produced an estrangement between them which was never dissipated.

Nevertheless Locke had now become the father-figure in my life. I trusted him utterly. He was my accepted tutor and mentor in the maze of correct grown-up social behaviour, and he had only to speak a few rare words of admonition for my fragile world to collapse entirely.

He devised a unique way of telling us children about the war. Almost every day after lunch he would regale Sheila and me with the latest details from the 'war career' of a Colonel 'Teddy Bear' who sat on the table wearing an impressive row of medals. Brought to life under the long, tapering fingers of the story-teller, Colonel Teddy would describe the battles of the Somme and Passchendaele or the blowing up of Hill 60, in unforgettable detail.

Colonel Teddy was later sent on a secret mission and succeeded by a Field-Marshal 'Bruin'. He was a real *man's* Field-Marshal. From time to time – when he was really wound up – he would lift a large champagne bottle to his lips and signal his pleasure with a deep growl. Close inspection revealed that liquid *did* apparently come from the bottle into his mouth, but where did it go? The question remains unanswered.

These sessions were sheer Locke. His works have been accused of being too sentimental and too whimsical, but this was a reflection of the man himself. He once confessed that he could never really create a villain; as he wrote, the character himself disclosed valid reasons for having left the straight and narrow path. No doubt this was due in part to the author's delicate health. Having been left tubercular, after a serious illness at Cambridge, he was physically frail and inclined to avoid 'turbulence' of any kind. Aimée, with her dominating person-ality, saw to it that he remained protected to the day he died.

In 1914, he converted a wing of Corner Hall into a hospital for soldiers.

Throughout the war he worked unceasingly, writing articles, and organizing help for the Belgian refugees.

During those war years the London theatre was working full out to produce shows for the troops on leave. This obviously meant musicals, pretty girls and comedy since the men's life in the trenches was tragedy enough.

Aimée and Will Locke were devotees of the theatre and always maintained close contact with stage people. In spite of wartime rationing they somehow managed to keep open house. Beerbohm Tree (who played *The Beloved Vagabond* on the stage), Charles Hawtrey, Arthur Bourchier, Cyril Maude, Clara Butt – the list was endless, and I met them all. Sometimes Sheila and I were allowed to stay up late when visitors came, and we quietly listened to the grown-up conversation. This was to stand us in good stead in later years, since we had to listen, without interruption, while innumerable points of view were exchanged between people of wit and intelligence.

In 1918 Locke wrote a children's play as part of an entertainment in aid of the Nation's Fund for Nurses. Sheila and I were cast in the leading parts, and the set – the interior of an Egyptian palace – was designed by the famous American artist, Benrimo. Among professional members of the entertainment were Viola Tree, Daisy McGeoch (composer of that slightly embarrassing song, 'My Bed is Like a Little Boat'), Miss Eva Moore in a play by her husband, H.V. Esmond, and a professional conjuror.

This was to be my first appearance as an actor – and a comedian. After the play I was recalled to the stage to aid the conjuror.

'Now sir,' said he in a whimsical mood, 'this bag is empty, I think you will agree. The ball has completely disappeared.'

'Then what is that bulge you're holding in the corner of the bag?' I inquired innocently. The conjuror was not amused but the Tommies in the audience roared with laughter. Immodestly, I took it that I was a success.

Back at school we had become used to weekly fire-practice. Weather permitting we would be called upon to leave our dormitories by the windows and slide down a canvas tube to masters waiting below. This was a reasonable precaution, as periodically German Zeppelins and bombers passed directly over Canterbury on their way to bomb London.

On one occasion, much to our excitement, anti-aircraft guns actually brought down a large bomber just outside the city boundaries.

Then came my last term in the junior school. I was dreading the change. Not only had I happily settled down at last, but the prospect of new rules, new masters and new surroundings meant facing yet another unwelcome break. True, I still had Mrs Reid to whom I was devoted, to soften the impact, but who else was concerned about my future? The Lockes, of course. But they were miles away and Will

Locke had been ill again. There was talk of sending him overseas to some warmer climate – that would mean leaving Corner Hall for good.

One thing was left for me to do. I *could* demonstrate my ability in the field of sport. I would win some prizes or bust. The world would see that I *had* benefited from my time in junior school. At the end of that sports meeting I had won the 220 yards, the 100 yards, the long-jump and the hurdles!

After spending considerable time and thought I made a secret purchase in the High Street. Came the moment to pay my final visit to the headmaster's study, where I presented Mrs Tower with a small, suede-covered copy of the *Rubaiyat of Omar Khayyam*. On the flyleaf I had written, 'Thank you for being so kind to us all (signed: L. Mitchell)'.

She and I met again in 1979 – over sixty years later. Mrs Tower had sent me a charming letter about a recent television appearance of mine. As a postscript she added: 'I would so like to meet you again with your wife.' We went. Mrs Tower is now a widow and, sadly, has lost her two children. But her charm is undiminished. Just before we left, she turned to me. 'I've still got it, you know – the book you gave me.' And she had. Inscription and all.

3. Growing Up

My experience of senior school at Canterbury was destined to be of short duration, but I was involved in a tragic incident before leaving.

Early one morning in the summer of 1918, I walked into the science laboratory in search of a pen I had left there. Suddenly I noticed a man's legs protruding from behind a desk. Thoroughly scared, I moved closer and saw it was one of the housemasters. He was lying, ominously silent, on his back. Running to the door I told a passing boy to fetch the Head (Algy Latter himself), as there had been an accident. Sad to relate, the poor devil was dead. A jury brought in an open verdict.

It was, of course, a shock to us all, but by now death was coming to lose much of its meaning. It had become normal to see familiar names in the mounting casualty lists – relatives and friends, King's scholars and masters among them. Unlike the Second World War, the real horrors of being under fire were seldom brought home to civilians. The bombs on London in the 1914–18 conflict had minimal effect. In spite of the appalling devastation in France and Flanders, the men on leave would seldom discuss the living hell to which they had to return. They came home to forget it – to enjoy all they could while they still lived.

I joined the Officers Training Corps. Before long it would be my turn.

November 1918. Out of a grey sky came the Armistice. The British people had been totally unprepared in 1914; now in 1918 they seemed momentarily stunned. Then everybody went mad – crowds dancing in the streets; carillons of bells; marching bands; fireworks and singing. We had been privileged to live through the war to end wars.

The school attended the solemn services of thanksgiving as well as the usual daily Cathedral services. We were also given extended holidays and half-holidays. And everywhere there were joyous reunions as demobilization took effect. Mary Whitehead Reid was informed that Douglas would shortly be demobbed, and would be returning to resume his practice. Early in 1919 came news that my mother was coming back from the United States. I began to worry about my own future. My elders and betters were obviously far too concerned with their own plans to discuss mine.

Eventually the moment came to meet my mother again. Mary Reid had taken me to London, and we were waiting for the arrival of the boat-train. I was over thirteen now. Would my mother recognize *me*? My pictures of her were years old. Would I know *her*? As more and more passengers got off the train, my excitement mounted. According to Mrs Reid, as any likely lady approached, I stepped in front of her: 'Excuse me,' I said, 'are you my mother?' At last one of them accepted the liability.

It was a happy occasion. We returned temporarily to the Reids' house and a gay reunion of old friends. There was so much to tell. It had been a long separation for all of us. Toys and presents for me, sheet music from the latest American 'hits' for Mary and my mother to play to us. News and anecdotes in a continuous stream well into the early hours of the morning.

It was wonderful having my mother back, but it took some getting used to. She was far from happy about the change in my appearance. 'You were such a darling little boy – what's happened to you?' she said teasingly. I consoled my ruffled vanity by reflecting that she didn't understand about the war and all that. Slowly we grew closer to each other but I was still aware that I didn't quite match up to her expectations; yet the pleasure of actually *belonging* to each other outweighed other considerations.

The school summer holidays came, and Mother decided to take me to the seaside – Littlestone-on-Sea. So off we went, both of us, I suppose, hoping that we could retrieve something more from the lost years of separation. But I was no longer a little boy, and she still seemed baffled by the change in me, in her friends, and in England generally.

Facing our hotel at Littlestone, about four hundred yards out to sea, was the wreck of a ship which had been sunk there during the war. One of my first impulses was to swim out and perch on the masts, still piercing the water-line. I was well on the way when loud hails from shore made me return. Apparently, not long before, two swimmers had made their way to the wreck, at which moment the local RAF station sent off a squadron of fighter planes on a routine battle-exercise. They had always used this particular wreck for target practice.

Also staying at the hotel was a widowed Canadian, Fred Ashe, and his daughter Anstice, some two years older than me, with her governess. Somehow we became formally introduced and the suggestion was made that Anstice and I should get the local golf professional to improve our game. Only three weeks later I discovered that I was to acquire a new stepfather, a stepsister, and an as yet unseen stepbrother. The wedding reception was in London at the Savoy Hotel. Anstice and I stayed the night in rooms adjoining the Honeymoon Suite. I was to become very familiar with the Savoy in years to come, but this was my first real taste of honey.

The following day I was informed: that my name was to be changed by deedpoll to Mitchell-Ashe; that I would be taken from King's School and sent to Storrington College – a cramming establishment for boys entering the Navy; and meanwhile I would go back to King's for a final term. I was somewhat overwhelmed by all these new developments. A stepbrother in the Navy; a stepsister to write to about plans for the holidays; news from my mother about how she was furnishing our new house, with lyrical descriptions of the gardens and the house itself. All very stimulating. I looked forward to becoming part of a promising idyllic family background for the first time.

Our new home turned out to be a large Edwardian riverside house near Windsor: Clewer Meade. Here I met my stepbrother, Gordon, for the first time. He was a twenty-one-year-old naval lieutenant, home on special leave. I stood much in awe of him in his uniform. I did somehow get the idea that he didn't exactly favour his father's remarriage; but he appeared to accept me, and I was equally prepared to like him.

The careless rapture of the early twenties held no hint of a revolutionary future. The war was safely over and gaiety had become the keynote. Summer picnics on the river – our punt and an electric canoe were in continual use; cocktail parties, dances and garden parties were the order of the day. And with two tennis courts, the query 'Who's for tennis?' had not yet become a joke.

As general manager of the Union Bank of Canada, Fred Ashe had close connections with a number of prominent Canadians. These included a Colonel Grant Morden at whose house we met Lord Beaverbrook, the great F. E. Smith (later Lord Birkenhead) and leading financiers and industrialists of the time.

The Reids were now happily reunited, and the Lockes had gone to live in Cannes, so I seldom saw them; but there was a growing collection of new friends from Ascot, Maidenhead and the surrounding districts. Anstice and I were quickly absorbed into the local younger set of the time – the Maidenhead Crowd. Luckily for me, Gordon had acquired a Douglas motorbike and sidecar which I was permitted to use while he pursued his naval career, so when I acquired a licence, I was able to take Anstice with me to visit friends under our own steam.

My days at Storrington College proved happy enough, and here too, I began making new friends. My term reports were improving and it appeared that I should have no difficulty in passing the Navy Entrance Examination in due course. Many of the boys were older than I, and there was an almost 'university' atmosphere about our schooling.

The Rev. George Gordon, our chaplain, was an interesting character, full of fascinating yarns about the war. A well-known amateur yachtsman, he had commanded his own craft in the Auxiliary Service at the beginning of the war, later obtaining a commission in the Royal Navy, from which he was newly retired. He had been connected with the development of the paravane, a torpedo-shaped weapon with an explosive head, which could be towed along at controlled depths to destroy enemy submarines. The invention had proved of considerable help to the Allied navies.

One friend of my own age was a good-looking young man, John Paul Scott, son of a leading figure at Lloyds Register of Shipping. I also struck up a friendship with 'Dod' Frankland whose mother, the Baroness de Zouche, lived at Parham House nearby. He was a keen horseman, and we would join him at meets of the Leconfield Hunt.

All seemed to be going well, then soon after my second term began, I developed severe pains in my innards. I was packed off to see a specialist in Harley Street, who decided that I must have an immediate operation for the removal of tubercular glands.

It was a major operation. When I came round, a sister came to warn me they would bring me a dose of castor oil. Protesting that I could never take castor oil without being sick, she waved the objection aside. 'We'll give it to you in lemon juice,' she said. 'You'll never taste it.' I was too weak to argue, and drank it. Shortly after, a second angel of mercy appeared with a glass in her hand. 'Would you like some cold milk, dear?' she inquired. Nodding feebly and inadvisedly, I drank it, and was violently and impressively sick. Half an hour later I was back on the operating table. My stitches had burst, and I had to be sewn up again.

The result on my youthful, clean-limbed torso gave privileged observers the impression of opencast mining. It at once became obvious that the Navy would certainly not be persuaded to adopt anyone in such inordinately bad trim. Medical advice pointed to the wisdom of any future schooling taking place in Switzerland. But first they insisted I should recuperate for some weeks.

My mother arranged that we should rent a villa with the Pitt-Chathams at Veulettes, on the Brittany coast, for a month. The holiday presented me with one quite unexpected development. My stepfather and I came into conflict for the first time.

We had arrived at Dieppe and went to sit on the beach. My mother and I were laughing together over some incident of my childhood. To my astonishment, my stepfather came purposefully over to where I was sitting and aimed a powerful blow at me. Surprised but resourceful, I tackled him rugby-style, and he fell heavily, breaking the pipe in his mouth. He got to his feet, purple in the face, and strode away without a word.

I was still weak from the after-effects of the operation and not at all prepared to take on physical gamesmanship. However, still mystified, I apologized to him later that evening. But my apology remained unanswered. It transpired that he was almost insanely jealous of everyone – including myself – who had known my mother before he married her.

Later in our holiday we received the tissue-thin foreign edition of the *Daily Mail,* and I was horrified to read that my friend Scott had been drowned. The chaplain at Storrington, with his long experience of sailing, had chartered a fishing lugger with a mate for the school holidays. They had set off with a master and five boys from the college, with the intention of sailing to Spain. They reached Vigo safely and, as there was a favourable wind, decided to return by the same route. In the Bay of Biscay they encountered rough weather, and a really violent storm blew up. Mr Gordon and young Scott were both washed overboard by a giant wave. Their shipmates managed to turn back to look for them, but in the conditions prevailing, the search was unsuccessful and they sadly made their way back to Little-hampton. Miraculously, hours later, the chaplain was spotted in the water and picked up by a Dutch steamer en route for Antwerp.

The loss of my young friend upset me considerably; an elderly friend of the Pitt-Chathams – Harry Bradish – was sympathetic enough to observe this. But the family was not unduly concerned since they had never met either the boy or the chaplain. The Pitt-Chatham children – Joan now a pretty fourteen-year-old and Paul who was twelve – and I resumed our old relationship, and we kept together most of the time, enjoying each other's company.

It was a fine summer, and we spent most of the days on the beach. I had been given a model sailing-boat which came with me when I bathed; attached to a large ball of string, it would battle bravely through the waves and turn only if I pulled the string connected to the rudder when it would make its way back again. This became a daily

game and attracted a friendly crowd of French youngsters. But one
day the string broke and the sailing-boat continued out to sea until
eventually it disappeared, even from the sight of my stepfather's
binoculars.

Four days later we arrived on the beach as usual to be met by an
excited crowd of boys. *'Regardez, monsieur. Regardez votre bateau. Il va
retourner.'* There, sails ballooning in the breeze was my beloved yacht,
heading for a nearby stretch of beach. How it survived four days in the
Atlantic seas or how it became so accurately re-directed, I shall never
know. On our return to Clewer, it was put on blocks as an exhibit in
the billiard-room.

Shortly after we got home, we were horrified to receive a letter from
Maria telling us that Paul had died. We just couldn't believe it. After
leaving Veulettes, they had stopped for several days in Dieppe before
embarking for England. Somehow Paul had contracted typhoid fever
and died in spite of all efforts by the doctors to save him. This second
tragedy so close on top of the first affected me deeply. Was all my
generation destined to die young?

This morbid depression was not helped by another manifestation of
Fred Ashe's uncertain temper. A friend of my mother's from America
had come to stay the weekend. She was sitting in the drawing-room
after dinner trying to draw me out about my plans for the future –
what did I want to be when I grew up, and so on. I was politely
answering her questions, Anstice standing beside me, when my stepfather seized me by the seat of my pants and threw me headlong under
the piano. Apparently he was also jealous about his daughter. Needless to say, our American guest left first thing in the morning.

I learned from my mother afterwards that Fred Ashe had been in
serious trouble as a young man when he nearly killed someone in a
fight. Also, she confided, his first wife had died in a mental home, and
she was sometimes worried that Gordon was not quite normal either.
On reflection I had noticed my stepbrother was in the habit of
standing with his arms akimbo and his fingers widespread as though
they were full of treacle. But after all, he *was* in the Royal Navy, and he
had no objection to my using his motorbike – he *must* be all right.

Then I learned that Anstice was in trouble. Evidently her school
report complained about her behaviour. Something about being
unruly in the dormitory – girls' stuff. While she was being given a
lecture about her misdemeanours, I hung outside my mother's
boudoir waiting for her; we had been invited to a tennis party at
Holyport. Anstice seemed a bit downcast when she came out. 'It's so
unfair,' she said. 'Why does she have to pick on me?' I commiserated

with her. Most grown-ups were a bit unpredictable, but school reports should not be allowed to interfere with summer holidays. Off we went to Holyport.

But there was an increasingly unhappy atmosphere at home, and we were all becoming involved. My stepfather would come home exhausted in the evenings, obviously suffering from strain. Our week-end guests were almost confined to bankers and businessmen with their wives. In fact, our real friends were invited less and less often. My mother, too, seemed preoccupied and had obviously decided not to take *my* part in any difference of opinion. I began to feel increasingly that I was being treated unfairly.

I realize now that my mother was probably trying to avoid rousing Fred Ashe's obsessive jealousy by paying less attention to me but, not being in her confidence, I began to feel more cut-off than I had ever been.

My spirits descended to a new low when I was lectured by my stepfather on slackness and lack of gratitude for what he described as a 'damned expensive relationship'. He further informed me that there was no possible chance of sending me to university later; he was not, he added, prepared to throw good money after bad.

This seemed to be the last straw. Slowly walking through the garden to the river bank, I sank into deepest gloom. What did the future hold anyway? Separated from my friends, no hope of getting into the Navy, no training for anything, not even fit enough . . .

There had been a fatal accident in the river only a few weeks before. Two youngsters had fallen out of a rowing-boat, been caught in the long reeds and drowned. I started cramming some of the big stones from the rockery into my pockets. Then, standing on the balustrade, I jumped into the water. The river was running fast and I swam with some difficulty into mid-stream. I began to sink under the weight of the stones and was being swept down towards Windsor Bridge. Suddenly the instinct of self-preservation took over. I swam slowly back to the boathouse and climbed miserably up the steps to the garden again.

Unfortunately our gardener had watched this idiotic performance. He ran in amazement to tell his employer what he had seen. When I got to the kitchen door (I was too wet to go to the front door), Fred Ashe was waiting for me. He actually broke his walking-stick on me before the butler diffidently interfered.

It was clear that the servants liked me well enough. I was often called in to share tea, or a cup of cocoa in the pantry. Bridget, the parlour-maid, was always around and would sometimes tip me off if there was trouble looming. But it was William, the butler, who taught me another important lesson.

I was beginning to enjoy the prospect of going to Chillon College. Never having travelled further abroad than the Belgian and French coasts, Switzerland sounded intriguing. I had read all about Chillon Castle and the 'Man in the Iron Mask' who had been incarcerated there, and gathered that the college was only a short distance away. So there seemed interesting possibilities for exploration. The time came for me to be off. My bags were duly packed, a new overcoat, hat and umbrella to go with them. The butler approached me as I stood waiting in the sitting-room.

'Good luck, Master Leslie,' he said. 'They'll have given you quite a bit of pocket-money, I suppose – you having to get all the way to Switzerland on your own?'

'Yes, they have, thank goodness, William. Nearly fifteen pounds.' His face fell. 'It's not all that much, is it sir?'

'I've got the tickets, of course – it's just for porters and food and taxis, really,' I added.

He looked round cautiously. 'You wouldn't like to make a hundred pounds this afternoon, Master Leslie, would you?' Evidently he was on intimate terms with the owner, the jockey, the trainer *and* the horse, who through their joint efforts would – so they had promised him – win the 2.30 at the adjacent Windsor race-course.

My doubts about this heaven-sent opportunity were calmed somewhat by his obvious air of integrity, and the fact that he had recently stopped Fred Ashe from beating me. With a conspiratorial wink I gave him £10. 'You know the school address, William, don't you?'

'There'll be no trouble, sir. It'll be sent off to you tonight.'

My mother took me to London and saw me off on the train. As it pulled out of the station, I opened the evening paper. 'Windsor – 2.30' – there it was. . . . My horse had won at ten to one! Good old William. What a wonderful pal! What a super butler! I'd have to send him a tip. Now I really could stand on my own feet for once – my future would be assured, at Chillon anyway.

The first letter from my mother told me that the impeccable William had been sacked out of hand for insolence. I never saw that £100. It was an impoverished introduction to another first term.

4. Cutting Loose

Chillon was a great new adventure. Snow was no new experience for me, I'd seen plenty in Scotland. But deep snow, the trees and the mountains piled thick with it – and the dazzling heights of the Dents du Midi reflected in the waters of Lac Leman – were a revelation.

The school house had previously been a hotel and boasted a lift in the entrance-hall. It was tempting, as I discovered later, to disengage the latch of the gate while the lift was in motion, thus suspending the masters or lesser victims between floors until their infuriated shouts brought help. The headmaster, the Rev. F. de W. Lushington, was a benevolent man with a kindly, artistic wife, and a shy, reserved young daughter; so the family were seldom called upon to suffer the pranks of the scholars.

It turned out that there were about thirty pupils in the college, most of them between sixteen and eighteen years old. As at Storrington, we were treated more like undergraduates, and enjoyed wider freedom than usual at school. Here I had time to make more permanent friendships, chief among them that of Edward Partington, later Lord Doverdale, who had the whole situation summed up in the first week.

He was the sophisticate who took me to my first experience of a *thé dansant*. He it was who claimed that he knew several girls at nearby Des Essarts, a finishing school for young ladies. So it was that on *his* money I began my social life in Switzerland. On the appointed days we would arrive at the Hotel Palace in Montreux and take a table near the dance-floor. When a girl he knew arrived with her parents, he would introduce me and I would be expected to dance with her. Like him, I was a good dancer, so, week by week, we added to our list of partners, becoming increasingly acceptable on the strength of friendships earlier. Soon we were expected to join the parents' tables, and *all* our expenses would be paid by them.

The Des Essarts girls went to the same church as we did every Sunday. On one occasion I saw a particularly attractive girl in the pew behind me and, pricking my thumb, wrote in my own blood, 'Meet Palace 3.30 Wed.' She was there, with a school friend's parents as chaperons. All innocent fun, but no less exciting for that.

It was possible occasionally to slip away by tram to Montreux and back without being noticed. And the older boys, like Teddy Doverdale, took full advantage of the fact. But I remember my amazement at seeing him early one morning, fully dressed and walking steadily towards the mountains. This was something I couldn't afford to miss. Teddy was not remotely athletic. Where could he be going – and why? Hours later when I had dressed and followed his tracks, I discovered he had climbed an exhausting snow-covered track to the Caux Palace Hotel where the Des Essarts girls had been taken by their headmistress on an outing.

I would not like to create the impression that our schooling was totally wasted. Work, in fact, had become much more interesting. Convinced that I had missed my chance of getting into the Navy, I decided to try for what I had always wanted – a short-service commission in the RAF. The stars seemed to favour me. My maths master had been working on airships in the design department of Vickers. Noticing my obvious interest in aeronautics, he would discuss with me various aspects of aerodynamics and aerodonetics between classes. Mathematics became also comprehensible. I had found someone with understanding who could really make me take it in.

His name was Neville Barnes Wallis, probably the most distinguished inventor of our time. His brilliant invention of a completely new structure for aircraft – the geodetic structure – stemmed from his earlier design for the R88. The growing future of British airships at this time had been halted by a decision of the RAF to discontinue using them. As a result Vickers naturally decided to stop producing them.

Barnes Wallis, disheartened by this turn of events, had left Vickers in 1922 and come to Chillon to teach mathematics. He was, as we all found, a quite exceptional master, and we were treated to lectures with models, which further stimulated my airborne ambitions. On the more peaceful side, he also invented a dimmer to make a very realistic sunset for the school play in which I played a leading part.

His later work before and during the Second World War, is historic, including the Wellington bomber, the Möhne Dam bomb, and the designs (taken over by the Americans), for a high-speed, retractable-wing fighter. At the end of the Second World War I wrote him, asking whether he would allow me to interview him in my series 'Close Up'. He wrote a charming note back to refuse. Since he held so many vital secrets in his head, he explained, he dared not risk spilling them.

At the end of my third and last term, I had settled in happily as a prefect; saved a vital goal with the football team; and become cox of our rowing eight (some indication of my size then). On one occasion we were caught some way out in the lake by a *Föhn* – a storm common to the Alps which would blow up suddenly and violently without warning. We almost made it to the slipway and sank in shallow water so we were able to save the boat by manhandling it to shore.

After this incident I found myself back in the doctors' hands. I was taken to a clinic in Vevey for a painful internal examination. Following X-rays it was decided to operate for stones in the kidney. Fortunately my mother came over and insisted on my being taken back to the King Edward's Hospital at Windsor. There they decided that the shadows in the Swiss doctor's X-rays were merely blood clots from my previous operation. I was put on a strict diet and sent 'home'.

There was now no question of my returning to Chillon. I was nearly seventeen and Fred Ashe had contacted a well-known firm of London stockbrokers, asking them to take me on as office-boy to learn the business. He told me of his plan and explained that I could hardly expect any money, but they had agreed to pay me £1 a week. The following month I would go up to the City with him, and he would introduce me. I had no choice in the matter; my mother seemed completely preoccupied with her own problems at which I could only guess. Eventually the doctors ordered her abroad for a complete rest and change. She went to Baden-Baden for an indefinite period.

So I began travelling to the City daily with my stepfather, and started my training as a Stock Exchange clerk with the leading firm of Panmure Gordon & Co. Needless to say, the engagement was due more to my being related to the General Manager of the Union Bank of Canada than to any belief the partners might have had about my business acumen. I started as a messenger-boy under the helpful guidance of a junior clerk who showed me where to find the innumerable banks and stockbrokers' offices concealed in the labyrinths of the City streets. I was a quick pupil, and before long was delivering and collecting stocks and bonds to the many clients of the company.

I was now getting rapidly taller and outgrowing my strength. My main difficulties arose from physical exhaustion and worry about the troubles at home, which tended to make me unusually absent-minded. On one occasion I took a bus for a short journey and jumped out at my destination, leaving behind thousands of pounds' worth of stocks and bonds in the blue bag I'd been carrying. Only catching a passing taxi saved me from hitting the headlines and the partners of the firm from hitting the ceiling. The taxi caught up with the bus and I retrieved the bag, but on £1 a week, it seemed a costly extravagance.

The situation at home appeared to be worsening. It had begun to dawn on me that the basic trouble could be financial. I had been promised at an early stage of our relationship that my stepfather would pay me £100 if I did not smoke till I was twenty-one. As a conciliatory gesture I waited till we were in the sitting-room together, took a cigarette from the box on the table, and lit it. Fred Ashe spotted it at once, but all he said was: 'I *thought* you were smoking on the quiet. That stupidity has just lost you £100.' It seemed unnecessary to explain that I'd just saved *him* £100. He would never have understood.

It was an uncertain, unhappy period for me. Anxiety about my mother and the new job intensified. There was a strangely dead atmosphere at home. One night no less than three portraits hanging in the dining-room fell from the walls. This was presumably due to the damp riverside air rusting or otherwise affecting the chains by which they were hung. But Bridget, the parlour-maid, with true Irish superstition vowed that it meant terrible bad luck for us all. My mother was still in Germany but wrote that she would soon be returning. Meanwhile Gordon, Anstice and I were left in the house with the servants for a time as my stepfather decided to stay in town at a hotel, presumably for business reasons. One evening, after we'd all dined early, I went up to have a bath. I must have spent some time there pondering the whole situation. Returning to my room, I saw Anstice had left her bedroom door open. As I passed, she called, 'Sonny, is that you? Come in a moment.' I went in; she was already in bed. 'What do you think is happening, Sonny? Do *you* think Daddy is going bankrupt? Do you think Mummy has departed for ever?'

I told her that I knew nothing. My mother had ceased to take me into her confidence, and I was only worried that she was ill. Anstice gave me a sympathetic look. 'Poor old Sonny, you are having a rotten time, aren't you?' Then, holding the sheets open, she added, 'Come in with me for a cuddle; why don't you?' I took it that this was a girlish effort to be comforting. 'No Anstice. I don't think *that* would be at all a good idea,' I said. With that I kissed her good night and went back to my room.

The following morning I went down for breakfast and began to help myself from the serving table. The door opened with a crash – it was Gordon, his eyes staring with rage. 'You dirty little bastard,' he said, 'I'll kill you for this.' He jumped forward to catch me, but I was too quick for him. 'What on earth are you doing, Gordon? What have I *done*?' I really was entirely ignorant of what this unexpected scene was about. But recalling my mother's stories of the family's mental history, I was frightened. Dodging round the dining-room table, I raced through the front door to the garden, closely pursued by Gordon. My training at King's School stood me in good stead. I managed to run gasping to the vicarage next door and rang the bell. I've always been ashamed of this reaction. But summing up my own physical weakness and Gordon's fitter and heavier advantages, it seemed possible he might have killed me.

The vicar received me with sympathy. By now I was trembling and crying with shock. I told him what had occurred and warned him of my fears that my stepbrother would be violent. Nevertheless he left me and went next door. Some twenty minutes later he returned. 'Young man. Your stepbrother tells me that last night you attempted to – well – er – rape his sister. Can that be true?'

Suddenly I became convinced. Gordon *was* mad, my *stepfather* was mad, the whole family was mad. True, Anstice had never seemed 'barmy' before but there must have been something odd in her make-up. I explained my theory to the vicar who calmed my suspicions by suggesting that it might all be due to a series of misunderstandings.

He finally arranged to come with me to the house while I packed my belongings. But first he asked where I would go and who would look after me. I remembered my understanding old friend, Harry Bradish, who'd stayed with us in Brittany. He now lived in a cottage near Maidenhead. The vicar telephoned him. True to form, Harry told me to catch the bus to Maidenhead where he would meet me and put me up until some plan had been decided upon.

Re-reading his letters now, I can more fully appreciate his kindness. My phone call came at an awkward time for him. Living in a small cottage and having few facilities for visitors in his bachelor abode, he had to disrupt his way of life entirely for my arrival. Food, blankets, heating – all had to be extended for me. Worst of all, he was for the moment nearly broke. But he welcomed me and lent a sympathetic ear while I poured out my story. Sensibly he put the whole business into perspective. After all, I had never been really happy at Clewer, had I? Now fate had taken a hand and provided me with a chance to start life on my own.

The following day he got in touch with Maria Pitt-Chatham who was now living in London. She was naturally horrified at the news and contacted my mother who was still in Baden-Baden. Otherwise she was in no position to help for the moment, but promised to think up something.

Harry brought me all the papers which advertised rooms to let, and together we combed through the details, making notes of the cheapest and the nearest to the City. I travelled to work every day by paying extra on the season-ticket my stepfather had bought for me at Windsor.

The walk from Paddington and back, allied to the day's walkabout in the course of my work, left me very tired, but Harry always had a welcome and a meal for me when I returned.

The day came when I made up my mind I had to stop relying on other people. We found an advertisement for a room with a gas-ring near Kennington. The price was eleven shillings a week, but I would no longer be commuting, and it was not too long a walk from the City. I took it.

There was a pitcher and basin; no bathroom; but the room itself was quite large and clean. The bedding was marked WD and looked as if it might have started as horse blankets, but by and large it was all one could expect for the money. The landlady was good enough to bring me a cup of tea on my arrival, so I determined to do my own house-keeping on the morrow and went to bed.

After work the following day, I bought at Woolworths a frying-pan, a cup and saucer, two plates, a knife, fork and teaspoon. Butter, bread, eggs and bacon at the grocer. Realizing my ignorance of *haute cuisine* – from the chef's-eye view – I would settle for a simple meal of bacon and eggs. But the expense was prodigious – I must have spent all in all 12s.6d. Unfortunately the handle of the knife, being inflammable, caught fire on the edge of the pan. This set the fat burning, and I had difficulty in extinguishing this *flambé* confection. Before long, my worried landlady groped her way through the smoke and helped to put the fire out. I am glad to say I've never tasted eggs like that before or since.

The room having been cleared by opening the window, I decided to take a bath. Getting hot water for the pitcher and standing stork-like with one foot in the basin, my mission was nearly accomplished when I noticed a growing puddle on the carpet. The basin was cracked. It was almost midnight before mopping-up operations were completed.

A day or two later my landlady's natural misgivings were somewhat allayed by the arrival of a gleaming chauffeur-driven Rolls-Royce. She came to my room in an obvious state of excitement. 'It's for you, Mr Mitchell,' she said. 'The man says, it's for you.' Looking out at the car I could think of no one likely to present me with a Rolls, so hastened to the door.

'Hello, sir,' said the chauffeur. 'I had a bit of difficulty finding you, but I was told to give you this with love from Mrs Cottingham.'

Mrs Cottingham was one of our Maidenhead friends and 'this' was a gargantuan hamper from Fortnum and Mason, filled with chicken-breasts, caviar, tinned peaches and all you would expect to find for lunch at an Ascot race meeting. I fell upon the contents but my stomach rejected them with bad grace. I was too hungry. Nevertheless I have always remembered Mrs Cottingham with special affection for a kind thought so quickly put into action.

As the weeks passed, inquiries from friends discovered my whereabouts, and I was invited to visit them or stay the weekend. Naturally none of them realized I couldn't possibly afford the train fares. I made excuses about 'pressure of work', which sounded grown-up, but was in fact a synonym for 'pressure of income'. Actually, most Sundays were spent walking about the parks and discovering London.

One fine day I decided to visit the Zoo and set out on the long trek from Kennington. Arriving at the turnstile, they informed me that Sunday was reserved for 'Members Only'. Feeling tired and a bit stupid into the bargain, I tried argument. 'I've walked a long way on my only day off, will you let me pay?' But the official was adamant and uninterested.

At that moment a middle-aged man spoke to me. 'So, you want to come in, young man? I am a member; would you care to join me and my wife?' I gratefully accepted the offer. It transpired that he was a Mr Lütiger, a Swiss sculptor, who had been a member for many years. He and his wife made a regular habit of visiting the Gardens since he modelled many of the animals there.

Altogether they were charming to me. Through his influence, I was able to see behind the scenes, and I particularly remember a keeper demonstrating how a rattlesnake injects its venom. We had tea together before parting, and he gave me his card with the instruction to let him know if I ever wanted to visit the Zoo again on a Sunday. It was a great kindness to a complete stranger, and I haven't forgotten it.

At length I received a letter from my mother posted at Windsor. She had returned home and, to my relief, after a terrible row Anstice had confessed that her accusation of rape was sheer invention. My stepfather was in serious financial difficulties; my mother had signed back the marriage settlement he'd made on her three years ago. They had made up their differences and were moving to a flat in London. She also wrote that Fred Ashe would pay for a small room in Cromwell Road where I could stay.

This last suggestion made life easier for me in every way. I was now earning thirty shillings a week, and would have no lodgings to pay. Swallowing my pride, I gratefully accepted the offer, said goodbye to Kennington and moved west.

The flat which my mother and stepfather had taken was off

Kensington High Street. I made no effort to enter it. My mother would meet me outside, and we would walk around Kensington Gardens in the evening or go to the cinema. Fred Ashe was deeply immersed in his future. The Union Bank was being quietly absorbed into the Royal Bank of Canada and he was eventually retired on half-pension. The house at Clewer he sold with everything in it. A journalist in *Country Life* was moved to express his regret at the unknown tragedy which could have brought the owners to leave such a handsome property intact with all its beautiful furnishings. It later became the Eton Country Club.

A few weeks passed, and I went as usual to collect my mother from the Kensington flat. I found her lying on the landing outside their front door, weeping hysterically. I picked her up and tried to comfort her. Apparently she had been telling Fred about her visit to Baden-Baden and mentioned the name of a man-friend she had met there. Fred with his usual reaction had hit her and thrown her out of the flat.

This was unforgivable. I rang the bell insistently. Fred answered. 'You must be bloody mad,' I said. 'Look what you've done. I've come to collect my mother's things.'

To my astonishment he said nothing, walked into a room and I heard him turn the key. My mother put some clothes in a suitcase and together we went back to my hotel where I booked a room for her. The following day she went to see a solicitor about getting a divorce.

As soon as an allowance had been organized for her, she decided to rent a furnished flat for us both in Brompton Road. The flat was small, but comfortable, and I looked forward to trying to look after my mother in spirit, if not in kind. The arrangements for a divorce dragged on, and the weeks passed uneventfully. We saw Joan and Maria Pitt-Chatham from time to time, and other friends of my mother's who discovered her whereabouts.

During this period Bobby Pitt-Chatham died tragically at the height of his career. Lord Rothermere, a personal friend, had financed the sequel to *The Beggar's Opera – Polly*. Bobby managed it and played the leading part. He had made a signal success with his charm and his fine voice, and was well on the way to becoming a star actor. Now, at only thirty-eight he was dead – a little over a year after the death of his son. This double blow to Maria and Joan was almost too much to bear. It was a period of disasters which seemed to affect us all.

One morning I took my mother a cup of tea as usual. She was lying in bed very still and breathing stertorously. As I could not wake her, I phoned a Harley Street doctor my mother knew and asked his advice.

He quickly contacted a colleague in the Brompton Road district. In due course the doctor arrived. After a few minutes he came out from the bedroom. 'Have you and your wife had a recent disagreement?' he asked. I explained that I was her son, not her husband. He altered his approach. 'I'm afraid your mother is suffering from an overdose of sleeping-pills,' he said. He called an ambulance, which took her to hospital. It was several days before my mother had recovered sufficiently to return to the flat.

At last news came from the solicitors. A divorce had been agreed and my mother would be given a more adequate allowance. She decided to live in Paris to take advantage of the favourable rate of exchange, so I found myself a room just across Hammersmith Bridge not far from the Playfairs and the Lyric Theatre. The Playfairs' son, Giles, and I had already struck up a friendship. Though he was younger than me he would invite me to the Lyric to see the current productions. I had also been given a weekend job by his mother, May. She and Maria Pitt-Chatham had recently opened a shop in Beauchamp Place – the Cottars Market. My job was to help paint furniture in the traditional Spanish and Portuguese style.

Giles was by way of being a budding author and actor, and had an astonishing hold on his family. I remember a dinner-party at his house when Nigel dramatically silenced the guests. 'One moment, ladies and gentlemen,' he said, 'Giles has something he wants to say.' I've forgotten what it was he said, but that was of no real importance. The fascination for me was that a young man could have parents who thought his opinion of any interest at all.

On another occasion Giles took advantage of his power over the family by displaying his dramatic temperament. We were staying the weekend at their house at Sandwich, when he suddenly began to tear his hair and shout. He left the room whilst the family took it in their stride and sat silent. But I was not to be outdone. Jumping up and unceremoniously knocking over my chair, I too began to shout and laugh hysterically. 'I can't stand another minute. It's all too much. Even *we* have to live and make something of our existence. The world's gone mad,' and similar gibberish.

Giles returned to the room with an air of astonishment. Equally astounded, the family looked at me. 'Leslie, darling, are you all right?' said May. 'I've never seen you like this before.' Nor had they. But at least I had out-acted Giles.

The Playfairs' helpfulness and interest at this turning-point in my life was a wonderful boost to my self-confidence. Back in London I became a frequent visitor to their house in Chiswick. It was a meeting place for current leading lights of literature, music and the stage.

Here I met Arnold Bennett, John Drinkwater, A. P. Herbert and Michael Arlen; and among up-and-coming designers Lovat Fraser, George Sheringham, Anna and Doris Zinkeisen, two young sisters whose paintings and stage designs had made them famous already. Then there were Hermione and Angela Baddeley. Hermione had already achieved stardom (at the age of fourteen) in *The Likes of Her*. And there was Edith Evans, toast of the town after her dazzling performance as Millamant in Congreve's *The Way of the World*.

I orbited happily round this star-filled constellation. My private existence was improved. The new digs were comfortable, and though I was still earning only £3 a week – with thirty shillings in the City and thirty shillings from the Cottars Market at the weekend – it *was* possible to eat regularly and take the occasional bus.

One evening I had an unexpected stroke of luck. I have always enjoyed painting and was finishing a series of landscape pictures when there was a knock on the door. It was my landlady. 'You painting again, Mr Mitchell?' she said. 'I've been talking to my husband and he's agreed these pictures would be just right for an empty wall we've got downstairs. We'd like to buy the three pictures you're doing. We could let you off two weeks' rent. Would that be all right?' To her embarrassment I gave her a kiss and accepted on the spot. I was an *artist*! I had a public. I began to dream of designing sets for the theatre. It was many years before I achieved that ambition.

My contacts with the arts took an upturn when my mother wrote to me from Paris, asking me to join her for my annual two weeks' holiday. She sent me the money for the journey plus £10 to buy a new suit. The Mitchell wardrobe had dwindled somewhat by this time. My most recent suit had been bought from government surplus stock and had cost £1. My shirt collars and cuffs showed signs of my amateur scrubbing.

After intensive window-shopping I plumped for one of the ready-made suits produced by Mr Mallaby Deeley, one of the first tailors to cater for the smart junior-clerk-about-town. With two new shirts and a tie to match, I felt confident that Paris and my mother would be overwhelmed.

Mother had booked a room next to hers in a small hotel off the Champs-Elysées. I had carefully guarded my new clothes for this special occasion. I shall never forget her horror when I thoughtlessly took off my jacket and exposed the sleeves of my new shirt. They had been neatly cut in half, the lower half being suspended by a series of safety pins so that I could show the accepted amount of linen at the cuffs. I was rather proud of my inventiveness. In those days it was considered *de rigueur* to show at least half an inch of linen. Even today they don't manufacture shirts with sleeves long enough for me. I was quickly taken to Sulka, one of the most expensive shops in Paris, where two more shirts were ordered. Meanwhile, I was swept into a round of social activities.

One of the most impressive was a reception given by the Grand Duke Michael of Russia. It was the period when refugees from the Revolution were flooding into Paris, making it a main rendezvous for survivors from the Russian *ancien régime*. Almost daily there would be joyous reunions as courtiers and officials of pre-Revolution days made their appearance in the capital. For the first time I was privileged to join in the drinking of a toast in the traditional Russian manner – the drinks quaffed in one and the glasses shattered on the floor. I thought wryly of my consternation at breaking a cup in my digs. This was the life – carefree, extravagant, and to hell with tomorrow! I am afraid for most of them the glasses ran out many years ago.

One particular acquaintance I made was a General Spiritovich who, I learned, had been head of the Tsar's Secret Police. My youthful imagination was stimulated by the fact that he was constantly shadowed even during our casual walks in the Bois, though this seemed to disturb him not at all. Like many officials of the Russian court, he was married to an opera singer whose art fortunately transcended revolutionary handicaps. She at least continued to earn a living. Not so the General, who, with only his rank to offer, had little chance of entering the labour market even as a member of the *Sûreté*. Before long however, an unexpected opportunity arose; a distinguished compatriot died suddenly, and the General was called upon to arrange an appropriately impressive funeral. It was, in fact, so impressive that he was immediately offered a permanent funereal position on the staff of a leading Paris undertaker. Sad to relate, his pride compelled him to refuse.

But this was only one side of the cosmopolitan set in which my mother sought refuge from her unhappiness. It became obvious that she had acquired a number of new admirers, and I wondered curiously which of them might be a future stepfather. Certainly one of the most amusing was Josef Stransky, a leading international conductor, whom she had met earlier in Baden-Baden. He was now conducting at the Paris Opera House to which he invited us on several occasions. He had a splendid disregard for the conventions and I was delighted by a story told me about him. Some time earlier, he had been conducting at Carnegie Hall and was invited by one of the leading hostesses in New York to join a celebration party after the concert. In due course, he arrived in an immaculate grey suit. His hostess was appalled. 'Mr Stransky,' she said, 'everybody here is dressed in formal evening dress!' 'Surely, Madam,' he replied, not one whit disturbed, 'you would not expect me to come in my *working* clothes.' He was admitted. I am aware that this story has been told about other conductors. But in 1924 I heard it for the first time.

During my hectic two weeks, he and other friends of my mother's invited us both to a number of dinner-parties and night clubs. The floor shows of that time starred many top-ranking American artists, amongst whom was Norah Bayes, the blues singer who always worked with an enormous ostrich fan. She had a compelling, not to say overwhelming, personality. She was charm itself to me; chiefly, I think, because she loved young people, and in fact adopted eight children in the course of her career. Sadly, years later, she died in poverty.

Among other stars I met and admired were the beautiful Leonora Hughes who had earned an international reputation in exhibition ballroom dancing, and Florence Walton, who was partnered by Maurice, Leonora's former husband and dance-partner. This early experience of wine, women and song prompted me to regard the opposite sex with a somewhat more appreciative eye, so I became increasingly self-conscious about the cut and style of my clothes, surrounded as I was by the *jeunesse d'orée*.

My first romance came shortly before my return to London. At one of the dinner-parties to which I had been invited, a very attractive Hungarian girl made a point of talking to me in fulsome, not to say flattering, terms. During the evening, I had shared fully the vodka and wines being offered, and became increasingly aware of the lady's charms. After dinner my mother played the piano while I sat next to my new friend on the sofa, in a haze of tobacco and other unaccustomed fumes.

When the party eventually broke up, I shook hands in a formal but despondent farewell to my companion and was thrilled to find a small piece of paper in the palm of my hand. With astonishing aplomb I managed to take the paper without dropping it and put it into my trouser pocket. Back at the hotel, I hastily unravelled the note. It read, 'Darling, meet me tomorrow at the X Bar on the Champs-Elysées 11.30.'

In my best suit, my best shirt and best tie I made my way to the rendezvous only to find I was an hour early – sixty endless minutes of sipping Grenadine syrup. Then at last a car drove up and my inamorata appeared. Following her out stepped a large and formidable gentleman who had also been at the party the previous night. She passed my table without a glance.

The following day I returned to London and my room in Hammersmith.

Maria Pitt-Chatham and the Playfairs were still keeping an eye on
me. They were far more worried about me than I realized at the time.
Apparently my mother had written to them, expressing her disappointment that I had not yet found myself a real job with a good
salary.

The fact was that the early 1920s were just the wrong time to be
thrown onto the labour market. Many thousands of men, recently
demobilized, were looking for civilian jobs. The lucky ones were being
accepted back in their pre-war employment, but the misfits with only
Service training behind them were lucky to get work of any kind.
Ex-colonels and other officers proliferated as chauffeurs, gardeners
and odd-job men. Most of them had a chip on their shoulders, as it
seemed damn little return for what they had endured in France and
elsewhere. Quite properly, young civilian nonentities without
influence were roughly shouldered out of the endless queue.

My own main disadvantage, of course, was not having a home in
which to shelter from the icy blasts of reality. This was all too well
understood by Maria and May Playfair, if not by my mother.

Quite out of the blue I received an offer from Nigel to understudy in
his forthcoming production of Sheridan's *The Rivals*. The pay would
be £3 a week. By this time I had become as convinced as my employers in the City that there was little future for me in stockbroking.
Yet here was Nigel, who not only believed in me, but was apparently
willing to pay me twice the money to prove it.

I snatched at the offer gratefully before he had time to reconsider.
Having worked out my notice with Panmure Gordon, I appeared
expectantly two weeks later at the stage door of the Lyric. Through
the door, past my old chum the stage-doorkeeper, turn left (follow the
arrow), onto the *stage*.

5. Bright Lights

So far my experience of acting had been limited to my appearance in school plays, and earlier, in the children's play written by W. J. Locke during the war. For the rest, my impressions had been gained solely from being a member of the audience in theatres to which I had been taken. It seemed to me obvious that the London stage would be the very centre of bright lights, stimulating colour, music and brilliant conversation. But looking round the dusty stage under the bare pilot lights I saw only a group of very ordinary-looking people sitting in a semicircle reading a script. My excitement grew as I was able to identify them. Claude Rains, that brilliant actor with the black velvet voice was to play Falkland – quite the most difficult part in the play. Miles Malleson, whose appearances in eccentric characterizations were enjoyed by playgoers over several decades, was David; the beautiful Isabel Jeans was Lydia Languish; Douglas Burbidge was Captain Absolute; and Nigel Playfair himself was the comic character of Bob Acres. The stage manager called me over and gave me a script. I was to understudy Claude Rains and Burbidge.

Through the daily rehearsals that followed, I studied them with lynx-eyed attention, and in the evening earnestly memorized the two parts. I was soon word perfect. But more was to be required of me. For some reason, during rehearsals Douglas Burbidge had to be absent, and it fell to me to take his place. Determined to prove my worth, I proceeded to play the part without the book.

It was most unfortunate that this early exhibition should have taken place in the presence of Nigel Playfair's stage director, Stephen Thomas, who had just arrived back from Australia to take over the production. After watching for a few minutes, he hastily made his way to Playfair's office. 'Nigel,' he said, 'I don't know who you've engaged to understudy Burbidge, but he must go. He hasn't the first idea of acting. Come and see for yourself.'

I was delivering my lines with increasing bravado when Playfair called me down to the stalls. 'I am sorry, my boy,' he said, 'perhaps it's my fault, but I am afraid it just won't do. You really have a great deal to learn.' So it was that I was fired even before the play opened.

The following day Playfair wrote a letter of recommendation in suitably evasive terms to Edward Knoblock, who was producing a revival of *Kismet* at the New Oxford Theatre. Here I was engaged as what was known as a 'super'. Alas for my £3 a week – now it was back to thirty shillings. In the crowded market scenes Mitchell was to be found carrying a heavy load of 'property' bananas on the end of a stick – something on the lines of an oriental version of Dick Whittington. At one moment I was halted by the voice of the producer who sarcastically begged me to avoid standing sideways if I wanted to be seen. At least I was acquiring a lean and hungry look.

On the strength of Nigel Playfair's introduction, the management had half promised me the understudy to Robert Harris, who was playing the leading part, but as soon as they had sized me up, it became obvious that this was not to be. I decided to take Fate by the scruff of the neck and try for something better. This time I sacked *myself* before the opening night.

It was dawning on me that I was no better suited to the stage than I had been to stockbroking. On medical grounds the Services were out of the question, but there was still the landlady to pay and food to be bought. Shamefacedly, I made my way to an employment exchange and drew my first dole. They gave me thirty shillings. It seemed that this was to be the height of my market value: thirty shillings in the City; thirty shillings on the stage and now thirty shillings for doing nothing. I made up my mind to double it at all costs.

An introduction to a London theatrical agency got me an interview with the leading partner. Having listened to my tale of inexperience he gave me a chit and told me to take it to the stage door of the Queen's Theatre, adding that if I landed the leading part, he would like to know as soon as possible since he would be entitled to 10 per cent of my salary. Undeterred by this shaft of irony, I hastened to the theatre and was promptly ushered onto the stage where a number of other young men, far more sure of themselves than I, and all impeccably dressed, were standing in the wings. One of them was Wilfred Hyde White, later to become a leading light of films and stage, and memorable for his performance in *My Fair Lady*.

In turn we were all asked to read lines from the script to the management, seated in the stalls. The chosen few amongst us would be required to act as a sort of Greek chorus. The play *The Beggar on Horseback* was an American fantasy woven round the life of a business tycoon. It included nightmarish dream-sequences in which identical characters appeared at unexpected moments as butlers, jurors in a court scene, businessmen at a conference and so on.

The producer stared gloomily from the stalls and pointed a finger. 'You there, – you look as though you can sing.' I admitted that I could. 'Okay,' he said, 'sing this,' and handed me a page of script. The lyric was short and seemed more than usually naive. It ran, 'You have broke my heart, like you broke my heart, so why should you break it again?' In brackets was the stage direction, 'To be sung in a ghastly voice.' I peered anxiously down into the stalls.

'Is there a tune to this, sir?' I asked querulously.

'Not that I know of,' he replied. 'Make one up.'

Desperately trying to look self-assured, I quavered in an appropriately ghastly voice, 'You have broke my heart, like you broke my heart . . . '

There was a howl of anguish from the stalls. 'For the love of Mike, I thought you said you could sing.'

Man-sized butterflies fluttered in my stomach. 'But it says here, "In a ghastly voice", sir.'

'Young man,' he said gravely, 'you may yet become another Henry Irving. That was certainly the ghastliest voice I ever heard. Now sing it straight.'

Smothering a swelling inferiority complex, I did as requested. There was an ominous pause.

'OK,' said the voice. 'Put him on the list.'

The salary was £4 a week – a sum exceeding my wildest dreams. At last I had become an actor.

On the strength of this, my first West End engagement, I collected my entire savings – all of £5 – for a celebration, and carefully thought about who to share it with. I decided on Angela Baddeley whom I met so often with the Playfairs. I went to visit her at the Lyric where she was currently playing in *The Duenna*, and gravely asked her if she would lunch with me the following day in a nearby restaurant on Hammersmith Broadway. Equally gravely, she accepted. Eureka! I had reached a position where I could play host to an up-and-coming young actress.

The next day I bought a rose from the flower-seller by the underground station, and made my way happily to the restaurant. At last she arrived. She looked sweet and very sophisticated in her tailored suit and white gloves. I presented the rose, and having already had a chance to study the menu, pressed her to choose some of the more expensive dishes. I did not want her to think I wouldn't be able to pay for this special occasion. I even ordered a bottle of wine, to reassure her. Altogether I think we enjoyed the meal and each other's company.

I was about to order coffee when she looked at her wristwatch. 'Oh, heavens, Sonny, I'm terribly sorry. No coffee, thank you, I've got to rush.' It was time to get ready for her matinée.

'I'll see you back,' I said. 'Just let me pay the bill.' The waiter handed it to me. I felt in my pockets feverishly. Oh god. I had forgotten my wallet.

Angela rose to the occasion with dignity. 'Let me pay it, Sonny. You can always pay me back.' My face was purple with embarrassment and shame. Gosh! She might think I did this sort of thing for a living.

Thanking her profusely, I saw her back to the theatre. Once there, I turned and ran round Broadway, over Hammersmith Bridge, and along to my bed-sitter. Thank goodness, the wallet was there. Pausing only for a glass of water, I returned at breathless speed to the Lyric. Angela was dressed for the stage when I found her. 'My dear boy, what *have* you been doing. You look exhausted. Sit down and get your breath back.'

Doing as she told me, I displayed my wallet and its contents. 'You see, Angie, I *did* have it. I wouldn't do that to anyone – least of all you.' Then I carefully paid back my debt. I noticed the rose was in a glass on her dressing-table. When we parted, she gave me a motherly kiss. She was, after all, two years older than I.

With the opening of *The Beggar on Horseback*, I had also been called upon to understudy Eric Maturin, an actor of considerable repute who played the villain of the piece. The leading part was played by A. E. Matthews, one of the most charming and most unpredictable of stars. Even then he seemed to me far too elderly for a juvenile, but through the years until his death some forty years later, he remained quite unchanged, an ageless example of the magnetic power of true star personality. When we last met I could not imagine how anyone his age could have remained so young.

The Beggar on Horseback had been an enormous success in America, but the all-American theme was lost on British audiences since they had yet to be introduced to the American way of life and conversation by the arrival of the Talkies. The critics were not kind. After a few short weeks, a notice went up on the board, warning us that the play was coming off. Matthews, convinced of its merit, decided to transfer it to Wyndham's Theatre at his own expense. But still the play failed to draw the public and a few weeks later it came off for good.

Part of the play took the form of a mime ballet in which the principal dancer was Kyra Alanova, daughter of the famous Adolph

Bolm, a leading star of the Russian Ballet in St Petersburg. She had come over with the show from America with her husband, and was bitterly disappointed at its failure, so she decided to present the ballet sequence as a separate act at the Coliseum, and she invited me to join her. So it was that I made my first and last appearance in ballet.

To any beginner, the vast size of the Coliseum stage with its great 'revolve', which allows for the turning of a whole scene together with the players, into or out of position, is a revelation. Even more impressive and frightening as the curtain goes up is the first sight of that vast audience in the auditorium, extending up to the 'gods'. Nature has provided me with hands of disproportionate dimensions, so none of my gestures were lost though, come to think of it, that may have been against me. In any case, we were only booked for a fortnight and Alanova was too soft-hearted to sack me. Luckily, I was not required to dance in the accepted professional ballet sense. That great dancer, Anton Dolin, told me that he had seen me at the Coliseum, but couldn't remember that I was particularly bad. At least he hadn't missed me altogether.

Meantime, Angela Baddeley, unknown to me, had recommended me to the Arts League Travelling Theatre with which she had herself worked for two years. They asked me to go and see them at their headquarters in Gower Street. Here I was auditioned by Eleanor Elder the organizer, Judith Wogan her number two, and Leslie Banks, the actor and producer.

I read from various poems and plays. They retired out of sight. I waited. At last Eleanor came back and said, 'We were quite happy about your reading, and would like you to join our company next week for rehearsals.' The pay was to be £3 a week, all found. Travel and lodging were provided. It was the equivalent of about £10 in those days. This time surely nothing could go wrong.

In the early 1920s there were only silent films in the cinemas – to which were added the variable talents of local pianists improvising suitable music to match the changing moods of the action on the screen. These films seldom found their way outside the towns and cities. Live theatre in the country communities was confined mainly to amateur performances in village halls. It was therefore something of a breakthrough when a determined group of actors managed to introduce a company of travelling players into these areas under the banner of the wealthy Carnegie Trust Fund.

The initial aim of the company (somewhat unfortunately christened the Arts League of Service) was to bring the arts – music, poetry, painting, ballet and one-act plays – to a far wider audience.

To the surprise of the cynics, the Travelling Theatre proved an almost immediate success. Permanent organizers for the tours were Eleanor Elder and her husband, Hugh Mackay, the famous singer of those haunting songs of the Hebrides, and two experienced actresses, Judith Wogan and Norah Balfour. They made a resilient back-up for the companies which toured Britain nine months of the year.

Transport was provided by a large Lancia van which carried an adaptable framework (for curtains and backcloths) which could be expanded according to the size of the halls we visited. Then, apart from the driver, there were members of the cast – some eight or nine in all – with their costumes, and the lighting, which included footlights, spotlights and floodlights.

The cast was picked in London and rehearsed by leading West End producers, amongst them George Bernard Shaw (producing one of his own plays, of course), Leslie Banks, Ernest Milton, Donald Wolfit, Harold French and Reginald Denham. Two of the many players to join the tours were Hermione Baddeley and her sister Angela. There were Donald Wolfit and Rosalind Patrick (later to become his wife), Vivienne Bennett, Andrew Cruickshank and Jon Pertwee. All of these achieved fame in the British theatre, whilst Ernest Lush, our pianist, gained a fine reputation in his own field.

Our entertainment was similar to that of the brilliant Russian Chauve Souris company in London some time earlier. Although we lacked the financial backing of their famous impresario, Diaghilev, with his inspired talent, nevertheless we aimed at the same colourful simplicity and international content. Costumes and backcloths were specially designed by leading designers – Marion Dorn and McKnight Kauffer, for example. Plays were by Irish, French and Russian authors; sea-shanties, ballets, one-act comedies and tragedies were all interchangeable at the preference of our hosts in each stopping-place.

And, of course, we had to know how to behave socially, since we stayed with local people. Our hosts ranged from the Marquis of Aberdeen at Tarland and the Duke of Montrose at Arran, to celebrities in the district and any local people with the necessary spare rooms.

It was altogether an almost perfect training ground for the theatre. Hard work with considerable variety; changing audiences from different environments; and a basic training in stage lighting and management, singing, dancing and acting. The only drawback was that the tours of the Travelling Theatre were not continuous throughout the year. So there was the problem of finding work and also somewhere to live in the intervals.

To me it was one of the happiest times of my life. I still hear from people in remote corners of the country who, like me, remember the Travelling Theatre with affection. Only the other day I heard from the daughter of a Scottish family with whom I stayed fifty-five years ago.

My mother returned to London from Paris early in 1926 and shortly afterwards invited me to meet a new friend, a Major Owen Davies. I think neither of us was particularly impressed by the other – in fact we had very little in common. He appeared to be a large, dull, back-slapping horsy type, whereas my mother assured me he was a most amusing companion and highly educated to boot. She told me that he could quote Latin and Greek with equal facility. I was anxious not to be caught out as I had no Greek and my Latin was confined to a sailor (*nauta*) at a table (*mensa*), who came and saw and conquered. I could do better with French, but he could *not*, so our efforts to appear bright and sophisticated were doomed to failure. We settled for just being amiable.

I set off once more with the Arts League after rehearsals in London. The tour was happily and successfully making its way to Cumberland, I think, when I received a letter from my mother asking me to return at once as she was going to marry Major Davies and wished me to be present. He had agreed to put me up at a hotel. Torn between contracts and loyalties, I wrote that, happy as I was for her, I was in no position morally or financially to throw up my new contract, since we travelled with no understudies, and anyway I had not yet amassed the necessary train fare. She replied in broken-hearted vein, accusing me of lack of feeling, responsibility and filial devotion, but I could do nothing other than send a dutiful telegram on the day, which I did.

My mother and Owen Davies left on their honeymoon just before the General Strike which brought me back to London. The General Strike was my first involvement with social problems other than my own. It looked as though the country was suddenly faced with another war – an internal war – a revolution if you like. It was up to all of us to take defensive action and protect our way of life.

The government appealed for volunteers so most people of my age were coming forward to help, driving lorries, buses and even trains. I set off for the recruiting station at Scotland Yard where I was quickly appointed to join a number of hefty characters with fast cars, many of them racing drivers from Brooklands. We were used as a Special police reserve. If trouble brewed, we would race through the streets to the danger-spot to help deal with it.

Later we were diverted to the docks area to guard a convoy of lorries on their way out. It was arranged that we should patrol each street on foot in pairs, always keeping in touch with the pairs at either end. Along came a convoy of lorries laden high with crates of bananas under netting. We watched them approach. Quite suddenly the street was full of strikers and their families.

The lorry nearest to me and my companion stopped dead. Two burly strikers got into the driver's cab and hit him with a brick; meanwhile two more hefty-looking men were letting down the tail-board of the lorry and trying to set the contents on fire by throwing lighted rags between the straw-packed crates. The time being ripe for action, we helped the driver out of his cab and went to the back, where the men made no attempt to stop us. I was holding the defensive weapon given to all 'specials' – a wooden chair-leg with a hole bored through one end and a short piece of cord threaded through by which to hold it. I jumped onto the floor of the lorry and started throwing out some of the blazing crates.

'What's the matter, son? Need help?' asked a face below.

'We could do with some water to douse this lot,' I said.

He was back in no time. ''Ere you are, mate,' he said, and emptied a bucket in my direction. There was a rush of heat and a smell of burning Mitchell. It was petrol.

I was irritated by this piece of treachery so when he started to climb up the tailboard, I hit him on the head pretty hard. Either I funked hitting him hard enough, or the chair-leg bounced because it had no weight in it. He looked up and started climbing again. 'Now you 'ave bloody asked for it,' he said.

As in all the best film scripts, there was a shout of 'Look out. Here come the rozzers.' The crowd evaporated into the neighbouring houses like magic.

Fortunately for me, apart from a smouldering overcoat and a burnt hat, minus eyebrows and lashes, I got away with it, and retired inside the nearby Guinness Brewery. We didn't need much refreshment; the heavy fumes saved us the trouble. But we were quickly relieved from our duties by the next shift. I've kept the wooden chair-leg.

At the Lyric, Hammersmith, *Riverside Nights,* a successful revue by A. P. Herbert, had been badly hit by the strikers who were using Hammersmith Broadway as a centre for their activities. Nigel Play-fair, having decided to move the show to the Ambassadors Theatre in the West End, invited me to join the cast to understudy James Whale. I also sang with two well-known singers, Cavan O'Connor and George Baker.

Although a *succès d' estime,* the revue had lost the impact of its early success. Then during the last weeks I arrived at the theatre to learn that James Whale had been taken ill. Like most understudies, I am afraid I was not saddened by the news. This would be my first chance to prove to Nigel Playfair how much I had learned since he had fired me from *The Rivals*.

By sheer chance it also gave me an opportunity to see the Lockes again. Just three nights before the show closed, they sent me a note inviting me to dine with them at the adjacent Ivy Restaurant – the famous theatrical rendezvous of those days. I was overjoyed and rushed over to meet them after the final curtain.

Locke was, as ever, amusing and congratulatory. 'My dear chap,' he said, 'to think that it was I who started you on your career! I always knew you'd turn out to be an actor, given half a chance.'

He was pleased with my efforts in the revue, and I thanked my guardian angel for having brought about this unexpected reunion. I had not met him for five years, and I sorely missed his influence. Sheila was now very grown up and social. Aimée had softened with the years, and I, of course, was now nearly twenty-one.

There was so much to talk about. And when it turned out that I had no plans for four weeks following the run of *Riverside Nights*, they insisted that I should return with them to holiday at their villa in Cannes. Needless to say, I jumped at the idea.

Before our departure, I carefully packed a large bottle of hair-cream in the folds of my dinner-jacket. From Calais we travelled south by car, visiting various places en route to view the battlefields and cathedrals still being restored – a legacy of the war. All went well until the night in Avignon when I unpacked my suitcase to find the contents smothered in broken glass and sticky green Anzora cream. Fortunately we stayed long enough for my clothes to be cleaned and generally put to rights.

Travelling with the Lockes was always rewarding since Will was a gourmet with a considerable knowledge of French food and wines. To me every meal was a revelation. As we progressed to the South, we travelled by devious routes since Will Locke was anxious to re-stock his famous cellar. This necessitated long talks with the owners of vineyards and much sniffing of this and sipping of that. I began to learn the rudiments of wine-drinking. I had a lot to learn.

The Lockes' villa in Cannes, Les Arcades, was set high on Californie, a hill overlooking the island of St Marguerite on which my old friend from Chillon, the Man of the Iron Mask is reputed to have been also imprisoned. The climate and the beautiful coastline were a joy to the senses and I revelled in the experience.

Cannes itself was very different from what it is today. Rich socialites rented villas there for the season, or stayed in one of the three big hotels on the Croisette. The whole coastline had been comparatively little built upon and social life was confined to a prolonged succession of parties given by the owners of the larger villas. The Lockes were among the paramount hosts of that time. They had gone to live there in 1919 on medical advice following Will's severe illness. Hardly a day went by without a luncheon-party, a cocktail-party and a dinner-party to follow. Will's popularity was by now worldwide, both as an author and as a host, and there was a constant stream of visitors from every part of the globe.

Nearby residents at Juan-les-Pins were the Lloyd Osbornes – Robert Louis Stevenson's stepson and his wife. They had a beautiful villa with a private beach where we all spent many happy hours. Here I met another penniless young man – Eric Maschwitz, who I was to encounter later when he had become Head of the BBC's Variety Department.

Amongst the neighbours were Mary Garden, the famous opera singer, and Richard Hudnut, the perfume king of America, whose daughter Natasha Rombova had been married to the late lamented Rudolph Valentino. I was invited no fewer than three times to see a private showing of the *Four Horsemen of the Apocalypse* at their house. Other visitors included Phillips Oppenheim, Somerset Maugham, Phillip Gibbs, Valentine Williams, Michael Arlen, the young Beverley Nichols, and Cyril Maude. I met the singer Clara Butt with her husband Kennerley Romford, and pianist Benno Moiseiwitsch. Here, I felt, one was at the very centre of talent, sophistication and luxury with on all sides the sweet smell of success.

Locke worked to a definite schedule. He would write in his study from 11 p.m. until 3 or 4 a.m. every night of his life, reappearing in time for the morning cocktail before lunch, always immaculately dressed. From then on he would perform his duties as a benign and sophisticated host until, sharp on the hour of 11 o'clock in the evening, he would retire to his study again. He was genuinely fascin-ated by his craft and worked largely for the joy of it. Being naturally modest, he was only too glad to have found a recipe for success and never forgot his early days of penury. Certainly his books could be, and indeed were, read by every level of society, young or old. His income at this time was reputed to be something in the region of £70,000 a year, in royalties from Russia, France, Spain, Italy, England and America. A vast amount in those days.

One evening we were all invited to a party given in honour of Marguerite d'Alvarez, the opera singer. The party, as usual, attracted leading lights from all the arts. It was a glittering occasion, and feeling rather out of it, I retired briefly to the garden to soak myself in the magic atmosphere of the moonlit Riviera. Suddenly aware of someone approaching my hideout, I saw it was Madame d'Alvarez herself. 'Young man, why are you so sad? Why are you not joining the party?' I explained diffidently that I was really very happy, but had little to offer in such distinguished company. She sat down beside me, and learning that I was interested in music, spent the next half-hour singing to me snatches from various operas in her rich contralto voice. Needless to say, I was entranced. That evening began a loving friendship which lasted to the day she died. But the party was breaking up in the absence of the guest of honour, and I was not exactly popular for having distracted her from her role as chief guest.

The days flew by until, alas, I had to return to London at the end of four glorious weeks with the Lockes. I left Cannes regretfully, promising myself that one day, somehow, I would return. Sad to say, I was never again to be a guest there. Will Locke died before the opportunity arose. My memories of him I treasure, bound up as they are in the manuscripts and copyrights of his work which Aimée later bequeathed to me.

My next tour with the Arts League took us all the way to Scotland. So by chance I celebrated my twenty-first birthday in my native land.

On my birthday I sported a new, bright blue-green plus-fours suit, made of locally woven tweed. When I made my entrance at breakfast, Vivienne Bennett, who was in the company, put her hands in front of her eyes and turned away. 'You *can't* wear that, Leslie,' she said. But I did, and I never quite forgave her.

My mother wrote me a conciliatory birthday letter. She was very happy at long last. Owen was a paragon among husbands and *so* amusing. I sighed a sigh of relief. At last everything was working out fine, and I was happy that she was happy. To my surprise I also received a particularly well-chosen present from my new stepfather and naturally wrote him a fulsome letter of thanks.

Later when we were returning south to play for several days in Oxford, I wrote to my mother, inviting them both to come and see the show. I would arrange a room at the Mitre Hotel for them. She accepted the invitation on her own, as Owen was otherwise engaged.

This proved not only a happy weekend for us both, but gave us a rare opportunity to talk intimately to each other about our separate lives. Mother explained that she was still very happy with Owen in his Queen's Gate flat. Perhaps I could find a room reasonably near them when the tour ended? Another point she made was that Owen had *not* sent me a birthday present. She had chosen and posted it to me herself in case he forgot – which he had. In view of our all-too-brief acquaintance I could hardly blame the man for forgetting my birthday, and I told my mother so. She seemed inordinately relieved. We parted affectionately with promises to join up for Christmas with her new relatives, Owen's sister and brother-in-law.

Back in London I found new accommodation near Queen's Gate as my mother had suggested. The room was large and comfortable, with a gas-fire and French windows leading to a balcony. Things were looking up.

Christmas with my new stepfamily was not the success my mother had hoped. Their world, it seemed to me, was far removed from the world of the theatre, and I longed to get back to work and away from family involvements. My stepcousin and I had little in common, but I liked Owen's sister Hilda and her husband, Henry Dutfield. He was a real cockney, with true warmth and kindness lurking behind a sharp business brain.

Nigel Playfair came to my rescue once again. He engaged me to understudy and play in *The Beaux' Stratagem*, another *tour de force* for Edith Evans. Also in the cast was Rupert Hart Davis, whose father was a director of my former city employers, Panmure Gordon. Rupert was a giant of a young man with a voice not even the new-fangled loudspeakers could have emulated. Not that he shouted. He never had need to – his lungs sufficed. I am very glad we met. He was to be extremely helpful to me later when he abandoned the stage and turned to publishing. I like to think we are still friends.

Dear Carleton Hobbs, of BBC fame, was in the play. In a scene where I played a lascivious highwayman, I had a line to a struggling female in my grasp: 'I'll *mousle* you!' After that he always called me 'Mousler', explaining that he never saw an actor give such a dark, fruity impression of evil as I had extracted from a single phrase. However that may be, the play came to an end and I embarked on my last tour with the Arts League.

6. Pride Before a Fall

By the spring of 1928 I felt the need to reassess my value in the light of experience. I had by now acted, sung, danced, understudied and played in six London plays and performed some fifteen different characterizations in the Travelling Theatre. I had recently played the younger Pitt in a Sunday Play Society production, and studied lighting and scene design. At least I knew *something* about my job. But the success of an actor's career is not dependent so much on experience or ability as upon unexpected twists of fate. A basic fact which I was about to learn.

After a tiring and depressing day visiting London's theatrical agencies, I gave up the unequal struggle and sat myself down in a tube train to South Kensington. A familiar voice addressed me. 'Hello, old boy, how nice to see you again. What are you doing nowadays?' It was Leslie Banks.

I told him frankly my plans were as yet unformed.

'Oh, damn,' said he, 'I wish I'd known. I've been casting the new Edgar Wallace play, but it's all fixed now.'

Ah well, another opportunity lost. My face must have fallen, but I politely thanked him for the kind thought.

'Wait a moment,' he said. 'I could give you the understudy to the leading man. And would you consider playing a very effective little part I haven't cast yet?'

I hastily confirmed that my chief ambition was to be seen in the West End in *any* capacity.

'Meet me at the theatre tomorrow,' he said, 'and I'll talk to Wallace about you.'

I turned up at the stage door bright and early the following morning and was handed two pages of script by the stage-manager.

'That's *you*,' he said, pointing to the bottom of one page and the top of the other. Leslie Banks was right; it *was* a small part. In fact, it wasn't a part at all – just a series of disjointed sentences. The character was a drug addict in the dock of a magistrates' court.

'How,' I asked myself, 'do dope fiends behave? What singles them out from the crowd?' I pondered this point in the wings, while the cast rehearsed on the stage. Then I remembered an article I'd read somewhere about the effects of 'snow' on addicts, and a reference to their habit of inhaling cocaine like snuff. Of course, drug-taking then was nothing like so widespread as it has since become, so I was completely ignorant about it. Finally I decided to memorize my few lines on the spot and improvise when called upon.

At last rehearsal ceased on the stage, and stage hands began to set the scenery for the court room. Leslie Banks came over to greet me. 'Do you think you can make anything of it?' he asked. 'I've arranged you can understudy the lead.' I gratefully acknowledged this kindness and put a bright face on the minimal size of my own part.

'We don't expect you to do anything with it this morning, just read it,' he said.

'Oh, I'm a quick study,' said I nonchalantly. 'I've learnt it already.'

The scene started, and before long two stalwart characters ushered me onto the stage where I climbed slowly into the dock. Came my first cue, and I started trembling violently, sniffing my thumb and forefinger spasmodically and looking vacantly round the courtroom like a lost soul. My lines delivered, the judge gave his decision, and the two stalwarts took me, protesting, out of the dock and off the stage. I was aware that the actors in court had been astonished at this *tour de force*, and I was not at all sure I hadn't grossly overplayed.

It seemed a long time before rehearsals finished. The stage-manager beckoned me over to him. 'Mr Wallace wants a word with you,' he said. 'Good luck, boy.' I made my way through the pass door to the stalls. Edgar Wallace was in deep conversation with Leslie Banks. Seeing me standing there, he turned round and offered me his hand. 'Well done, Mitchell,' he said, 'very good. That character could be developed considerably. I've decided to write it up. I'll let you have a new script tomorrow.'

True to his word, at succeeding rehearsals he produced many more lines for me, and in due course we set off for a six-week tour before the London first night. At this time, to be taken up by Edgar Wallace was an almost certain guarantee of success. He had three plays already running in London. Also, he promised I would be given a much greater opportunity in a future production he had in mind. Heady stuff indeed.

The tour was a great success, though I had some difficulty in reconciling my cheap theatrical digs with the refined pleasures provided by kind hosts and hostesses of the Arts League. I received favourable notices from the critics. And I still have a copy of the book, *Are They the Same at Home* by Beverley Nichols, which Giles Playfair presented to me. Dated 11 March 1928, it is inscribed, 'To Leslie

Mitchell – in memory of a superb performance at Oxford.'

In the final weeks of the tour I decided to buy a second-hand motorcycle. I found a Levis two-stroke for £15. Now at last no more long-distance walks to visit scattered friends; no queuing at bus stops; no arbitrary curtailment of parties to catch a last bus. I would be my own master, free as the air, and my worries about the future began to recede.

During the last week at Lewisham Hippodrome there was very nearly a nasty accident on the stage. The scene was in a warehouse which had become the headquarters of a gang of crooks. The chief crook, played by Bill Cronin Wilson, was awaiting the arrival of one of his henchmen, played by Tarva Penna, who had been secretly acting as informer to the police. The suspense of the scene depended upon the two men circling round a desk in front of which was a carpet concealing a trapdoor with a straight drop to the river below. The trap could be opened by a secret mechanism in the desk itself – all typical Edgar Wallace stuff. Unfortunately, the scene had only just started when Tarva Penna disappeared down the trap taking with him not only the carpet but a nearby chair which he must have grabbed in passing. The audience, expecting something dramatic, were suitably impressed by the realism of his performance. Meanwhile, the horrified Cronin Wilson stood over the hole – revolver in hand – making up lines such as 'You won't get away with this, you little rat'; then, *sotto voce*, 'Are you all right, old chap?' While from the river below stage came a confused burble of voices and distant moans.

For some reason the curtain failed to come down. It seemed a long time before Tarva Penna once more made his entrance in a valiant effort to start the scene all over again. As he was covered in dust, out of breath and obviously very bruised, even the audience came to the conclusion that all was not well. At long last the curtain *did* come down, to confused applause.

I remember nothing about the accident that followed. All I know is that after the performance I left the theatre, collected my motorbike, tied my suitcase on the carrier and drove happily off. In the following months I gained practical experience of the effects of dope. Too late, alas, to incorporate into my performance in the Edgar Wallace play.

My poor mother – called from her bed at dead of night – spent a horrifying few minutes peering into the faces of patients in the Lewisham Hospital casualty ward, and quite failed to recognize me. Finally she saw my hand with the signet ring she'd given me. Of course, my head and shoulders were heavily bandaged and I was still unconscious.

Me – and my mother

My father (see top hat) with his staff at Holyrood House

Right: W. J. Locke
Above: Myself when young

Corner Hall,
the Lockes' house at Hemel Hempstead

Dr Whitehead Reid
joins up

Mrs Reid, myself and
a friend of the family
in 1918

'The Flying Doctor'
Douglas, and Mary Reid

Clewer Meade, my home, 1920

Belowstairs (far right), with A. E. Matthews, Wilfred Hyde-White
and others in *The Beggar on Horseback*

Left: Dear Angela Baddeley!

Below: Sir Nigel Playfair,
my benefactor in the theatre

Playing Lomov in Chekhov's *The Proposal*

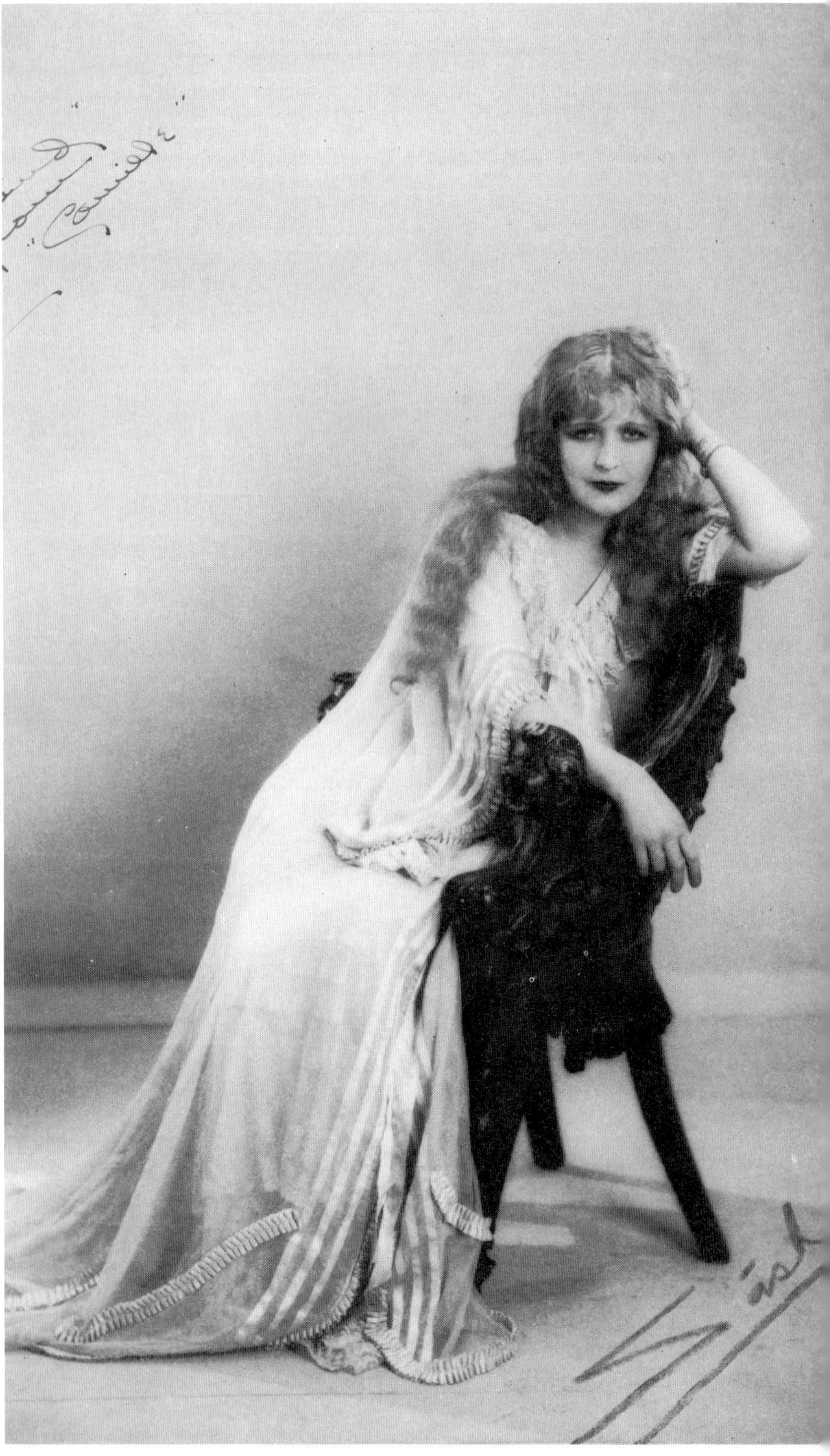

Far left: Margaret Bannerman as *La Dame aux Camellias*

Left: Dad when I met him again after twenty years

As Stanhope in *Journey's End*

Below: The letter scene in *Journey's End*, with Pat Curwen as Osborne

On the air, 1936, with Donald McCullough and
in the air – fire-fighting at Ally-Pally

Live outside broadcast with Joan Miller

good leg, threw myself on him. The ward sister rushed to the rescue as a general scene of disorder reigned. She got us back into our respective beds and sent for the house surgeon to repair any damage.

Little did that unhappy man know that he scared me into getting better. A week later Sir Charles Gordon Watson examined my leg. 'Do you know, young man, I believe there's some sign of improvement.' This time I became more interested. And he was right.

Eventually I was well enough to leave the hospital. I had become devoted to the nuns and nurses who had looked after me so well. But the time had come to look forward again.

Sir Charles came to see me. 'I'm rather bothered about a small matter, young man. Perhaps you could explain for me. I sent my account to your father and he returned it to me. He says that he is *not* your father, and the responsibility is entirely yours.'

I went cold with dismay, then hot with embarrassment. 'I don't know how to apologize, sir,' I whispered. 'He's my *step*father, and I have no money at all till I get work again. I'm most terribly sorry. I had no idea he'd be like this.'

Sir Charles was not only a great surgeon, he was also an exceedingly kind man. 'Let's leave it like this, Mitchell. When you become a star, send me a cheque for twenty-five guineas and we can forget about the whole thing.' I promised gratefully. I learned later that my stepfather had arranged a fee of £3 a week with the hospital, as 'he had taken an interest in a young man who had no money'. Charmed by his obvious desire to do good, they had admitted me for the minimum fee.

When I was about to leave, they wheeled me into the grounds and left me in the fresh air and warm sunshine. It was wonderful to be out and about again. I thought once more of the future. My face was still scarred, but rapidly improving; my leg was still in plaster. I decided to try and walk. As I took my first unsteady steps, it seemed the entire hospital emptied. Nuns, nurses and doctors racing towards me. 'Stop, Mr Mitchell.' 'Don't get up. Stay in your chair.' 'Do be careful.' A tearful sister helped to handle me back into the chair. 'How could you? After all we've tried to do for you. How *could* you?'

But I *had* to get back to work again; I *had* to make my leg work.

Since then it has become accepted medical practice to make patients walk on their damaged limbs at the earliest possible moment.

The doctors insisted that I should have a reasonable period of convalescence, and somehow my mother persuaded my stepfather to take me with them on a three-week holiday to the Belgian coast. In due course, they collected me from hospital and we set off for Le Zoute. I was bothered by being so much of an encumbrance. I was not yet capable of walking unaided, so had to be manhandled on and off the ship, in and out of taxis, and up to my hotel room which adjoined theirs.

It was a fine summer's night and we all retired to bed early. I was awakened by sounds of confusion and loud voices, the slam of a door and the noise of running footsteps in the corridor. My mother came to my room. 'Are you awake?' she said. 'Poor Owen, a terrible thing has happened.' I looked at her in alarm, but she was choking back the inclination to laugh. It turned out that my stepfather had carefully placed all his French notes on the dressing-table in the corner of their room between two french windows. A sudden breeze had whisked the money into the street below. For more than an hour he was away scrabbling in the dust and sand in search of the missing money. When it became light enough to see more clearly, he found he was still short.

He came to my room in a furious temper and gave me a lecture about the expense and trouble that I had caused by my selfishness and stupidity. What was more, he made it clear that after this holiday was over, I must support myself whatever the circumstances. I agreed, and set about getting myself fit with wholehearted dedication.

One of my favourite sports was swimming so, having placed my gown on the beach in a sandpit, I hobbled into the water and started swimming vigorously. I had gone about fifty yards out to sea when there was a sudden tremendous pain in my arm and shoulder. Finding it impossible to use the arm, I somehow managed to make my way back to the beach. From the nearby crowd, a complete stranger ran towards me, threw me on my back, sat on my chest, heaved on my arm savagely, slapped me hard on both cheeks, and went on his way. I can only suppose he was a doctor. Nobody had warned me that I had a permanently dislocating arm.

Nevertheless, by the time we returned to England, I *was* capable of walking without crutches. My mother took a room for me. Once again I started my search for work.

Naturally, one of my first visits was to the Lyceum Theatre where *The Flying Squad* was still running. My part in the play had been taken over by none other than my old school friend Carol Reed. I was given a great welcome by the stage-manager who decided, as a joke, to smuggle me in as a member of the jury. Although Carol had not been warned of my reappearance, he was far too professional to be put off when I suddenly caught his eye.

I had hoped Edgar Wallace might have another part for me as he had promised. Unfortunately, the time was not yet ripe. So once again I turned to Nigel Playfair who offered me a job as assistant stage-manager and understudy to the leading juvenile in the Lyric production of Martinez Sierra's play *A Hundred Years Old*.

The production was notable in many respects. The producer was Harley Granville-Barker, whose name in the theatre had long been internationally recognized. The stage-manager was James Whale, who also designed the scenery. James was, of course, an old friend, as was Angela Baddeley who played a leading part. She was later succeeded by Celia Johnson, playing her first major role in London. Another up-and-coming young actress, Peggy Ashcroft, was also in the cast. One of the understudies, knitting inconspicuously in the wings night after night, was Margaret Rutherford, later to become the international darling of stage and films. That fine old actor Horace Hodges played the central character of the centenarian.

This was a remarkably lucky engagement for me as I still bore marks of my accident and had little self-confidence in my appearance. The business of stage-management kept me happily employed whilst I used the breathing space to study the sensitive production methods of Granville-Barker.

Shortly after the first night, I was called upon to play the juvenile lead. After the performance, Granville-Barker came to the dressing-room. 'Congratulations,' he said, 'that was exactly how it should be played.' Although I only appeared for that one performance, his words did more for my morale than any medical treatment.

There was another booster to my ego at this time. I fell in love with a young actress in the play, Bunty Cobb. I realize now how difficult it must have been for her to put up with my constant aches and pains, but we were both young and happy together. Bunty's mother, Gladys Cobb, also worked in the theatre in stage design and was a close friend of Leslie Banks and Edith Evans. She accepted me with affection as a suitable escort for her daughter, and I became almost as fond of her as I was of Bunty.

In due course Bunty and I became engaged, although the prospect of marriage remained steadfastly out of reach. One evening we started a quarrel about nothing. A typical lovers' tiff. When she had gone, I poured myself a large double whisky and drank it, followed by yet another.

As it happened, my mother came round to visit me and found me crying like a child. As it was impossible to stop me, she rang for a doctor. 'This boy has hysteria,' he said, 'and he seems to have been drinking. Has he been ill recently?' After being given my medical history, he expressly forbade me ever to drink whisky again. 'He's probably had severe concussion,' he added. And nobody denied it.

I never drank whisky again – and me a Scot.

One day, towards the end of the run of the play, James Whale casually handed me a manuscript. 'You might read this, Leslie. Tell me what you think of it.'

I took the script back to my room and started to read it. Then I read it again. I phoned him. 'This play,' I said, 'is terrific – absolutely wonderful. It has only one drawback, it's all about the war.'

'That's the whole point,' he replied, 'there hasn't been a really good play about the 1914–18 war, and I think this is it. How would you like to play the lead?' He went on to explain that it was being put on by the Incorporated Stage Society for a Sunday night performance – to allow London critics and theatre managers to see it. It wasn't to be produced until the following month; so he told me to keep the script and take time to study the part.

My spirits soared. It provided an opportunity to appear in a beautifully written leading role – the sort of opportunity any actor dreams about. For two weeks I sat studying the script in every spare moment, memorizing, and trying to improve on my interpretation.

Some days later James and I met as usual at the theatre. 'By the way, Leslie,' he said, 'about that play. I'm terribly sorry, I'm having second thoughts about it – just met a young man I believe might have the edge on you for that part.'

My heart sank. 'Anyone I know?' I asked.

'No, I don't think so,' said James nonchalantly. 'I think the fair thing is to invite you both to lunch on Sunday so that I can see you together and make up my mind. Would you come?'

Baring my teeth in what I hoped was a smile, I accepted.

For me the lunch was not particularly enjoyable, but the other young man seemed completely at ease. He exuded charm and self-assurance; in fact, he showed all the characteristics which I felt I lacked. Nevertheless, we parted cordially enough and I returned to my rooms.

In the evening James telephoned me. 'I hate doing this, Leslie, but I really think the other chap must play it. It's essential for me to get this play absolutely right. But I promise you, I'll make it up to you later.'

The play was *Journey's End*, and my successful rival – Laurence Olivier – then comparatively unknown.

I need hardly dwell upon my disappointment, but the torment was not entirely over. Two weeks later, there was another phone call. James Whale again.

'Leslie, do you remember anything about *Journey's End*?'

'I should,' I replied evenly. 'I studied it hard enough.'

'Well, Larry's lost his voice,' said James, 'and may not be able to play. Can you come to rehearsal straight away?' I raced out and took a taxi to the theatre. But on the Saturday Larry reappeared – his voice in perfect melodic order – and on the Sunday night I moodily paced the wings standing by for the emergency which never came. Looking up the original programme for that performance, I now realize that I *did* play the very small part of 'a soldier' – a fact I had completely forgotten, remembering only how I lost the leading part.

Shortly afterwards, Leslie Banks engaged me to understudy him and play a part in *The Lady with a Lamp* with Edith Evans, who as Florence Nightingale was to give yet another memorable performance. We were busily rehearsing the play, and a week before the opening night I received yet another urgent call from James Whale. *Journey's End was* to be put on in a West End theatre. Laurence Olivier, on the strength of his performance on the Sunday night, had been snapped up by Basil Dean for a production of *Beau Geste*. James had decided I was the only possible replacement for him, and told me the part was mine if I wanted it.

I listened, torn by indecision. After all I had been engaged for a play which looked like being successful. It would be base ingratitude to leave it at such short notice, so soon before the first night. Quite apart from earning a reputation for being unreliable, I owed my loyalty to Leslie Banks for his kindness to me in the past. This time the position was reversed. I turned the offer down. So *Journey's End* entered on its long and brilliant success with Colin Clive playing the leading part.

The Lady with a Lamp ran smoothly and successfully for six months. During the run, Leslie Banks was taken ill, and I played his part. This led to one of the more embarrassing moments of my career. There was a touching scene in which I was carried on a stretcher into the hospital at Scutari, delirious and badly wounded. In the play I had been Florence Nightingale's unsuccessful suitor, so it was a particularly dramatic situation for her to discover me there after years of separation. She bent over me. As I lay on the stretcher shouting incoherent military commands in my delirium, the dental plate which I inherited from my accident fell with a clatter to the floor. I wished I could have died. Fortunately, the part demanded that I should.

This was not my only mishap. I was also playing the character of the Jewish purveyor of stores at Scutari and while dressing for the part, dislocated my shoulder. This had become a permanent hazard, and the shoulder could only be put back by a doctor. The theatre doctor was called and, taking little notice of my explanation, he proceeded to push the arm further out of the socket instead of returning it there. Then realizing I knew what I was talking about, he tried the correct method, and it went back like a cannon ball.

At the close of the performance, I went to apologize to Edith Evans for my non-appearance. 'My dear boy, what happened?' she asked. I explained about my shoulder. 'Ah, is that all?' she said. 'I was afraid it was something serious.' Of course she was a confirmed Christian Scientist.

On the last night of *The Lady with a Lamp,* I received a visit from the manager of the Prince of Wales Theatre. 'Are you free on Monday?' he asked. 'Colin Clive is leaving *Journey's End* for three weeks for his honeymoon with Jeanne de Casalis. We've had a cable from James Whale telling us to get you for the part.'

The following Monday found me playing Stanhope in *Journey's End* – at last. One of my proudest possessions is the programme with my name surrounded by those in the original production whose performances are still remembered by countless theatregoers.

Shortly afterwards, an agency put me under contract, then sent me to Elstree for an interview with a director who was casting a war film. The great man was seated behind a battery of telephones and signalled me to sit down. He carried out an impressive number of telephone calls in which the names of stars and quite astronomical sums of money were loudly mentioned. Eventually, the last receiver replaced, he turned to me and asked me what I wanted. In the film he was casting, there was the part of a young army captain. This was the role the agency had in mind when they sent me to see him.

After I had explained this to him, he half rose from the desk to get a better look at me. 'My dear fellow, you were never in the army, were you? Frankly, you're nothing like it. We are looking for a chap who looks like the real thing. You know, Cavalry Club, Sandhurst. Shoulders back, chin up and all that.' Hastily springing to my feet, I demonstrated that this was well within my capabilities. 'I am afraid not,' he said wearily, 'not really you, is it? Come and see me again some time, there might be something.'

Desperate not to miss the chance, I stood my ground. 'Would you mind taking my name?'

He looked up apologetically. 'My dear fellow, how very rude of me.' I told him, and his jaw dropped. 'You're not the chap from *Journey's End*, are you? Good heavens, why didn't you say so? We're waiting to give you a test in the studio.' I got the test, but not the part.

Elstree in those early days was at the beginnings of the British film boom, and was run by two entirely separate camps. In one the directors who had spent their life in the theatre and knew very little about film people. In the other, people who'd spent their life in films and knew very little of the theatre.

Type-casting has always been the bugbear of the actor. Once an artist has been particularly successful he or she is doomed to play the same type of part for years afterwards, unless they have a lucky break and make an equal success in something quite different. So it was no great surprise when I was invited by the BBC to play in *Journey's End* for what I believe was their first 'international hook-up' on Armistice Night, 1929.

Radio was a new experience for me and on this occasion a little unnerving. One missed the atmosphere of the theatre and the reactions of an audience. Most difficult of all, Howard Rose, the producer, was insistent that all swear words should be deleted from the play. As he explained, radio was heard by 'the family' in the privacy of their home and the family might very well include old ladies, parsons, young children and others whose sensitivities might be offended, were we to use the original script.

Obediently trying out this regulation at rehearsal, it seemed to me that it made the character sound more and more effeminate. Lines like 'You b . . . .y little swine' sounded very watery without the b . . . .y. Anyway, when it came to the actual broadcast, my enthusiasm and my knowledge of the part made me revert to the original lines. Even worse, rehearsals had imprinted the word 'bloody' on my mind, which made me say it even more often than it occurred in the play.

In spite of the success of the broadcast, it was some years before I was invited to broadcast for the BBC again. However, the fame of *Journey's End* had spread throughout the world and there was a steady stream of touring companies leaving London for America, Canada, Australia, and other English-speaking countries. So when I was invited to go to South Africa with the play, I readily agreed. It was a chance to see a new country, and to get the part of Stanhope out of my system.

7. A Glimpse of the Sun

On 11 July 1930 we sailed from Southampton in the *Kenilworth Castle*. The second day out I developed an abscess in my jaw. There was no dentist on board, so for two days I made no appearance in the dining-room. On the third night I retired early to my cabin, undressed and rested on my bunk. Before long, there was a gentle tap on the door. Outside stood a charming young American girl. 'Mr Mitchell,' she said sweetly, 'you don't know me, but *we-all* have been so unhappy about you and this terrible pain you are having. I want you to know we have just been praying for you!'

In my dressing-gown and pyjamas I felt slightly on the wrong foot, but invited her in. 'Well, how nice,' I said rather feebly. 'Tell me, who are *you*-all?'

'Why, the Group,' she said, 'the Group.' Absolutely mystifying. But she was a very attractive girl, and it wasn't long before she had persuaded me to kneel down and say a silent prayer.

Visions of our innocent occupation being disturbed by the steward decided me to make a move. 'This is very charming of you,' I said, with a sort of swollen leer, 'but do you think God would approve of attractive women envoys visiting a bachelor's cabin at this time of night?'

'It's not like that,' she said firmly. 'I must go now.' It transpired that she was one of a team from the Oxford Group, now known as Moral Rearmament. The following night her husband replaced her and we-all became friends. We met up on a number of occasions in South Africa when our tour coincided with theirs.

Another member of the Group with whom I became friendly was Campbell Mitchell Cotts who, from his family's shipping connections, knew most of the leading South Africans, and provided a number of introductions for me while I was touring. In fact, through our friendship, I was invited to stay with the Gwelo Goodmans when we arrived in Cape Town. One of South Africa's foremost painters, Gwelo and his wife were among the leading hosts of Cape Town society. Among their close friends was Princess Alice, whose husband, the Earl of Athlone, was then Governor-General. They were frequent visitors to the Goodmans' house at Newlands.

Princess Alice personified that royal gift of being able to put everyone at their ease. In spite of her simplicity and charm, one never forgot that she was a representative of the Crown. And even while she was chatting with you privately, it was obvious that little happening elsewhere escaped her attention. How few of us appreciate the heavy strain placed on members of the royal family: names to be remembered, precedence and protocol to be observed, and every moment of the day under the critical eyes of strangers, who expect them to be smiling and gracious whatever their private feelings or state of health.

A small example of this almost incredible attention to detail came when I drove Campbell to Government House where he went to leave his card. In spite of my having already being 'presented', Campbell gave me to understand that it would not be accepted form to leave a card myself, since I was only an 'actor' – traditionally bound up with rogues and vagabonds.

At our next meeting a few days later, Princess Alice turned to me quietly and said, 'Mr Mitchell, I thought I saw you drive up to Government House the other day. I looked for your card and couldn't find it.'

Colouring with embarrassment, I blurted an apology. 'You see, Ma'am, it occurred to me that since I am only an actor ... '

'Mr Mitchell,' she interrupted, '*you* are a professional man. Mr Cotts, your companion, is after all, in commerce. We should be pleased to receive your card.'

The Goodmans gave a ball at which the Athlones were present. It was, of course, impossible for me to be there until after the performance of the play in Cape Town. When I eventually joined the festivities, it was a pleasant surprise to find that a dance had been officially reserved for me with their daughter, Lady May Cambridge, to whom I was formally presented. We danced together, and as the music stopped, I turned to her and invited her out into the garden. 'Do let me show you the new Jersey calf,' I said. 'She's in the barn here – I call her the Jersey Lily.' We had gone no more than a few steps before we were halted by two young attachés who 'invited' her to return to the ballroom. Not for the first time I had stepped out of turn.

The press notices for *Journey's End* were unanimously good. The general comment about me was astonishment that such a convincing performance could be given by someone who had been too young to take part in the war.

I have mentioned that owing to my head injuries the doctor advised me never to drink whisky. Unfortunately, the part of Stanhope demanded that I should drink whisky in copious amounts throughout the performance. Luckily, it was in reality only coloured water, so no great harm was done, but on the night of my twenty-fourth birthday, the cast arranged that only the *real* stuff should be provided (we were regularly provided with it by the distillers as an advertisement). I innocently drank the first mouthful, spluttered, coughed furiously and shouted for my batman. 'Mason,' I yelled, 'bring another bottle, this tastes filthy.' He promptly produced yet another bottle of Haig. How I got through three acts of this, I cannot remember, but there was whisky on the floor, over the table, and slopped all down my uniform. I only hope the audience did get the impression I had been drinking it.

The time came to continue the tour. The next date was Johannesburg. The city stands some 5500 feet above sea level, and the innocent traveller is liable to find climbing stairs or making any kind of physical effort something of a strain until he becomes acclimatized. We had most of us thought of Africa in terms of Livingstone and Stanley, hacking our way through jungle paths with native bearers, sweating under tropical sun. Several of us had prepared for these discomforts by buying pith-helmets, shorts and bush-jackets in London. Arriving after an interminable train journey, we found the streets of Johannesburg blanketed in snow. We were assured by everybody – 'This *never* happens!' It *did* for us.

The fame of *Journey's End* had spread from Cape Town and once again the play received ecstatic reactions. At a party we were given, I sat next to a rather gushing young woman who inquired how I found it possible to keep up with all my fan mail. Under the impression she was joking, I replied flippantly that it would require the services of at least half a dozen secretaries. I should have known better. The lady was a reporter on the *Rand Daily Mail*. My remark was quoted in her column the following morning. Needless to say, the rest of the cast diligently set about writing imaginative love letters and pleas from love-lorn secretaries which continued to swell my mail for weeks afterwards. One of them, I remember, said, 'I feel I might appeal to you; I work in a bacon factory and am used to hams.' I knew better than to reply to any of them.

One night, in the bar of the Carlton Hotel, a diffident little man approached me. 'Excuse me sir, are you Mr Leslie Mitchell?' he asked. 'I have a message from your father.'

'From whom?' I asked incredulously.

'Your father, sir,' he repeated.

'I'm afraid there's some mistake, my friend. My father was killed in the war; it must be a case of mistaken identity.'

He went away with no further comment, and I forgot about it.

The following evening the same man approached me again. 'Your father wants to see you,' he insisted. 'He told me to show you these.' There in an envelope was a picture of my mother, together with letters in her handwriting and a photograph of myself when young.

Still suspicious I began to think this was a new line of blackmail. 'If it's really my father wanting to see me, he only has to come here. Why should he send you?'

He tactfully lowered his voice. 'He thought you might not want to see him in view of the trouble with your mother.'

Still not knowing what he was talking about, I arranged that 'my father' should meet me outside the broadcasting station from which I was to give a talk the following day. Sure enough, when I left the building after the broadcast a man was standing there, his face in the shadow. I stared, prepared for anything from a thug to a complete stranger. As he approached there emerged an older version of the face I knew only from pictures in my childhood. He smiled and drew me to him. 'My boy,' he said, 'my boy.' His voice was choked.

Unbelievably it *was* my father. There could be no mistake. As we stood there, grasping each other's hands, there were tears in our eyes. Memories from my childhood and questions about the years between filled our minds.

Over a late dinner after the show that evening I learned for the first time *his* account of the break-up of his marriage to my mother. He'd been astonished to learn from the messenger that I thought he was dead, and even more surprised that I knew nothing about the divorce.

'I suppose you were too young to take it in,' he said.

'I've just worked out I must have been about seven at the time, Dad,' I replied. He enjoyed me calling him 'Dad'.

As we talked I noticed that several times he gently stroked his nose between his thumb and forefinger.

'That's a habit I'm always being ticked off for. Where on earth did you pick that up,' I inquired.

He stared at me with a smile. 'Where on earth did *you* pick it up?' he asked meaningly. For a moment I'd forgotten he was my father in fact.

Like my mother he had remarried. He wasted no time in introducing me to Rose, his wife, and Thelma, her attractive fifteen-year-old daughter by a previous marriage. We all quickly became firm friends. Much of my spare time was spent with my new-found family. I hired a car, they would bring the picnic basket, and we would make sightseeing tours through the Transvaal.

It was Rose who told me much about my father that he was too reserved to tell me himself. Apparently after my mother had left him, taking me with her, his business went slowly to pieces, as he did himself. He had always bitterly regretted losing us, but life had become too much for him, and he began to drink. When war broke out, he joined up, like the majority of men of his age and responsibility. After the war, having lost everything, he decided to emigrate to South Africa where one of his elder married sisters lived. Since that time he had completely lost touch with England. From what I learned, my father now had little money, but he certainly had many devoted friends. Some of them, like him, had fought in the war.

The week before Armistice Day, a lively group of characters arrived at the stage door and demanded to see me. With them was my father. I settled them in my dressing-room with appropriate refreshments while I returned to the stage for the last act. On my return they introduced themselves as members of the MOTHS. I took this to mean they had some connection with the De Havilland Aircraft Company which produced the famous Moth light aeroplane. There was some misunderstanding until they explained they were members of the South African Ex-service Organization – the Memorable Order of Tin Hats. They went on to say they had decided I was to lead their ceremonial parade to the Johannesburg War Memorial on 11 November, Armistice Day. It was obvious they had been celebrating, to say the least, and in spite of all my objections, they man-handled me, still in my uniform, into a waiting car, in which I was driven to a nearby drill hall. Luckily I called for other members of the cast to join us, which they did as soon as they were changed.

Here I was, still in stage uniform and make-up, embarrassed and rather angry. The hall was in darkness, but for a solitary lighted candle stuck on the top of a tin hat on the table in front of the officer in charge. I stood there helplessly. After a few moments he looked over in my direction.

'Captain Stanhope?' Playing with the tide, I stepped forward three paces. 'Captain,' he continued with heavy solemnity, 'in view of your distinguished record, it is my honour to inform you that we have decided to initiate you as a member of our ex-service organization.'

Panic began to overtake me. 'Sir,' I replied, 'I must explain at once that I was never in the war.'

'Never in the war?'

'No, sir, I was too young.'

'Well, you can't have been too young to earn the ribbon of the MC you've got up there.'

By now the ceremony was taking on a nightmarish quality.

'My name is not Stanhope, sir, it is Mitchell – and the uniform including the MC is worn by me as an actor who has been called upon to perform the part of a captain.'

Confusion reigned.

'But,' I went on, 'other members of the company *did* serve in the war and those of them here would be only too glad to accept membership.' I then slunk back into the darkness and watched my fellow-actors go through the drill.

We met with an extraordinary lack of sophistication among South African audiences. In many places, hypnotized by the realistic atmosphere of the play they took acting for reality. Many of them had travelled hundreds of miles to see a performance which was often their first visit to a professional theatre. I had quite a number of letters chiding me for the bad example I set young South Africans by allowing myself to become drunk on stage. My part in the play also provided a fund of rumours concerning my private life. One story going the rounds was that the men under my command during the war had decided to shoot me when next we went over the top; but I had been hurriedly transferred. I was also credited with a wife and an unknown number of children who had been treated with great brutality during my frequent bouts of drunkenness. This grew to be a current source of gossip in the smaller communities out there.

For my birthday, my stepfather had sent me an uncashable cheque for £1 drawn on an English bank. I decided to equate his generosity with a suitable Christmas present. During the many halts on our train journeys, groups of natives offered animal skins and wood-carvings for sale to passing tourists. I chose a splendid, but uncured skin and sent it off forthwith with seasonal greetings. In its raw condition, it could have well made part of the journey on its own. With some satisfaction I learnt later that it cost my stepfather £15 to have it cured and mounted as a rug for the car.

We toured Rhodesia with equal success visiting Umtali, Bulawayo and Salisbury, where our mail from England caught up with us.

All in one packet I found (a) a letter from my mother telling me of the imminent failure of her third marriage and threatening suicide as the only way out of the situation. This worried me particularly. I well knew she was prone to carry out the threat, and there was absolutely nothing I could do about it; (b) a letter from Mary Reid in Canterbury, telling me in heartbreaking terms of the death of Douglas in a flying accident; and (c) an apologetic letter from my fiancée breaking off our engagement, as she had decided to marry someone else.

I went through the play that evening automatically. The combined effect of the three letters stunned me. As the last curtain fell, I was only grateful the play was over, and I had not done anything untoward. When we took the curtain calls, I was astounded to see the audience standing to applaud and calling for me by name. This is a pretty rare experience for any young actor. Could my nervous tension have been so reflected in my performance that it actually improved it? The character of Stanhope is, of course, under a considerable strain through the three acts of the play. But normally the temptation on stage is to get your effects by using tricks of the trade. Anyway, that is an evening I'll never forget.

We returned to Johannesburg. Here at a party I met K., an amusing and attractive young Italian woman. Being footloose and rather conscious of it, I took her to the door of her suite in our hotel. We were both tired, but she invited me in, and I joined her for a last drink.

Being short of cigarettes, I asked her if I could order some. She rang for the waiter who quickly brought some. Before leaving I pursued the mystery of her nationality. It transpired that she was English, but separated from an Italian husband to whom she had no intention of returning. Out of politeness I asked if I might pay for my cigarettes.

'Don't be ridiculous, my dear man,' she said, 'everything is paid for.'

'By whom?' I asked.

Her reply put paid to any plans I might have had about our relationship. Her bills were being paid by one of South Africa's leading millionaires. I soon made my excuses and went my way to my room. What a fool I was. Of course, she couldn't look like that or live like that without a rich boy friend.

Two days later there was a phone call to my room. It was K., my young Italian friend. 'What happened to you,' she inquired.

'Oh nothing,' I said airily; 'been rather caught up with this and that.'

'No, I mean why did your whole manner change before you left the other night. Was it something I said?'

I explained it hadn't occurred to me that she was going round with Mr X.

'Going *round* with him?' She screamed with laughter. 'He's my stepfather!' It was only good manners to join her again after the show to apologize. This time I stayed a little longer.

In due course we met again in Cape Town; as it turned out, we sailed together in the new *Winchester Castle*.

On board there was a letter waiting for me from my father. In it he wrote: 'My dear boy, . . . It has been a great delight and event for me to be reunited to you, and I trust things will improve for all of us and that I may be able to help you in the near future. . . .' But Fate was against us both.

My mother met me at the boat-train on arrival in London. She seemed well, but preoccupied. Before long she explained she had left my stepfather, and there was a room for me at the hotel in which she was staying.

This time it was obviously up to me to try and do something about the situation. The following day I went to see my stepfather. In due course he and my mother were reunited and decided to go on an extensive holiday cruise. My mother suggested I should act as care-taker in their London flat while they were away, which seemed to suit us all admirably.

They had been away less than a week when I found myself without gas, light or telephone services. My stepfather had omitted to pay the bills before he left. However, with the aid of numerous candles, I decided to carry on regardless.

It was 1931 – the year Gracie Fields made *Sally in our Alley*. Anxious to get my foot back in the door in any way I snapped up a tiny part in a dance scene. Basil Dean's casting director insisted I should provide full evening-dress – top hat and tails, the lot. All the white articles, he demanded, should be sent to the studio wardrobe for treatment. 'It's nothing much,' he said blithely. 'We dye them yellow to stop them "flaring". It all comes out in the wash.' But it didn't. I was paid £5 for the day, but a new shirt, tie, collar and waistcoat cost rather more.

Years later they showed the film on TV. I had lots of letters asking if it was me dancing with Our Gracie. It was.

Shortly afterwards I got another offer to appear in a film as an extra. The scene involved a crowd of businessmen at a station, and we all had to wear bowler hats and overcoats. Having no bowler, I borrowed my stepfather's and shot off to the studios for the day. We were all lined up before the take and a studio hand sprayed us, one by one, with a mixture of paraffin and water, so that the 'rain' would show up on the film. My borrowed bowler looked a bit worse for wear when I guiltily placed it back on the hatstand.

These jobs didn't exactly improve my financial status, and the return of my mother and stepfather meant I had to leave their flat, and explain why the premises were in total darkness, without light, gas or telephone.

Friends encouraged me to have another go at making my fame and fortune in films. So when I found myself one day at Walton-on-Thames facing a large placard inscribed 'To the Film Studios' this seemed a good omen. The gatekeeper was helpful. 'Left at the end of the building, sir, second on the left.' The office he had indicated was empty, but seeing a chink of light under a door, I knocked and went in. I found myself face to face with Michael Powell, yet another film director with whom I had been at school.

'Good Lord,' he said. 'Why on earth didn't I think of you? You're absolutely right for it.' It transpired that the part he had in mind was a 'red herring' in the plot of a whodunit; in fact I was supposed to look and behave villainously before the real villain was unmasked. The film was called *Rynox* and the leading man was Stewart Rome. I remember little about it except (having been warned that microphones reacted to false teeth by producing a whistle), I pronounced all my S's like Z's which may have added to the villainy of my performance, but little to its distinction.

In spite of this, I got a part in Basil Dean's film production of *From Nine Till Six* with Elizabeth Allan. Some of you may remember this famous all-woman play about a dress-shop in Mayfair. Like all film scripts, the story was changed and two *men* were introduced into the plot: me and Richard Bird. So I can claim not only to have appeared in an all-*male* production – *Journey's End*, but in an all-*female* production as well!

Meanwhile I got another understudy – this time to the leading man in *Grand Hotel*, an old chum, Hugh Williams. During the run of the play I got to know a young Russian actress in the cast, Nina Bucknall, and her boyfriend Gordon Latta who was working on the adaptation of a French comedy. *Grand Hotel* eventually ground to a halt after six months. It was what might be called a 'mass' production, with what seemed like hundreds of small parts and consequently overcrowded dressing-rooms. Somehow it lacked the personal atmosphere of theatre. One had the impression of spending one's evenings at Liverpool Street railway station.

Gordon Latta's translation of *The Heart Line* was by now in rehearsal and being produced by Komisarjevsky at the Lyric Theatre. It was a small cast with Maurice Evans, Ann Todd and Jeanne de Casalis as the stars. So I was thrilled when I was asked if I would meet Komisarjevsky to discuss a part in the play. They were having difficulty in casting Jeanne's middle-aged husband. To my surprise, he immediately agreed to engage me. They had been rehearsing for some time, so I had to learn the lines very quickly. By the third day I was standing by ready to rehearse with Ann Todd and Jeanne de Casalis.

Komisarjevsky, however, seemed to have lost interest and continued to concentrate on other parts of the production. Eventually I was compelled to appeal to him to rehearse me, since my own scenes were not particularly easy and the opening night was fast approaching. It was only then he revealed to me that he had earlier decided the part had little value in the play, and had thoughts of cutting it out altogether. Fortunately he changed his mind, so I duly appeared.

The play was an amusing trifle in the French idiom, very well translated. But although it had a prestige success, it was a box-office flop and they had to take it off after only a few weeks.

Since getting back to England from South Africa, my romance with K. had blossomed in spite of all obstacles. So when she decided to buy a runabout, I was on hand to advise her. Although she was related to a millionaire, she was rich in prospect rather than in fact. Meanwhile she had to live modestly on a small income. Thus I picked for her a neat little car which would suffice for her needs – the Wolseley Hornet, a fabulous little bus.

K. herself did not really enjoy driving, so when *The Heart Line* came off prematurely early in the summer of 1932, she suggested we might go on a holiday trip if I was willing to drive the car. I agreed to this idea without much persuasion.

We decided to visit Spain and Morocco. Setting out from Dieppe, we went through France to the Spanish border. The Spanish Revolution was over, King Alfonso had left his country the year before and we continued with no difficulty to Burgos. Before we left the town, we found a knot of Spaniards standing fascinated by the smallness of the car. K. was able to speak quite fluently with the locals. I was then at the stage of *'No comprendo'* or *'Buenos dias'*. French was not generally understood any better than English.

In Madrid I remember being charmed by a notice left over from the Revolution advising citizens to keep off the streets as there would be machine-gun and rifle fire between 4 and 6 p.m. Presumably this was to allow opposing Spanish parties to finish their lunch, which traditionally starts well after 2 p.m.

K. decided to go luxurious in Madrid and stay at one of the best hotels. We were both tired and rather dusty, so I agreed. Having dropped her with the luggage at the main entrance, I drove the car round to the garage. When I returned to the reception desk, the manager gave me an ingratiating smile. 'The lady has already gone up, sir,' he said.

I rushed to the room. It was a double room as I had feared. 'Darling,' I said, 'have you gone barmy, You've left your Italian passport with the management! Your husband can easily cancel it and force you to return to Italy! Especially if he finds out you're not alone.'

Fortunately in the foyer I met a character whom I had always imagined was something in MI5. We fell on each other's necks. 'How extraordinary, Leslie,' he said. 'Fancy meeting *you* here. Seems like a day of coincidences. Guess who else I just met from London?' I had already guessed.

We all met for drinks. I found he was well known to the hotel manager so he agreed to persuade him that my passport had been temporarily mislaid. We made our way to the car early next morning and drove off south.

Our next stop was a medium-sized town, which was in the throes of a fiesta. There seemed to be no accommodation available; every hotel was full to overflowing. Eventually at a reasonable hotel, they offered me a room. I jumped at it, but there was a snag. It was only a single bedroom. Fine by me – I would look elsewhere; our experience in Madrid had taught me a lesson.

The proprietor was not optimistic. 'There is nowhere, señor; I know. Other clients have told me. There is nowhere. The fiesta is a big occasion for us. You will find nothing.'

Having this time introduced K. as my married sister, I found it hard to convince him that we insisted on separate rooms. 'Señor – I will arrange something specially for you! It is a large room. Wait, and I will show you.'

When I arrived, the room certainly was very large and very long. At the distant end was K. seated on her bed; in the middle were two confessional screens in open lattice-work over which large Spanish shawls had been discreetly thrown to conform to my social sensitivities. At the near end was a bed for me. The niceties were satisfied.

Spain is such a glorious country, the landscape is ever changing. The life is hard, even harsh for its people, but they have a dignity and moral code which compels admiration. They react fiercely to double-dealing, but once they accept you, they treat you and yours with generosity and friendship.

Our AA route suggested at one point that we could save a needless fifty-mile detour by going a few miles along a dried-up river bed. It was the appropriate season, so I determined to take the river route. Half an hour later we came across a dam of mud and rocks, stretching eighteen inches high from bank to bank. Getting out to investigate, in the barren emptiness of the valley, I realized that at one point there was a slight incline towards the top of the obstruction. I removed some projecting rocks, then telling K. to stand clear, I got into the car and attempted a running jump. There was a very nasty bang. We were over, but the engine had stopped. The battery was torn from its brackets. Before we could discuss what to do, the river bed was alive with Spaniards – heaven knows where they had been hiding – who told us to stay put, and they 'would fix.'

We got back into the car. In due course a horse was introduced, attached to a rope. Half an hour later we were sitting at a table drinking sherry, while from a nearby garage came the exclamations of astonished mechanics. They, too, had never seen so small a car. Before leaving the following morning, I asked for the bill from the garage, but they firmly refused to accept payment. *O hasta la vista* – courtesies like that are rare indeed today.

The most interesting part of the tour was to Marrakesh, and it certainly was the most testing part for the Wolseley Hornet. From Ceuta we drove to Tangiers which we explored for a couple of days and visited the Sukh. It was my first experience of an Arab country, and I was learning fast how to barter for everything you wanted to buy. We drove through Rabat, that interesting old fortress town, to the shining modern city of Casablanca, immortalized by Ingrid Bergman and Humphrey Bogart. The dusty roads gave way to more sandy tracks as we drove further south, eventually reaching Marrakesh, tired and exhausted. But it was worth it. Marrakesh was a revelation, particularly the royal palace and its lovely grounds. This of course was long before it became a regular haunt of tourists, or a wartime meeting place for heads of state!

And I shall always remember the young native girl – about twelve years old – who helped me to barter for a pair of *babouches* (open leather slippers, decorated with coloured designs). She had attached herself to me in the bazaar and dragged me from one merchant to another. They were all asking too much, she explained, and I could not resist her great, olive eyes as she finally commanded, *'Demain ici, à six heures'* (tomorrow here at six o'clock). I turned up, and we finished back at the very first stall where I finally got my slippers for a song. My guide's eyes nearly popped out when I gave her the money she had saved me. She kissed my hand and skipped away into the crowd.

Another unforgettable part of our motoring tour was, of course, Granada. I have always loved Spanish music, and everywhere we went I could feel the throbbing pulse of de Falla's *Nights in the Gardens of Spain*. The wondrous mosaics and graceful arches, the blue of the pools, the symmetry of the pillars, the velvet heaviness of the nights. Gypsies singing and dancing into the night. Everywhere a brooding Moorish sensibility. Here is a place for dark imaginings and passionate inaction.

Wishing to see the interior of a church in the town, I was startled, having rung the bell, to find it answered by a gentleman who smiled politely, and said, *'Dias señor,* I am the Virgin.' I think he meant verger; but I have kept the postcard of the church's beautiful virgin in my wallet ever since.

We got back to England, tanned and grateful for the break. We had driven some 3500 miles – not bad for those days.

Although K. and I had eventually to part – it was inevitable I suppose – we still keep in touch. A happy continuity of friendship.

But for the moment it was back to work again. This time in a play by an up-and-coming author, Phillip Leaver. Phillip and I had been friends in the days of the Arts League Travelling Theatre, and we had kept in touch. During my long months in hospital, he was the most loyal of visitors to my bedside. Now he was enjoying the distinction of having two plays produced simultaneously in the West End – *The Way to the Stars* at Wyndham's with Douglas Fairbanks Jr and Gertrude Lawrence, and *Tomorrow will be Friday* at the Haymarket with Marie Tempest, Celia Johnson and Leon Quartermaine, whom I was to understudy.

The atmosphere of the Haymarket was stiff with tradition. It has been a theatre since 1720, and Marie Tempest, who had known me for some years through the Playfairs, saw to it that protocol was properly preserved. During the run, Leon Quartermaine was taken ill, and I was called upon to play his part. While I was getting ready in the dressing-room, the manager Charles La Trobe made his appearance. 'Mr Mitchell, as soon as you have completed your make-up, you are to come and be presented to Miss Tempest.' Rather airily I explained we had met on many occasions. 'Nevertheless,' said he firmly, 'Miss Tempest wishes you to be presented before appearing with her in the play.' She had not yet been created a Dame of the British Empire, but she was treated with considerable respect.

Gravely the presentation was accomplished. 'I hope you know your lines, young man,' she said graciously, 'it's not an easy part.' This little exchange did absolutely nothing to help my nervous system, but fortunately all went well on stage.

Shortly afterwards I was commanded to escort Miss Tempest to an engagement at Selfridges, where she had consented to appear at a demonstration of a new development of the wireless, as it used to be called. We arrived at the wrong entrance, and apparently we were not expected. A manager was summoned who sent minions to find Mr Selfridge and inform him of our whereabouts. Miss Tempest was not amused. After a short wait Mr Selfridge appeared, and amid profuse apologies we were conducted to the third floor where the demonstration was to take place in the wireless department.

An area at one end had been curtained off from the passing shoppers; inside several chairs had been placed in front of a contraption resembling a miniature Punch and Judy theatre with a frosted glass window in place of the proscenium arch. This was the Televisor (the world's first television set). As we seated ourselves we were briefly introduced to the inventor, who was obviously much too concerned with the placing and arranging of his equipment to cope with mere social niceties. I quite failed to realize how much I would be seeing of John Logie Baird in years to come.

Now a floor manager explained to us that this was a historic moment in the development of communications. For the first time, thanks to Mr Selfridge, there would be a public demonstration of television which would also be seen by shoppers in the wireless department.

At last a face appeared on the Televisor screen to announce that members of the cast from the Haymarket Theatre, led by Miss Marie Tempest, would be appearing in person. Watching the picture intently she turned to me. 'You, Mr Mitchell, will appear first.' Her decision was understandable: with one's face in close-up, the slightest movement of the head produced a mountainous eruption of the cheeks, jaw or forehead, which, as they swelled, disappeared outside the picture – something like the effects of a distorting mirror at a fair. However, I sat as instructed in front of the camera and nattered about nothing much for a minute or two, then hastily made way for somebody else.

Miss Tempest beckoned me to her side. 'Well, at least,' she said, 'your *voice* was very clear.' In due course she was persuaded to appear herself. With all that self-discipline which only experience can provide, she sat rigidly immovable and made a gracious little speech, so avoiding all the errors made by the rest of us.

In the taxi back to the theatre she turned to me. 'I liked that Mr Baird. Nice little man, but I don't think his invention will get anywhere, do you?' I was inclined to agree with her.

After Phillip Leaver's play came off, I went to the Embassy Theatre in the try-out of a play by Peter Garland, *White Lies*, appearing once more with Jeanne de Casalis. In the course of the play, Jeanne and I arrived at a hotel in the South of France. We'd run off together, unmarried, and she was beginning to regret her decision. She finally repacked her cases and ran out. When I reappeared, thinking she was still in the adjoining room, I talked to her about plans for the evening. It was some minutes before I realized that she had left. Then the curtain came down.

One night I duly reappeared and foolishly closed the door with my hand behind me. There was a thud and a tremendous pain – I had dislocated my arm yet again. Sweat pouring down my face, I went through those long minutes before I was meant to notice her absence. Casually I lit a cigarette with one hand – fortunately I had a lighter; casually I went to the sideboard and poured a drink, and still talking, looked into the bedroom. Less casually I looked over the balcony as a taxi started downstairs, only then, when I ran for the door, the curtain came down. The stage-manager was sympathetic. 'Better look at your make-up, old boy. You seem to have got a bit hot!'

Next a chance meeting with Owen Nares, another chum, led to my playing in Warren Chetham Strode's *Man Proposes* at Wyndham's Theatre. Owen was kindly disposed and told me there was a very good part he wanted me to play in a later production, so I gladly accepted the opportunity to join him at Wyndham's.

Not for the first time I fell foul of stage superstition. Driving in the country one evening, a white object hit my windscreen with a re-sounding thud and fell into the road. After a search I discovered the body of a large barn owl. The bird was so handsome I took it with me to the theatre to ask if anyone knew of a taxidermist to have it stuffed. 'Cor, that's done it, the play will be off at the end of the week, you mark my words.' The stage-doorkeeper was right.

Even more unfortunate, the play in which Owen had promised me a part never went into production. So when he asked me to under-study him in *Double Door* with Sybil Thorndike it seemed a good idea. We went on tour for a few weeks. One day Owen telephoned the theatre. He had been involved in a bad car accident and doubted whether he could be at the theatre on time. I had, of course, rehearsed the part during the tour, and was told to get ready to play.

Breathlessly I stood in the wings waiting to go on. There was a polite hand on my shoulder. It was Owen, sticking-plaster well made up on his face and neck. He gave me that famous smile. 'You don't think I could afford to let *you* take over, Leslie,' he said, and walked on.

The show came to London at the Globe Theatre, but ran for only a short season.

Later, whilst living in a cottage near Andover, I suddenly had a call to Elstree Studios. The producer – an American I had met with Mrs Locke months previously – had promised to give me a part in a film with George Grossmith. I quite thought he had forgotten about it, but hastily prepared to start at 6 a.m. on the morrow.

There was frost and a thick mist. After some difficulty in starting the little car, I set off through the gloom. It was hard work, my nose was almost against the windscreen. As I neared Basingstoke a cyclist appeared from the shroud, wobbling violently and warning me to slow down. I applied the brakes. There was a slithering sound as the car skidded and ended up in the ditch. He had been trying to warn me there was ice on the road. I had to leave the car where it was.

By devious means I got to Elstree, arriving about two in the afternoon. Luckily they had stopped shooting and were waiting for me. After make-up I was sent to the studio where I joined a lot of other young men at the barrier of a railway platform.

'What are we supposed to do?' I asked.

'Just shout: Can I have an interview, sir. We're reporters seeing Grossmith off. He's a foreign prince.'

While he spoke, the effects men started up a choking wall of mist. As it spread, we became all but invisible to the cameras. We all shouted our shout.

'Cut the lights,' said the director. 'OK, boys, come and collect your money,' said the money-man. He offered me £3.

I looked at him in astonishment. 'What's that for?'

He laughed. 'You don't expect a fortune, do you? That's your lot.'

I told him the story of my day.

'What's your name?' he inquired. 'Oh, Lord, they've got it wrong again. We thought you were Lester Mitchell.'

The producer was astounded when I found him. Over a drink, he explained there *was* a part for me – in about three weeks' time. And I got it.

My years as an actor had gained me a lot of experience. I had been fortunate in my friends and opportunities, but there seemed little chance of achieving the success of contemporaries – John Mills, John Gielgud, Laurence Olivier, Jack Hawkins, and the rest – and if I was not going to make it I would rather give up. After careful thought I decided to find out whether I had it in me to be successful in some other sphere.

As it happened, I was able to round off my career on the stage very happily when that doyen of Shakespearean actors, Balliol Holloway, offered me the part of Faulkland in a revival of Sheridan's *The Rivals* – the very part for which I had so brashly understudied Claude Rains in my first days at the Lyric, Hammersmith. True, it was for the usual limited run at the Embassy Theatre, but it was a splendid production which included Lady Tree as Mrs Malaprop, Balliol Holloway as Sir Anthony Absolute, and Eric Portman as Captain Absolute. Bob Acres, the comic country squire, was rather surprisingly played by Lionel Marson, whom I was later to join at the BBC. By now I had learned enough to realize that Faulkland was a very difficult part indeed. This time I was determined to make a success of it. My ego was rewarded by one leading critic who described my performance as 'quite brilliant', although I could wish he had left out the word 'quite'. But I began more than ever to doubt my capacity to stay the course. Apart from the fact that I was in almost constant pain, the equally constant threat of unemployment was getting me down. One day I read an advertisement inviting applications for the post of advertising manager on a trade paper in Covent Garden. On the spur of the moment I decided to try my luck. The managing director agreed to see me.

'What previous experience have you had in advertising,' he asked.

'None,' I replied honestly.

He gave me a startled look. 'What then?'

'I've been an actor, but I thought if I could get to see you, you might have something else to offer.'

He pressed a button on his desk and a clerk appeared. 'Smith,' he said, 'take Mr Mitchell downstairs and try him out on a few advertisers, see if he can bring in some business.' If he winked, it wasn't noticeable. In due course, Mr Smith handed me a list of addresses in the East End, and explained that all I had to do was to visit them and sell advertising space for the magazine. As sheer effrontery had stood me in good stead so far, it seemed best to continue with it. Payment was to be a percentage of whatever sales I made.

My first choice of address was a large fruiterer and greengrocer in Lewisham. Having explained my business, I was told the manager was very busy and unable to spare time to see me. I stood my ground. 'Look,' I said, '*my* time is valuable, and it won't be possible to come back, but I wouldn't like him to miss a good thing. Tell him it's urgent.' It worked. When he came out, it was obvious he expected some salesman he knew. I plunged straight in and as representative of an important journal on the point of going to press warned him that there wasn't much time for him to make up his mind. He either wanted to take a full page and have his wares widely advertised or he did not. Eventually I left with his signature for a half-page advertisement which cost him £50.

Fortune was not so kind in every case, but by the end of the week, having sold £200 worth of advertising, I returned to Mr Smith.

'Never thought I'd see *you* again,' he said. 'You were supposed to come back and report every day!' I showed him the signed order-book. He looked and his eyes opened. '*You* got *these?* I didn't think you'd go through with it.' It became obvious that he had given me a list of firms with whom his regular salesman had already failed. Still, I had made myself £20.

They offered me a job on salary plus commission, but my heart was not in it. To this day my deepest sympathies are with door-to-door salesmen. It's a tough and disheartening life.

I was discussing my lack of future plans with a friend. 'Why on earth don't you apply to the BBC for a job as an announcer?' he suggested. 'Your voice is all right and once you're there, all sorts of opportunities may come your way.' The idea seemed a good one, and suited my experience, so I duly applied through the usual channels. The application was formally acknowledged, but I heard nothing further.

Meanwhile, another idea occurred to me, which involved a product I both liked and understood – books. Surely there must be a market in schools for historical novels, biographies, books on architecture, travel, and so forth. It seemed that leading publishers had never attempted to break in to this part of the market, except under the specialized heading of textbooks.

It was worth a try, I felt, so I put the idea to my old friend of Lyric, Hammersmith, days – Rupert Hart Davies, who was now working with Jonathan Cape. He good-naturedly took the idea further, and eventually Cape, in collaboration with Chatto & Windus, offered me a job at £10 a week plus commission to tour the schools of Britain and test reactions.

I went to most of the leading grammar and public schools armed with copies of Professor Neale's *Queen Elizabeth,* Francis Hackett's *Henry the Eighth*, Duff Cooper's *Talleyrand*, and a wholesome conglomeration of other volumes dealing with history and the arts. There was an awful lot of ground to cover, and there were some interesting reactions, outstanding amongst them a history master who, having examined my wares, exclaimed petulantly, 'Good god, man, what are you trying to do, upset the whole educational system? I don't require my pupils to take an *interest* in history, I want them to memorize our textbooks.' Another comment came from a master at my old school, King's at Canterbury, who said sadly, 'The pleasure it would have given me, Mitchell, to see you applying yourself to books when first we met!'

Nevertheless, I did sell a considerable number of books during the next few months, particularly to girls' schools, where it appeared they had a more liberal outlook on the dangers of interesting sixth-formers in history. I continued to press on.

Nearly six months passed before I received a summons from the BBC to attend an audition in London for the post of announcer. I went to Broadcasting House and joined a roomful of earnest young men waiting to share the ordeal.

We were required to answer one or two general questions, speak for a short time on a given subject, and read a list of announcements which were booby-trapped from beginning to end with French, Italian and German names and titles – not forgetting a number of English names which are spelt one way and pronounced entirely differently. Having fallen down badly on Gianno Schicchi whose name I pronounced 'chi chi', followed by a hollow laugh – more to reassure myself than my unseen listeners – I left in confusion and returned to my schools' safari.

Three months later it astounded me to learn that the BBC would offer me a job as an announcer on probation starting in three weeks' time. The salary was £5 a week, rising to £7 after a probationary period of three months. I had to make up my mind whether to take the chance with the possibility of a secure job for life, or continue my gadfly existence in perpetual search of a stable career.

With a hopeful heart, I chose the BBC and said farewell to the stage and my publishing friends.

8. Airborne

It was with some apprehension that I entered the imposing new Broadcasting House at Portland Place and made my way to the announcers' room. Fortunately I was not the only new boy; there were Alvar Liddell, Frank Phillips, Lionel Marson (with whom I had acted in *The Rivals*) and Robert McDermott.

Among new friends I made was Aunt Sophie – Sophie Dixon, the BBC pianist who had been with the Corporation since its Savoy Hill days, when all announcers and personalities were named Aunts and Uncles in the regular 'Children's Hour' broadcasts. Uncle Mac still ran the children's programmes.

Sophie and I were in the canteen to which she had just introduced me. We had met a number of times in studios, but this was the first time we had a chance to talk. 'Leslie,' said she, 'Why did you join the Corporation?' I gave her my reasons – a broken love-affair, ill health, and even more – lack of steady income. 'You won't last more than a year, my dear,' quoth she; 'you haven't the necessary civil-service ingredients. Want to bet?' She lost her bet. But she knew something! In the following years Sophie generously insisted on being my accompanist for a number of records I made as a singer.

Curiously, Eric Maschwitz made a similar prediction for me. I was sitting in his office, reminiscing about our earlier meeting in Juan-les-Pins with the Lockes. 'You haven't got a hope in this outfit,' he said. 'You are too much of the gent.'

'I'd *rather* be a gent,' said I, 'but I can't afford it.' Eric, who had also had many months of penury, saw the point.

In every broadcasting studio there is a button which has to be pressed by the announcer in charge, signifying to the engineers that his particular studio is ready to go on the air. Amongst our probationers was a gentleman who made BBC history through starting a programme by pressing the fire-alarm bell in error. The resulting confusion can be left to the imagination.

At this time, Sir John Reith (Lord Reith as he became later) was Director-General. He it was, of course, who built up the unrivalled reputation of the BBC. A stern disciplinarian, his very name was sufficient to strike terror into the hearts of most of the staff. It was customary for new announcers to be taken and personally introduced to the great man, but for some reason the moment was delayed for me. Then one evening the telephone rang in the announcers' room and a voice said, 'This is Reith; who is that?' I nervously stuttered out my name. 'I'm afraid we haven't met, but I know about you, Mitchell. I have just discovered that we're sitting down at Beaconsfield thirteen to dinner tonight; my wife is superstitious, so I thought we would invite a presentable announcer.'

I found my own availability somewhat affected by the terms of the invitation. It was, I think, Lionel Marson who dutifully filled the gap. Anyway, he owned a better dinner-jacket.

The chief announcer of those days was, of course, Stuart Hibberd; one of the kindest of men, he went out of his way to be helpful to us all on our daily rounds. At that time news-reading was not a specialized art, but merely one of many functions of an announcer on duty, although reading the news was certainly the most important part of his job.

Then there was Professor Lloyd James, whose unhappy task was to see that announcers enunciated clearly and conformed to the BBC standards. He would take a recording of our interpretation and play it back to us in order to point out how monstrously incompetent we all were; and if you think news-reading is easy, it's obvious you have never had to do it. If you ever get the chance, borrow a news bulletin from somebody in the BBC and record it for yourself. You will soon find out. To begin with, few people recognize their own voices. We have all got tricks and mannerisms of speech which are horrifying at first hearing. Tongue-twisters, family names and place-names (foreign or otherwise) – the simplest words become misleading under the strain of reading to a vast, unseen but critical audience. As one simple example may show: I think it was Lionel Marson who quoted a Minister in the House of Commons as stating 'that he had been completely mizzled by another member of the House'. The word, of course, is 'misled', but it looks like 'mizzled' when you are working under pressure.

On another occasion when he was reading a speech from the Commons, Lionel Marson quoted Mr Churchill as saying, 'It would be an utter impissibolity. . . .' And Stuart Hibberd it was who carefully pronounced for a concert, 'We are now taking you over to the Bathroom at Pump.'

There are two schools of thought about how to deal with such emergencies. Either you stop dead in your tracks and say 'I am sorry.

I will read that again' – which infuriates a number of people – or you go smoothly on as though you had not noticed, and leave it to the unfortunate BBC telephonists to cope with thousands of discerning listeners who have spotted the mistake which you so obviously had not.

I had my full share of errors. In the announcers' room there was kept a log-book into which the announcer on duty could place his report on incidents connected with his programmes. Unhappily, just before I was given my first big concert to announce, somebody had criticized the musicians for making an undue clatter in the studio. Quite unaware of this, I stepped bravely into the concert hall at the appointed time.

The clock ticked slowly round, and in due course I called for 'Quiet, please.' Immediately the place became a bedlam of noise – cellos scraping, violins being plucked, drum-skins tightened, and a great deal of 'school-boy' coughing took place. I looked round wildly. 'Quiet, *please*,' I yelled. The conductor – quite as surprised as myself – took some time to restore order, but at last I pressed the button, the red light went on and I started my first announcement. My nerve had been rather shaken by this unusual demonstration – my confidence was not at its highest. With a despairing nod of appreciation to the conductor, I began, 'Our concert today begins with an excerpt from the well-known French comic opera *Les Sittimboncs*. . . er . . . *Les Saltimbincs*. . . *Les Biltim* – I'm so sorry . . .'

I pointed unhappily at the conductor who released me from this dire situation by going into the piece I had been trying to describe. With perspiration streaming down my face I again studied the announcement. A perfectly simple piece entitled *Les Saltimbanques* – French, of course, and I could speak French – really, I must pull myself together – *Saltimbanques* – nothing to it! All too soon the piece came to an end. I forced a smile into my voice and said, 'I must apologize for having become tongue-tied over my opening announcement. As most of you will of course have realized, it was an excerpt from the well-known French comic opera *Les Siltimbanks* . . . *Les Bottimsanks* . . .' I never did get it right. Having abjectly apologized once again, I continued on safer ground.

Nervousness, of course, is a terrifying factor on occasions like this, and yet I have never known any good performer who was not nervous to some extent on each and every appearance.

Another time I was introducing an early-morning talk by a Miss Monica Dickson on 'Shopping and Cooking'. 'Here,' I said, 'is Miss Monica Dickson to give you another talk on "Cocking and Snooping" – I beg your pardon – "Shocking and Cooping" . . . er . . . I'm so sorry: Miss Monica Dickson.'

At the end of six months my probationary period was extended for a *further* three months. Finding my £5 a week inadequate, I had been looking forward to achieving the £7 a week promised on confirmation of my appointment. I decided to subdue my nerves and adopt a new devil-may-care attitude to the whole thing. The results of this were not conspicuously successful with the Corporation.

It was early in the morning. I had read the weather forecast and the forthcoming events of the broadcasting day. I finished the early-morning news and went down two floors to introduce the early-morning talk. Outside the studio stood a woman in distress. As producer of the talk, she was there to welcome the speaker. But the speaker had failed to arrive. 'What can I do?' she asked tearfully. 'Don't worry, my dear,' said I reassuringly, 'I'll explain the circumstances and read it for him.' I glanced at the clock – three minutes to go.

Hastily she explained, 'I'm *so* grateful, Leslie – the Professor is Swedish and the talk is about the lingonberry.'

'The what?'

'The lingonberry – it's Scandinavian.'

I took a quick glance at the script. Yes, that was all right – typed clearly. The engineer started flashing the signal to stand by for transmission. I pressed the red button. We were on the air. The first two pages were fine – I was doing well. Came page three – a whole half-page had been cancelled out with M. Thus MMMMMMM! At the side, in pencil were lengthy notes in Swedish. It was a fifteen-minute talk, and I managed to invent seven minutes of it.

Back in the announcers' room I found the duty-officer had just arrived. 'Did you hear the talk just now?' I inquired. 'Why? Was it all right?'

'No, I had to make up a lot of it.'

'You had to – *what*?'

'Well, look at the script.'

In a fever the man phoned up John Reith's secretary. 'Did you happen to hear the early morning talk? What did you think of it?' He replaced the receiver and turned to me. 'God, Mitchell, you certainly have the luck. She said she thought the Professor very interesting!'

On another occasion, reading the late news, I discovered an account of a debate in the House which had been written like a play-script. The protagonists were in a heavy argument with each other, and the words they spoke prefaced by their names; for example, *Mr Smith*: Does the Right Honourable Member *really* believe what he is saying? It has never before been my misfortune to listen to such a dishonest interpretation of facts in my long connection with this

House.' (Cries of 'Withdraw')

'*Mr Robinson:* I very much resent the imputation that I am misinterpreting facts. If my Right Honourable Friend were to study facts instead of dwelling in the realms of his fancy, he would have to admit the truth of my statement, etc. etc. . . .'

This was something to get one's teeth into! I hope and believe that my account of this debate sounded no whit less hot-headed in the solitude of the studio. I gave it all my experience had taught me. The news over, I returned to the announcers' room. There, glowering at me from behind a desk, was the man upon whom my BBC future depended. He it was who would say whether or not my probationary period would ever end.

'Good god,' he said with supreme distaste, '*you've* come back.'

'Oh, yes,' I said brightly, 'just finished the news.'

'Mitchell,' he said, with a wealth of meaning in his voice, 'this may very well be the last time you read *anything* for the Corporation! Are you mad, or do you just not care?'

'What have I done?'

'Done! You have probably provoked leader-writers all over the country into scathing indictments of the BBC for its partisan attitude in politics. I got the impression that you had gone stark, raving mad. Have you not yet learned that the news, as we give it, is completely impartial? This is not a playhouse. We do not ask for *performances* from our announcers!'

'But,' I said, 'it was written like a play-script. I thought that was a sure indication it should have been quoted with full expression.'

At that moment the telephone bell rang, and I sadly picked it up. 'Oh,' said the voice, 'could I speak to the announcer who just read the news?'

Here it comes, I thought, and braced myself. 'Yes, sir,' I said diffidently, 'it was me.'

'May I know your name?'

'Mitchell – Leslie Mitchell,' I said.

'Oh, Mitchell,' the voice continued, 'I just wanted to congratulate you on your account of the debate. I happened to be in the House myself. I thought you reconstructed it magnificently. I've never rung up the BBC before. Just wanted you to know.'

'Oh,' said I – unable to resist the opportunity – 'would you be kind enough to repeat that to the gentleman here . . .' True, he was the *only* person who telephoned, and I forgot to ask him his name.

But of course, the BBC was right and I was wrong: once announcers decide to interpret the news, individually, anything could happen, and it *would* sound far from impartial. The Corporation was then and still is generally acknowledged to transmit the most unbiased news-broadcasts of any radio organization in the world.

Deciding by now that I might as well have fun, since it obviously wasn't going to be for long, my next effort was in the announcement of a programme of gramophone records. Faced with the label on one of the records (they were chosen in advance by the department concerned), I found myself saying, 'As an announcer on probation I think I should pronounce the next number: I cahnt dahnce; I've got ahnts in my pahnts – it's from America, of course!'

One day I was mysteriously summoned to the office of Reith's second-in-command. He explained that he'd been playing squash with members of Jonathan Cape and Chatto & Windus the publishers who surprisingly had expressed belief in my intelligence and efficiency. Which was why he had decided to ask me what was wrong with the announcing department.

I asked whether this was an official or a personal inquiry. 'Oh, official, of course,' he said. I broke into eulogies about international reactions to BBC announcing. How was it possible to weld ten or twelve men from different social and educational backgrounds into a team which had earned such world-wide appreciation? Only the Corporation could have worked the miracle – I thought it was unbelievably brilliant. There was a pause.

'Then between ourselves,' he said. I told him of the dissatisfaction about our contracts. In every case the probationary period for us newcomers had been twice extended. We were all still receiving the minimum £5 a week. It seemed like a ruse to save money for the BBC and quite unfair to those who had to live on it.

As I watched him, I noticed he had begun to sweat. The next day I went to visit Eric Maschwitz. 'Could you use me in *your* department?' I asked.

'But you are doing so well, Leslie. Everybody says so.'

'Frankly, I want to stay in London,' I said.

'Well, I'll gladly have you if you really mean it.'

'Thanks, Eric,' I said. 'You might say I approached you *before* your last departmental meeting, but it had slipped your mind?' He agreed good-naturedly.

My transfer to Belfast arrived on the same day as my transfer to the BBC Variety Department at St George's Hall. Someone must have made a mistake.

I took up my new duties. Looking around I discovered that there were very few aspects of variety which were not already being handled extremely competently by others. There was, however, the matter of dance bands. Dance bands were announced rather inadequately by the conductor or a member of his orchestra. It had become necessary to make improvements. So dance bands it was.

Looking back on my own announcements, I am not so certain. To avoid facetiousness was almost impossible; strained linking announcements from one number to another left much to be desired, but for some reason they were accepted, not only by the BBC, but the public. It was a new approach. Eric Maschwitz made me producer of a highly successful series with Geraldo called 'Romance in Rhythm', and wrote an excellent script. It was the English variant on America's Paul Whiteman Show, and became immediately successful. Another big orchestra making its BBC reputation at that time was conducted by Louis Levy – 'Music from the Movies'. And I introduced the young Joe Loss and his orchestra on the air.

I settled down to writing scripts, and the production and presentation of shows which included Anona Winn, Tommy Handley, Ronald Frankau, and the first radio performance in this country by Rawicz and Landauer. I also remember being approached by a theatrical agent who offered me 10 per cent on the salaries of anybody I engaged through his good offices. I was not tempted to accept the offer, and I must confess that – if anything – it forced me to avoid his artists. It was not always so. Some producers fell for the temptation.

It was about this time that I first met Joan Gilbert, who worked in the Variety Department as assistant to W. H. Hanson, originator of the famous 'In Town Tonight'. A favourite in the department, she had that ready smile, and all the charm which made her one of television's post-war stars. At that time neither of us imagined we would be so closely associated years later in television's 'Picture Page'.

I was gradually being given more productions to do outside the confines of dance band broadcasts. On one occasion, I was in charge of a musical programme featuring Noël Coward and Gertrude Lawrence. Noël decided, before the performance, that he and Gertie should have a glass of port to tone up their voices, and he asked me to arrange this. Unfortunately, the BBC canteen didn't run to port and my inquiries through other departments met with a definite refusal to provide anything of the kind.

I decided to take the matter in my own hands. Running across to the nearby Langham Hotel, I purchased a half-bottle of port and on my return, asked the studio attendant to bring me a tray and three glasses. (I was in need of lubrication myself by this time.)

My request was met with some suspicion. 'Three glasses and a jug of water, you mean, sir?'

'Never mind about the water,' I said, 'just three glasses.' In due course, pouring a generous libation into each, I ensured that the Coward, Lawrence and Mitchell larynxes were toned up before we went on the air.

The show was successful from every point of view, so I was mystified some days later to receive an internal memorandum, addressed to me and headed 'Introduction of Strong Liquor into BBC Studios' – going on at some length to explain that the rule against supplying alcoholic refreshment in the studio had never before been broken. An immediate explanation was demanded as to why as an official of the BBC I had been party to this unheard-of exception.

I patiently replied that my experience of singers led me to understand that there were two forms of vocal tonic commonly used by singers from grand opera to musical comedy: one was the glass of port which had already been noted – the other, the raw egg. In the circumstances, it had been impossible for me to procure the alternative to port, and in any case, eggs being by nature fragile, I might well have cracked them in transit and ruined my only dinner-jacket. The correspondence continued for weeks. My facetious reply was no doubt included in my annual report.

At last after so many false starts, I was losing my constant fear of unemployment. I was working hard and learning fast. New opportunities seemed to be coming my way. Meantime, elsewhere, preparations were being made for the opening of the BBC Television Service at Alexandra Palace; then, as now, television made the headlines.

9. A New Vision

My appointment to television came as a complete surprise. One morning, splashed across the front page of the *Daily Mail*, I saw the headline: TELEVISION ADONIS FOUND'; a photograph of my ugly mug stared from the surrounding context. It was a long time before I was allowed to forget that headline, and even now over forty years later it still crops up. In actual fact the appointment had *not* been made. There had been some six hundred competitors for the job, but without my knowledge, the powers-that-be had selected me as a semi-finalist.

With less mystery, but equal publicity, two charming young women had already been selected as announcers. One of them was Jasmine Bligh – a young and attractive society girl with good looks, a strong personality and a mind of her own. The other was Elizabeth Cowell, a lovely brunette with features ideally suited to the television screen. These two were to be the official representatives of glamour in the world's first public TV programmes.

As producer and compère of Geraldo's 'Romance in Rhythm', it fell to my lot to introduce them to the public for the first time over the air in June 1936. They were told to report to me for the requisite rehearsals. Elizabeth Cowell – rather more serious-minded about it than her colleague – faithfully attended on time. But Jasmine dug in her toes and steadfastly refused to appear for the afternoon rehearsal as she had a most important 'date' with the hairdresser.

That night, just before we went 'on the air', a young woman with an immaculate hair-do, but a very apprehensive look, sidled up to me and seized my hand in a vice-like grip. 'You will *help* me, Leslie, won't you?' she pleaded. 'I'm absolutely terrified.' She was, and I didn't! We've been firm friends ever since.

Finally my appointment was made official: Senior Television Announcer, Grade C (Temporary). Meanwhile publicity about the new medium grew like a snowball. Although the press seemed to take an inordinate interest, it was not yet regarded very seriously by the inhabitants of Broadcasting House, and very few of them realized that television would become a serious rival to sound broadcasting.

A few weeks later. Here it was – Alexandra Palace – a vast near-dilapidated exhibition building, set in a park at Wood Green, three hundred feet above sea-level. The south-east wing, taken over by the BBC, was surmounted by a towering television mast.

On the engineering side much had already been learned through experience on closed circuit. But the complications of producing visual programmes of any but the simplest kind had yet to be explored, since the main activities of the Corporation had been confined to the spoken word.

I was still learning variations of technique for different types of audience. In a theatre, it is necessary to exaggerate one's appearance and performance by means of make-up, a louder projection of the voice, and gestures which can be clearly seen by the audience sitting some distance from the stage. Cabaret artists, with the audience sitting only a short distance away, concentrate on the intimate approach. Whilst in films a performer is so magnified by the camera lens in close-up that it is necessary to reduce gesture, facial expression and body movements to a minimum. Microphones can magnify a whisper so that a large audience can hear every cadence.

Radio and television present quite different problems. Although they have audiences of up to several millions, the performance is distributed to individuals or small groups in the relaxed atmosphere of their homes.

I found myself more and more often being pressed into service as an interviewer, an art which had long been practised on radio. But those interviewers relied, of course, on scripts *written* for them by reporters and talent scouts. It was immediately obvious that one could hardly stand and read from a piece of paper in front of television cameras. As a result, I insisted on being given headlines containing only essential information about my victims, which I would memorize before meeting them in person. The strain of interviewing half a dozen people in quick succession from memory was considerable, but it did introduce a naturalness and informality upon which television then depended.

In 'Picture Page' – the magazine-type programme with which I was mainly concerned – the majority of people to be interviewed had little or no experience of acting or public-speaking. They could hardly be expected to learn their lines like trained performers, so in fact a scripted conversation was quite useless. Under these conditions, the first necessity was to put the individuals concerned at their ease so that they would be willing to rely on me to guide them into the required order and length of discussion. This was made doubly necessary by the fact that often they brought with them inserts of film to illustrate their subject. As film takes some seconds to run up to speed, it meant cueing the producer verbally whilst continuing our conversation until such time as the film appeared on the screen. Objects, which had to be displayed in close-up to the camera, required careful handling to get them in correct perspective or lighting conditions. These I handled myself since experience taught me the angles at which they showed to best advantage.

Meanwhile one had to lure unsuspecting performers away from pools of shadow where their features would be lost, whilst talking away coherently and easily. In those days we moved about during interviews. These difficulties were increased by any temporary break-down of the camera. This called for instant recognition of the situation and an unflurried move to another camera as it positioned itself to take over. The problems of constantly looking all ways at once and trying to maintain an even flow of conversation can be imagined. Nowadays, of course, the majority of interviews are conducted from a fixed position where the lighting is pre-set. Objects to be demonstrated are placed in front of separate cameras. And a script can be *read* from a giant tape-machine affair – the autocue. In the early days, our work was further complicated by the fact that two competitive systems of transmission were used alternately – Baird and Marconi EMI – one in the afternoons, the other in the evenings.

Each transmission system involved different personnel and equipment. For the performers it demanded different clothes and even different make-up. Unattractive make-up – dark blue lips and yellow faces – made even the girl announcers odd to look upon, and dyes on different materials, including women's hair, were likely to register black on one camera and near white on another. I found that the lapels on my dinner-jacket looked white, so had to buy another.

Film experience had taught me that with the hot lights, greasy make-up and abnormal wear-and-tear of cleaning, my existing wardrobe would be unlikely to stand up to the strain for long. Since my salary was still less than £9 a week, I persuaded the BBC to advance me £50 out of salary, so that I might lay the foundations of a wardrobe equal to this historic occasion.

It was essential to memorize names, dates, places, camera and lighting positions – in fact, all the particulars of each and every show. As well as rehearsing for the two alternative systems, we would also sit in for lighting, make-up and wardrobe tests and rehearsals.

On one occasion the lighting men were exploring the possibilities of back lighting (the effect of bright lights behind the subject). I was called upon to sit in for the experiment. As the floods were brought closer and closer behind me, I started to burn mentally and physically. Jumping from my chair, I stroked the back of my head and the hair came off in my hands, burned to a frazzle.

At an early stage in our preparations, I was proudly shown the lighting for the main stage. Lights had been set at equal intervals along the front and two strong floodlights at each side of the area. I pointed out, as an erstwhile producer and stage-manager, that this would 'burn up' the pictures of the performers if they moved anywhere out of centre to right or left, just as in the early days of the cinema, when film stock was far less sensitive. The acting area needed to be lit brilliantly over the whole frame, taking most of the character away from the faces of the performers, but cameras *and* lighting had to be moved for shots from positions other than the centre. I was told to mind my own business as an announcer and let the experts get on with it. But it did happen as I had predicted.

One of the first requisites for announcers is to have some visual signal that their camera is on the air. There was no such signal at first, so I soon suggested a small light-bulb which would operate as the camera came into action. One was otherwise left on the screen with a wide meaningless grin before getting the signal to speak. The engineers were hilarious. Me and my mad ideas – the additional power would break up the picture and put the camera out of action. All cameras have such a signal today as standard.

Incidents like these demonstrate just how ignorant many of the staff were about the techniques and methods of professional film-making. Moreover they started without most film requisites – not even camera-dollies and cranes for variable travelling-shots, until we had visited Pinewood and Denham Studios to see them actually at work.

On the production side however we had people of considerably wider experience. Stephen Thomas, from the Lyric, Hammersmith, was now an internationally known lighting expert and Dallas Bower an experienced film-maker. Peter Bax from the West End stage was our scene designer. And I myself had studied theatrical and film lighting during my years on the stage.

The shows were to vary from talks to outside broadcasts; from classical music to dance bands; from drama to variety acts; so it was obvious that life was not going to be altogether uneventful.

Jasmine, after one look at the terrors in store, was stricken with appendicitis, which left Elizabeth Cowell and me to shoulder announcing responsibilities for a ten-day transmission to 'Radiolympia'. Elizabeth too succumbed with laryngitis before the opening day. So I was left to hold the fort alone for the first five days.

It was during these hectic pre-opening experimental days that I came upon Baird's 'Spotlight Studio' for the first time. Here, I was seated on a high music stool in complete darkness. Behind me crouched two studio attendants, who up to this point I had taken for personal friends. From the wall in front of me was a blinding light playing over my features. When the appropriate red light prompted action, one of my friends hit me hard on my left kidney. This was my cue to smile (a rather unconvincing smile); then his mate gave my right kidney a similar violent blow, which was my cue to start talking. I only hope their crippling enthusiasm was because they neither of them knew their own strength.

Our first ever programme, on 26 August 1936, was a variety show called 'Here's Looking at You'. It included Helen McKay, the singer, Pogo the Horse, whose inner anatomy was provided by the two Griffith Brothers (they, with Miss Lutie, their 'trainer' had long been favourites in pantomime and on the variety stage), a close-harmony trio – The Three Admirals – from Cochran's show *Anything Goes*; and Chilton and Thomas, two dynamic young Chilean dancers.

For those ten days we put on a show, morning and evening, with off-beat variations which included trick camera shots and unrehearsed fooling from the conductor of the Television Orchestra, Hyam Greenbaum. Among players in the orchestra were an up-and-coming young violinist, Eric Robinson, and Sidonie Goosens, harpist member of the famous musical family.

From closely observing the reactions of people watching the screens at Alexandra Palace during those hectic rehearsals, I had got the feeling of the effectiveness of TV. It seemed to be taken with intense seriousness by viewers. Now, with a 'real' live audience at Olympia, I perpetrated a private experiment.

'Do forgive me,' I said, during one of the earliest transmissions. 'But *would* the lady with that lovely hat mind removing it? The people behind you are unable to see the screen. Thank you so much.' Naturally I could not see my audience, but it was reported back to me that the request was taken absolutely seriously. A number of women started to remove their hats.

Since they were completely experimental, these beginnings were naturally inclined to be rough, but we quickly learned that spontaneity covered over many deficiencies.

For some time the BBC's indefatigable Cecil Madden had been conjuring up programme ideas for the future. It was he who devised 'Picture Page'. A permanent feature of the programme in those early

days was a young Canadian actress, Joan Miller. Sitting at a telephone switchboard, she would announce each celebrity in turn for the
interviews. Joan, later the wife of Peter Cotes, the theatrical producer,
was to make a considerable name for herself as an actress in the
London theatre.

On 8 October, 'Picture Page' made its first appearance. I introduced amongst others, Squadron-Leader Swain; who had just broken
the world altitude record for the RAF, Prince Monolulu, the race-
track tipster, familiar to all racegoers, Dinah Sheridan, the actress,
then a very young advertising model, and Mrs Flora Drummond,
who had been closely associated with Mrs Pankhurst in the Suffra-
gette Movement.

During that first year alone I interviewed an impressive list of
celebrities: they varied from HH the Aga Khan to Pop-Eye the Sailor
Man! The effectiveness of Pop-Eye's visit to the studio was somewhat
dimmed by the fact that he had succumbed to laryngitis and could
barely talk above a whisper, but we managed to play an excerpt from
one of his films to back him up.

Through succeeding weeks we three announcers (Jasmine had now
recovered from her appendix operation) alternated between trying to
find somewhere quiet in which to memorize details of the programme
for the following day; and rehearsing afternoon and evening transmissions of the current day for the benefit of producers, artists, cameras
or lighting men.

The official opening of the television station had been arranged for 2
November 1936. There was an imposing array of participants, in-
cluding the Chairman of the BBC, Mr R. C. Norman, the Postmaster-
General, Major Tryon, the Chairman of the Television Advisory
Committee, Lord Selsdon, the Chairman of the Baird Company, Sir
Harry Greer, and the Chairman of Marconi EMI, Mr Alfred Clark.

In view of my greater experience, it was decided to make me
announcer of the day. In introducing this gathering I had to
memorize not only their names and titles, but a varied collection of
honours and decorations which they had accumulated during their
distinguished careers.

Also to be included in this official opening programme were two
coloured American dancers, Buck and Bubbles, Adele Dixon, the
singer and another edition of 'Picture Page' which introduced Jim
Mollison (fresh from breaking new flying records), Kay Stammers,
the tennis star, and Algernon Blackwood, the famous author and
playwright. Then – perennial favourites – a pearly king and queen
from London's East End, and finally, a formal introduction of my two

colleagues, Jasmine Bligh and Elizabeth Cowell.

Already my nerves were beginning to show signs of strain. On 1 November a senior official approached me with a fistful of closely typewritten pages – my announcements for the official opening, the result of a considerable amount of thought and preparation by the Governors of the BBC. As I looked, the pages seemed to multiply in front of me.

'I can't do it,' I said desperately. 'Tell me what to say and I'll say it to the best of my ability. But memorize that? No!'

'Mitchell,' the official said, 'if this is your attitude, I must remind you that your job is only temporary.'

I took the pages from him and tore them in half. Mind you, in the short time left, there was little opportunity for him to find anyone who *could* take it on.

The following day, having memorized the names and decorations I improvised the rest. Great was my elation to find in *The Times* the following day my first television notice – still one of my proudest possessions. 'The very successful transmissions of the male television announcer,' it reads, 'suggested that there is a technique to be learned by those who wish to be well televised.' So I kept the job.

Following the opening ceremony at Alexandra Palace we settled down to a regular routine of afternoon and evening programmes. Three to four and nine to ten were the appointed hours, though sometimes we over-ran considerably, when there was a particular reason. Many technical problems were being solved, but we had had little chance to learn much on the programme side, though we were already getting public reaction to personalities and ideas we presented.

The maximum guaranteed distance for good reception at that time was a radius of only twenty-five miles from our new transmitter, but when you come to think of it, the population of Greater London alone was nine million people, so potential audience was considerable. Programmes were regularly seen in Brighton, and many other places officially out of range, but this was impossible to guarantee.

Television sets were installed in London pubs and shop-windows, apart from private houses, but the sales stayed at a low level in the early stages. Just before the arrival of the television set, the radio-gram had been launched. It could only be bought by the well-off in the first months, but the manufacturers were soon able to reduce the prices by a considerable percentage. This deterred many people from buying television sets as they imagined these too would quickly become much cheaper. Some people explained they were waiting till they could have a full-size cinema screen. How on earth they imagined a screen that size could be fitted into an ordinary house they did not explain.

Our showing of the Boon–Danahar boxing match in 1939 was relayed on large screens in West End cinemas. This probably spurred figures towards some 25,000 licences. But the threatening undertones of war kept sales from climbing further or faster.

Cecil Lewis, a pioneer of radio, had rejoined the BBC to take charge of Outside Broadcasts and Talks. Poet, and author of a best-selling novel about the Royal Flying Corps – *Sagittarius Rising* – he had imaginative qualities which quickly produced results. One of his first successes was an Armistice Day programme on 11 November 1936. His series of talks with John Hilton on social and industrial problems of the day set a pattern which has been followed ever since.

Unfortunately, he left for Hollywood early in 1937 to write a film version of his book, and never returned to us. Mrs Mary Adams came from radio to take over the Talks Department. For the moment, it was left to me to take over many outside events.

At that time the transmitter vans which were to extend the range of outside broadcasts so greatly were not yet in commission; we were limited to the length of cable that producers could spare from studio productions. This meant that all outdoor programmes had to be confined to the grounds of Alexandra Palace. The shows I presented were dubbed 'Inside-Outside Broadcasts'.

Ingenuity offset the limitations. We were fortunate in being surrounded by many suitable amenities – a bowling green, a railway station, a large lake, a boxing arena, a skating rink, a dance floor, and some acres of grass. There we laid out a miniature golf course which was the scene of demonstrations and matches introduced by Bernard Darwin. Among the early players were such masters of the game as Archie Compston and Henry Cotton. It was Compston who, having accidentally putted his opponent's ball into the hole, followed up unthinkingly with a truly professional swearword – very properly described in the *Radio Times* as 'a grunt'.

A series of riding lessons was given by Major Faudel Phillips, with the occasional help of Jasmine Bligh. They even took hurdling in their stride. He could hardly have claimed to rival David Broome and certainly Jasmine made no pretence of being a Pat Smythe, but they made an excellent moving picture. A later appearance by Gene Autry and his horse Champion reminded me of the time that Tex McCleod arrived with *his* famous horse, which bolted at the first sight of the television camera. We watched Tex career after it, balanced

precariously on the running-board of a car. They got back just in time
for the programme.

I presented the first television amateur boxing-match from the arena
in a nearby hall of the Palace. Just before the match started, two lights
fell in the centre of the ring and exploded, throwing glass everywhere.
By a miracle, the staff had cleared the mess and replaced the lights in
less than three minutes.

The programme started thirty seconds late.

The first programme on cricket I presented in April 1937, with
Andy Ducat at the nets. There were also sheep-dog trials; and archery
contests in which my only fear was that some innocent bystander
would be felled like Harold at Hastings.

The TV gardening expert of those days was C. H. Middleton,
whose talks were illustrated in week-by-week construction of a
miniature garden with a wide variety of flowers and shrubs, a rockery
and even a lily pond. Jasmine and Elizabeth were additional attractions in the programme.

For my own benefit the railway authorities brought to Alexandra
Park station one of the new streamlined Golden Eagle class locomo-
tives. The resulting fanmail from railway enthusiasts and model-
makers of all ages was an eye-opener to most of us, and led to
demonstrations of model yachts and power-boats on the lake, some of
them completely to scale – even to the ship's cat. On one occasion,
Philip Dorté produced on the lake, with models, a most effective
reconstruction of the famous Zeebrugge Raid of the First World War.

Sir Malcolm Campbell gave us a close-up of his famous racing car
Bluebird on the terrace outside the studios. In spite of the scoffing of his
friends, he was already concerned at what he called the inevitability of
war. When we visited him later at his house in Surrey, he showed us
with pride the deep underground shelter which he had already constructed, with its own larder, electric light and air-conditioning
system – and this in 1937.

Anxious as we all were to publicize this new and exciting medium, the
announcers were constantly involved in stunts of one kind and
another. This breaking away from the conventional dignity of the
BBC had many critics at Broadcasting House, and of course the
stunts were not always successful.

One day I decided to row into shot on the lake for the opening
announcement of a programme about model boats. Immersed in the
business of keeping my proper distance from the cameras, and back-
paddling at the appropriate moment, I was suddenly faced with a

horrible thought. 'I am terribly sorry, sir,' I yelled across the water to the demonstrator, 'I have completely forgotten your name' . . .

Also about this time, the London Fire Brigade gave a working demonstration of its equipment – ancient and modern. I decided to give the public an impression of how it felt to be hoisted to the top of the newest 90-foot extending ladder. This meant holding the microphone with one hand and hanging on with my damaged arm. Three cameras were used – one on the ground, one on a balcony halfway up, and another on the roof. A 70 h.p. engine raised the ladder and me towards the top of the building. On the way up I suddenly became aware that all was not well. The knees of my trousers had caught between the sides of the extending ladders. It is not easy to argue with 70 horses, but by a tremendous effort, I pulled myself free; there was a sound of tearing cloth and the remaining trouser material was slowly ripped from me. Gamely I stuck to my description of the surrounding countryside, gesticulating wildly as a warning to the balcony cameraman to avert his all-revealing camera. Apparently he was too intent on the *focus* of his picture to bother about the content. Passing him with a moan, I continued to the maximum 90 feet, there to be televised by the other camera on the roof. Pictures taken by an early viewer from his set at Brighton are adequate comment on my feelings. But I suppose I can claim to be the first-ever streaker on television.

The fire brigade lowered me at a dignified speed quite unsuited to my trouserless condition. A thoughtful commissionaire stepped forward and wrapped a rug round me. As I slunk out of sight of the assembled bystanders, an official stopped me. 'You're insured for this,' he said. 'You'll be permitted to put in for replacement trousers. Send us a claim.'

Cheered by this unexpected generosity, I went back to my tailor, showed him my remnants and he agreed to make a duplicate of the original pair. The jacket was still intact. As I seldom got the chance to visit him I also asked if he would make me a pair of flannel trousers. 'And,' I said, 'let me have the bill for the replacement pair now. I have to send it to the BBC Insurance Department.'

Some weeks later I was summoned to see the Head of Finance.

'We have had this memo from Broadcasting House,' he said, 'I'll read it to you.' In so many words it accused me of dishonesty, and suggested I should be carpeted for having attempted to misappropriate BBC funds.

I listened open-mouthed. Then I got angry. 'Can I have that memo, please?'

'No, Mitchell, you *can not*. I have been instructed only to read it to you.'

At the first opportunity I went to Broadcasting House to deal with the writer. My way was firmly barred by an earnest secretary. 'I'm afraid Mr Wade can't see you,' she said. 'He has already written a memorandum on the matter.' I knew *that*.

What I *did not* know at the time was that the tailor had given me the bill for my flannel trousers. There was a thirty-shilling difference.

The success of my programme led to further fire-fighting demonstrations in the cause of public safety. Jasmine Bligh sportingly agreed to be rescued by a professional fireman from one of the higher windows of Alexandra Palace. It was obvious that gossamer feminine underwear would be inadequate for the occasion, so we exchanged a number of internal memoranda on the subject of 'Miss Jasmine Bligh, drawers black, for the use of'. These were duly issued and became virtually the first noticeable bloomers of her television career.

Which reminds me of the rat-and-mouse catcher who dwelt somewhere in the precincts (I know they are called 'pestologists' nowadays). Entering my office one day he stared fixedly at my new and timid secretary and asked, 'Any mice in your drawers, Miss?' Apparently rodents had been living on the contents of our filing-cupboards.

Another momentous occasion was a demonstration of fire-walking by a Mr Ahmed Hussain. We dug a long pit in the grounds outside, filled it with wood and fired it until nothing was left but hot and glowing embers. I can assure you, it was *very* hot indeed. With deliberate unconcern, Mr Hussain walked slowly across in his bare feet and came through apparently unscathed. A cameraman, convinced that this was a simple demonstration of mind over matter, insisted on following suit. He had bad burns and blisters for a long time. All of us in those days would do *anything* once.

I also presented a fun-fair on the Saturday before August Bank Holiday. There was indeed to be a fair in the grounds of Alexandra Palace, but it was not open to the public until the Monday. We invited friends, relations and any passers-by to join the fun, and in order to give the impression of a real Bank Holiday crowd, persuaded them to move from place to place with the cameras – sometimes with coats, sometimes without, sometimes hatless, sometimes not. The cameras ploughed through happily till we came to the swingboats. I had carefully prepared the camera shot from an angle which gave the impression that the boats, in their flight, would break through the television screens. We sustained it for the appropriate length of time and went on to other amusements. Almost immediately the camera man signalled to me that he had been ordered over his headphones to return to the previous shot. Since we were in no position to argue, I told him to do as he was asked. The crowds, of course, had moved on elsewhere, and astonished viewers saw only the row of swing-boats, empty and stationary with not a soul in sight. Later the explanation was given me that a newly appointed official had been so impressed by the effect of the swingboat shots that he had taken it upon himself to turn remote armchair producer.

Another effort of mine was an attempt to reproduce the atmos-phere of the beer garden in a German university town. I had written a slight story to bind the show together, and my intention was to have the BBC Chorus singing student songs (in German), with a typical brass band to accompany them, all of course dressed in traditional costumes. The location was ideal – the garden of the nearby refreshment bar. Beneath the blossoming trees were a number of small tables; the setting up of a rostrum for the band was comparatively easy; beer was readily available. I engaged the services of the BBC Chorus well in advance, and chose half a dozen artists as principal singers and actors.

Unfortunately, the chorus master was taken ill, my memorandum mislaid, and for the first rehearsal there arrived a gaggle of singers who spoke no German, and had been given no instructions. On top of this, the engineers suddenly discovered that from the nearby tramway they got electrical interference which would almost obliterate the picture.

In despair, I withdrew to the studio, together with a few battered branches of blossom, called upon D. H. Munro (as always) to help, and started the transmission with a personal introduction.

'How many of you have been to Heidelberg?' I asked cautiously. 'I never have, but we are about to present a curiously English impression which we do hope you will enjoy.' Thank goodness, they apparently did.

About this time I was informed that as I was getting too much publicity, not only would all my productions and presentations be anonymous, but I would be introduced in future as the 'male announcer'. I was rather stung by this, having been trained in a hard outside world where one accepts responsibility for whatever brickbats and bouquets come one's way. However, the ruling was made. It was only abandoned after a number of people followed my introductions with an opening phrase which varied very little, 'As Leslie Mitchell has just pointed out . . .' they would say.

It was in 1937 D. H. Munro produced the first outside broadcast to take place after dark – a demonstration of the latest anti-aircraft defences with the new 3.7 anti-aircraft guns, spotters and a searchlight battery to pick up a single plane making a mock attack on Alexandra Palace. It was during the ominous days of preparation for war and the Army personnel, made up of Territorials, were still learning their business. The 3.7 anti-aircraft guns had just gone into production and training was not yet complete.

The RAF, being too busy to participate, refused the appropriate loan of a bomber for the occasion, and we had to be content with a fairly aged civilian passenger aircraft. Time after time the plane staggered over Ally Pally. Searchlights wavered uncertainly, stabbing the night sky, but finding nothing. The pilot decided to come lower.

As he passed over again, spotters swung dizzily in their chairs, fieldglasses at the ready. The guns barked realistically from the ground. But plane and searchlights failed to meet. The plane made a yet lower approach. Again the guns burst and barked at everything and nothing. I became scared they might bring down the mast. Eventually the pilot decided to call it a day and flew off while he still had sufficient petrol.

The gun crews in their inexperience seemed to have caught nearly every part of their anatomy in the breeches. There was blood everywhere. Loading and unloading a heavy ack-ack gun needed a lot more training. On the way home I pondered the possibility that we had lost the war already.

BBC personnel, like eggs, are graded. I was still officially Senior Announcer, Grade C (Temporary). As the outside broadcast mobile vans came into commission, it became obvious that it would be impossible to continue my duties in the studio and deal with presentations of outside events at the same time.

Soon many other regular BBC commentators came into the picture. It was interesting to note how sound broadcasters fell into the trap of using the techniques of Broadcasting House. Trained to describe a scene for listeners, in a desire to use the right phrase they would wait perhaps fifteen to twenty seconds after the event before passing comment. This was infuriating to viewers who had already been able to see the action for themselves. But they learned fast – you have to in television. And it was always a pleasure to listen to the masters like John Snagge, Freddie Grisewood and Howard Marshall, forerunners of the inimitable Richard Dimbleby of post-war years.

Meanwhile, Philip Dorté had taken charge of Outside Broadcasts. By the end of the first year, viewers had seen polo at Hurlingham, Test matches, Wimbledon tennis, the Cup Final, the Boat Race and a host of other sporting events. They continue to be among leading attractions of television today. And how many people remember that television was there for the coronation procession of King George VI and Queen Elizabeth in 1937? It rained on that occasion too.

Dorté – a man of considerable experience in the film world – also arranged an extremely popular series of visits to the film studios. We went to Elstree, Denham, and Pinewood, calling on directors, producers, stars and technicians for explanations and demonstrations of their work, with myself as interviewer and commentator. Viewers met most of the stars and directors of that time, amongst them Maurice Chevalier, Margaret Lockwood, Valerie Hobson, Marlene Dietrich, René Clair, Basil Dean, Sir Michael Balcon and Alfred Hitchcock.

Alfred Hitchcock was a really wicked practical joker. The story goes that during the shooting of *The Thirty-nine Steps* he allowed the stars, Robert Donat and Madeleine Carroll, to remain handcuffed together for the whole of a long day, having ostensibly lost the keys. One of his least successful efforts was the occasion when he manoeuvred a large cart-horse into the dressing-room of Sir Gerald du Maurier during the run of a play. Sir Gerald – also a master of practical jokes – came off-stage and opened the door with some difficulty to find himself faced with the outsize flanks of his visitor. Without flickering an eyelid, he patted the animal gently. 'Hello, horse,' he said, and sat down to refresh his make-up while Hitchcock was left waiting outside for the reaction that never came.

I was one of Hitch's early television victims. We were watching the shooting of an important scene in his current film. When it was over, I joined him in the television picture for a discussion about film-making in general. The questions I asked him were met with a bland stare; his mind was obviously elsewhere. Suddenly he started to question me about my personal affairs. Was it true that I was grossly underpaid? Did the BBC overwork me? Did I regret leaving the stage? Knowing full well that the programme was being watched by the VIPs of the BBC, I tried unavailingly to return to the subject of films and ended by having to publicly reject the offer of a leading part in his next picture.

A film department under Major L. G. Barbrook was running at Alexandra Palace from the very beginning; its primary object was to produce film sequences for studio programmes which required exterior scenes. There was no *television* newsreel as such but Gaumont British News and British Movietone News were shown alternately. Mickey Mouse Cartoons – constant favourites – and a number of documentary and feature films were ours for the hiring. By sheer coincidence the very first documentary to be shown on the small screen was a story about paper-making – Alexander Shaw's *Cover to Cover* for which I had been the commentator.

It was as a direct result of television that I became associated with British Movietone News. They invited me to comment on the opening programmes of the television service which was naturally headline news at the time. Following this, they invited me to comment regularly on other subjects and the BBC gave their blessing, provided my work at Alexandra Palace was given priority. As my Movietone commitments increased, it became obvious I would be unable to continue fitting in enough spare time during the hectic hours of rehearsal and television programming. So eventually, I found myself working late through the night at Movietone's headquarters in Soho Square *after* I had finished uninterrupted days of television at Alexandra Palace.

In 1937, I had been invited to the first night of a new play – *Wise Tomorrow*, presented by Firth Shephard. The distinguished cast included Martita Hunt, Norah Swinburne, Diana Churchill, Esmond Knight, and Naunton Wayne making his first appearance as a straight actor. After the show, Norah Swinburne introduced me to Firth Shephard's daughter, Phyllis, who made an instant success with me by admiring a diminutive basket of flowers on Norah's dressing-table. In fact, it had come from me, and I was rather self-conscious about it, surrounded as it was by so many larger and more imposing bouquets.

We met again on a number of occasions and I learned about the tragic death of her young husband after less than a year of marriage. She was still deeply unhappy, and I did what I could to distract her from her sadness. We found we had a lot in common – love of the theatre was just one aspect. We also shared many friends, and we laughed at the same things. Phyl had an unusually perceptive sense of beauty and great personal integrity. I slowly realized I was really in love for the first time.

Marriage had at last become a possibility; my future was showing signs of stability. I decided to ask her to marry me. But after having proposed twice and been twice rejected, it became plain that Phyl was not for me after all. Eventually we decided not to meet again. I was heartbroken. But two days later she changed her mind and telephoned me at my flat. 'Is that the Adonis of television?' she asked. 'I will, I will, I will!' I was back in the Firth Shephards' flat almost before she had finished speaking.

At this time Firth Shephard was at the height of his career. In partnership with Leslie Henson he had been producing successful, long-running musicals at the Gaiety Theatre. Now he decided to go into management on his own and turned back to straight plays as well.

I approached my future father-in-law with suitable apprehension. 'Could I have a word with you, sir, it's about Phyl.'

He looked at me nervously – he was in fact a very shy man. 'Oh God, that! I suppose you'd better come in here.' We sat down. He got up again and went to the drink table. 'Better have a drink first. . . . Gather you want to marry my daughter. . . . Sounds like a bad line from a play, doesn't it?' There was an awkward pause. 'Well, I don't know anything about you, Leslie. What sort of future have you?'

'Firth, we're both in the same line of business. You're at the top. I'm only starting. What's *your* future?' I asked.

'That's damned impertinent,' he said. I agree. But I am sorry to say he eventually died in debt.

However, Phyl and I became unofficially engaged. Not that there was much time to spend together. Television was an all-absorbing business, from early morning to late night every day of the week, except Sunday. But we made the most of my days off. I had acquired a sports model of the little Wolseley Hornet which made it possible to keep up my daily commitments at Broadcasting House, Ally Pally and Movietone.

One morning, arriving at Alexandra Palace, I settled down to work in my office as usual. D. H. Munro, came in to see me – he was obviously upset.

'Leslie,' he said, 'I'm terribly sorry about your car.'

I looked at him blankly. 'What do you mean?'

'Oh God, haven't you seen it? Come over to the window.'

There, several terraces down, a crowd was gathering. They were looking at an object hanging brokenly from the lowest branches of a tree. Some kids playing round with my open car must have released the brake. My Hornet was gone for ever. As I was only insured for third-party risks; it was a dead loss.

That evening several engineers in turn offered me a lift back to the West End. I think they all knew what I felt. We lived very close to each other in those days. It made for a warm relationship.

Phyl too was very upset when I told her about it, but insisted that I go out and find myself a good second-hand replacement. I found myself a beautiful aristocrat – an Alvis Speed 20. It had belonged to a rich woman who owned several cars, it had been chauffeur-maintained, and used very little. It was only three years old and it would cost me £180. I was still young enough to believe the salesman – and the price. I just about had the money to buy it on HP, which I did.

Some weeks after Phyl and I became engaged I got a hysterical telephone call from my mother. My stepfather had died quite suddenly; could I come at once and help her? I managed to get compassionate leave and drove down to Friston Court, their house near Eastbourne.

My mother was distraught; Owen had apparently died in his sleep. After the various disagreements and upsets of their married life I had been assured that my stepfather had made a new will leaving everything to my mother. He had told me so; she had confirmed it; his sister Hilda and her husband Henry Dutfield had told me; all his close friends had been let into the secret.

His will was locked in Henry Dutfield's office safe in the City, but Henry and Hilda were on holiday in the South of France. On their return they discovered the unpleasant facts. Owen had specifically left my mother one hundred pounds. He left debts in every direction. A business which he had inherited was losing money. He was personally overdrawn. In fact he had been living entirely on the proceeds of his partnership with his brother-in-law. Henry was general manager of the firm of contractors which provided the delivery vans and lorries for the Post Office.

Poor Phyl chose this moment to enter the London Clinic with acute appendicitis. I hardly knew which way to turn. The more I thought about it, the more hopeless the situation became. I would obviously have to support my mother and that put paid to any ideas of marriage.

As soon as Phyl was better I forced myself to explain these unpleasant circumstances to her. It was more than she could be expected to bear. The death of her first husband had been a tragic and overwhelming experience. I tried desperately to make it sound a sensible decision and, in fact, there was absolutely no alternative. I left the hospital in suicidal mood.

Henry Dutfield had invited me to dinner that night, and was in communicative vein. Owen, he told me, contributed little to the partnership. He was more interested in living the good life. Before he married my mother, he had been a gay bachelor, and for years boasted a manservant, a chauffeur and two cars, two hunters and a Queen's Gate address. He had left the Army as a major, and tried to make up for the discomforts of the First World War in every way. Henry had not been impressed.

He changed the subject: what was I doing about Phyl? I told him of my decision to break off our engagement.

'Good God, Leslie, you can't do *that*,' he said. 'I realize you have to think of your mother, but we can't allow poor Phyl to suffer for Owen's failings. Look, I've had an idea. I'll make your mother a sleeping partner in the business. We'll pay her £500 a year, tax free. How would that be?'

My eyes filled. I just couldn't speak. This was a totally unexpected turn of fortune; the past weeks had been a nightmare of apprehension.

We decided to bring my mother back to London and I found her a small flat near mine in the block to which I had just moved, where Phyl would join me when we were married. The house at Eastbourne was sold, as Clewer Meade had been, lock, stock and barrel. My mother was in a state of shock, but gratefully accepted Henry's generous offer. She became upset later when she discovered some of her treasured possessions displayed in Hilda's house. It made their friendship just a little stilted. But Phyl and I remained close to the Dutfields to the last.

When the dust had settled, our engagement was officially announced on 25 April 1938 and made headline news. Phyl was taken aback to find herself pursued by press and photographers. She never really enjoyed personal publicity. We arranged to get married as soon as possible and she chose 2 June. I asked Gerald Cock, Head of Television, if I could have the day off. Looking through the programme commitments, he replied it would be impossible to spare me as it was one of the busiest days of that week. But in any case, I was not required until the afternoon programmes began. I was a bit put out at this lack of interest but made arrangements for a morning ceremony at Marylebone Registry Office.

My chief impression of the occasion was that my wife made her responses in the sepulchral tones of a Paul Robeson and mine came out as a pathetic squeak, like Mickey Mouse. Afterwards we drove off in the Alvis to the Savoy Hotel where Phyl was to enjoy a wedding lunch with the family. After a quick glass of champagne I had to rush to Alexandra Palace in time for the afternoon rehearsal.

Late that evening, Gerald Cock asked me why the hell I had not explained I was serious about my marriage. Not believing me, he had just read about our wedding in the evening papers. Nevertheless, the moment the television programme closed down for the night, I raced off to the newsreel to complete my work for *them*. I eventually joined my bride at 2 a.m.

Through the years Phyl did become acclimatized to this sort of treatment. At least the extra money did contribute to a blissful honeymoon in the South of France some weeks later. We chose the South of France, partly because I was anxious to return to the scene of

my happy visits to the Lockes, and also because Phyl's mother was
now living there.

We motored all the way in the Alvis, enjoying the scenery and the
views, stopping as fancy dictated. This was the height of all my
ambitions – to enjoy the good life and pay my way in the company of
my wife. We both savoured every moment. But on the last morning of
our honeymoon I was worried to find that Phyl was running a high
temperature and having difficulty getting herself dressed. She tried to
reassure me and would not hear of my calling a doctor. 'No darling,'
she pleaded, 'just let me take things slowly, and I'll be all right.'

I knew she suffered from migraine, but this was the first time I had
seen the results of a bad attack. I found it very alarming. We set off for
Dieppe and the cross-channel ferry. I went aboard and spoke to the
captain, explaining that we were honeymooners, and my wife had
been taken ill. With true Gallic reaction, he insisted that she was
looked after during the voyage. True to his word, he had a bunk made
up in his cabin and made several sympathetic calls there en route for
Newhaven.

Phyl's doctor diagnosed too rich a diet as the main cause of her
trouble, and I became aware for the first time of the medical ignorance about the origins of migraine. Some experts regarded it as a
purely nervous affliction; others believed in a dietary origin; yet
others thought it a purely physical disturbance. Certainly it seemed
that each sufferer reacted differently to treatment – there was no
overall cure.

Throughout twenty-six happy years of marriage I believe this
created a closer bond than usual between husband and wife; we each
understood the physical disabilities of the other, and shared our
burdens.

On our return to London we settled down in the small furnished flat
which Mrs Locke had so generously let us take over from her. Having
had some trouble with the Alvis during the tour I sent it back for a
check-up. The engineers' report was disheartening. The salesman
had sold me a pup. The car required massive attention and what was
to all intents and purposes a complete new engine. But it *had* looked
good on our honeymoon. So I sold it and bought my first brand-new
car, a Ford V8 drophead, again on the never-never.

I was still obsessed by the desire to achieve security. And I was not
sure that my future in the BBC would ever lead to that desirable state
of affairs.

I woke one morning to find that my voice had all but gone, just at
the start of a heavy day. On my way to work, I stopped at a chemist
who diagnosed laryngitis and offered me some very unpleasant pills

which, he said, should do the trick although they would not make me *feel* very good. The pills were to be taken every half-hour in water. Arriving at Alexandra Palace, I made my way to the men's room for a drink of water and took my first dose. In my office, we were coping with a series of announcements, preparing a studio presentation and planning the outline for a forthcoming outside broadcast.

At the end of half an hour, I trailed along to the cloakroom once more for water with which to take my second pill. After the third journey and third pill, I decided to telephone for a glass and a carafe of water to be sent to my office.

'Who is that,' said the voice. 'Ah, Mr Mitchell, I'm afraid you are not *entitled* to a carafe of water and a glass, sorry,'

I slammed the receiver down and called up the Head of Television. 'You got me here, Gerald,' I croaked, 'and I really have just about had enough. I've just been told that I'm not entitled to a carafe of water in spite of the fact that I'm sitting here with laryngitis, preparing and writing two programmes and will be on duty for the rest of the day. If I can't have a carafe, you'll have no announcer!'

Smoothing me down with his accustomed understanding, Gerald promised me that if I could keep my temper, the carafe would arrive. As indeed it did – on a small circular tray, carried by a diminutive office-boy. Behind him loomed the head of the department. Waiting until the boy had left, he stared at me with a smouldering eye and announced, 'Mitchell, as you see you now have a carafe of water and a glass to which you are not properly entitled. I want to make it clear that this is solely because *I* have changed my mind.'

It was moments like this which made me wonder how long I could last in the Corporation. However, the decisive moment came when I applied for a rise in salary. Not a surprising move in view of the fact that I was performing the duties not only of Senior Announcer, Grade C (Temporary), but scriptwriter, producer and programme presenter (unpaid). Apparently my claim *was* discussed at some length. The suggestion that I might be made a junior producer with a resulting increase in salary was vetoed. At that time as the senior male announcer, my experience was too useful to allow my transfer. On top of this, it was decided that I must discontinue my work with the newsreel since it was patently becoming a second regular job rather than an occasional extra.

It was further pointed out to me that in less than four years my salary had been nearly trebled. From the original £260 per annum, I was now receiving £675 per annum, and had reached my salary ceiling. This was the final straw. I resigned and accepted Movietone's offer of three times this amount to become their permanent commentator. My letter of resignation was received by the BBC with 'regrets and good wishes'.

I did, however, arrange with Movietone that I would be free to work as a freelance for radio and television at any time, subject to my commitments with the newsreel. From then on, I worked with the BBC throughout and after the war only as a freelance.

The first offer I received from television was to appear once a week in my programme, 'Picture Page'. The fee offered was £1 10s. per show. I replied that since I had now returned to my former status of artist with an 'e' on the end, I could not afford it. We eventually settled for £10 for two shows.

I was glad to be with the newsreel, but sad to leave television. It had been a fascinating and exciting experience, but as Sophie Dixon had warned me when I first joined the BBC, I was certainly not cut out to be a civil servant.

10. Under Fire

With the outbreak of war in 1939, the days of television pioneering were brought to a close. Quite apart from the ominous future, all of us were desperately sad that this new and exciting medium should be discontinued just when it was beginning to make progress both publicly and technically. We went our separate ways with heavy hearts.

Movietone's headquarters were in Soho Square. Soon after the war began we were ordered out of London, and moved to the laboratories attached to Denham Film Studios, famous birthplace of the early Korda films – *The Private Life of Henry VIII, Fire over England, The Lion Has Wings,* and many other successes. But the period of the phoney war, 1939–40, decided the newsreel to return to London, leaving their large library of inflammable films in Denham. So we managed to get *back* to town in time for the start of the really *heavy* blitz from 1940 to 1943.

Anxious to get Phyl out of the capital in 1939, I had left the London flat and rented a cottage on the side of the Grand Union Canal at Harefield, just across the way from Denham Studios. Our landlord, Commander Dudley Colles, was a charming man attached to the royal family as Deputy Treasurer to King George VI. He willingly let us take the cottage for the duration. Little did any of us know how long 'the duration' would turn out to be. But it was certainly one of the happiest decisions I ever made. At first, my mother joined us, but she was never one to allow anyone else to take charge of her life. She left, with her attendant maid, after six months.

Meantime, Constance, Phyl's mother, had been stranded on the Riviera in Cannes, where she had gone to live after our marriage. She remained there after the Germans entered Paris, but was persuaded to escape in one of the last boats to leave the Riviera as the enemy made their way south. And it was Constance who replaced my mother in the cottage. Fortunately we were very fond of each other and we settled down happily, *en famille*. As a protector I had bought Charlie, a red bull terrier, and as a pet a Siamese cat called Flute. Sometimes these two would exchange jobs, but it was never more than a temporary aberration.

The cottage was small, two up and two down, but could be kept reasonably warm. Before long I had built a bomb-shelter as an extension to the brick garage. In it were four bunks and an oil heater plus a small cupboard for a kettle, cups and tea. Later we used it quite a lot when the enemy bombers were looking for nearby Northolt Aerodrome. There was gossip in the village when my wife shared the shelter with a Canadian Air Force officer, a personal friend of ours on leave, while I was detained for the night in London. Frankly I worried more about what the Siamese and the bull terrier were up to.

With my medical history, none of the Services would take me as a combatant. As a RAF doctor informed me when they turned me down, 'It's not you, old chap. It's the plane and anybody else that might be in it.' Anyway I was informed that my work with the newsreel placed me in the category of reserved occupations. Certainly the newsreel *did* become an important contribution to morale later on, but during the phoney war one was very conscious of the fact that most of one's friends were in the Services, and my civilian contribution to the war effort seemed useless indeed. I tried to make up for my omission by approaching the Ministry of Information with an idea for film propaganda.

At this time, of course, the Germans were convinced that they had beaten us already, and that the RAF was all but obliterated. This was largely due to the success of Dr Goebbels' propaganda machine and the overwhelming victories of the Luftwaffe from Poland to France. My idea was to record interviews with English-speaking German prisoners-of-war, together with newsreel pictures showing, for example, RAF fighters taking off from different British airfields, and the wreckage of German planes they had brought down. The pattern could be extended in various forms, and in each case pictures could counter the statements of the prisoners and go some way to disproving them.

The MOI received the idea with interest and invited me to submit it in script form. This I did, and was told that the matter was being urgently attended to. Some weeks went by before I heard that the Head of the Film Department had resigned – would I kindly send another résumé for his successor. I presented the idea again with new scripts, and was informed that the matter was being discussed at high level; would I be available to start producing material at short notice? I agreed to do so. More weeks passed, and I again phoned to ask what progress had been made. To my astonishment they informed me that they had no trace of any communication from me. A soothing secretarial voice explained that there had been yet another change in the department, and the outgoing chief had taken all the files with him. At this point I decided to mind my own business.

Some months later I was invited to make a commentary for this same department. The film, obviously made in peace-time, showed various aspects of Cambridge University and happy relaxed students enjoying their hours of leisure. Not a sign of barrage balloons, tin hats or gas masks. Presumably neutral countries were intended to believe that our traditional *sang-froid* allowed us to completely overlook the Blitz. The pictures seemed very remote in the desperate situation of 1941.

My own *sang-froid* covered an increasing worry. What best to do for my wife, my mother-in-law and my mother for their safety? Would my job with the newsreel work out? Would I be blacked by the BBC for leaving their staff? The biggest worry was would my health stand up to it? My back, my dud leg and my dislocating shoulder were all playing me up. For three years I had been working an almost unbroken fourteen-hour day from morning to late night. The results of my accident had become exaggerated by sheer nervous exhaustion.

But my luck held. Cecil Madden, who had instituted television's popular 'Picture Page', invited me to take up a radio interview programme which he called 'Close Up'. It started under the BBC Variety Department as a series of visits to stars of stage and screen, and was transmitted on the new Forces programme. At least, if I could not join the Services, I could help to entertain them.

One of the first of these radio interviews was with Jessie Matthews at the dress rehearsal of *Come Out to Play* in March 1940. Sonnie Hale was producing, and while my broadcast from Jessie's dressing-room interfered with the timing of the show, he accepted it as good publicity.

Jessie had to make a quick change before I left her and asked me to look the other way. As I did so, everything went black, and I collapsed on the floor. Jessie poured brandy over my face and generally tried to do the right thing, as did her dresser. Eventually I was sent back home in a hired car. The doctor called it a breakdown and ordered me to rest up for a fortnight.

Luckily Peter Fry, a young friend in the RAF, turned up on a three-day leave and at once offered to drive Phyl and me to Brighton. We gladly accepted and he drove my car. I was astounded by the fact that he drove all the way at about twenty miles an hour. Not the normal behaviour of a dashing young RAF officer in my experience.

Having delivered us safely at long last, he explained. 'Well actually, old boy, I had my licence taken away the other day. Bit of trouble in London!' While Phyl and I were grateful to him for taking us down, we were horrified he had taken such a risk. Tragically he was to lose his life shortly afterwards in a RAF training exercise.

After my enforced rest, I rushed back to the newsreel and to 'Close Up'. After a time a note of monotony had begun to creep into the show. Really there are only two forms of success story in show business – the long uphill climb to eventual stardom, or the exciting success of a young performer who makes the grade overnight. I wanted to enlarge on this pattern in the programme. I put forward the idea that 'Close Up' should include people from all walks of life and cover a variety of subjects. The idea was immediately vetoed.

Ruminating over this setback, another idea occurred to me. I knew Harold Nicolson whom I had met on several occasions. He was now a member of the BBC's Board of Governors. I phoned him.

'You may remember me, Mr Nicolson? I'm now working in the BBC and conducting a series of interviews.' He said he'd actually listened to some. 'Well, I'm desperately anxious to attempt something more serious. Could I perhaps persuade *you* to be my first subject?'

'My dear chap. That's very nice of you, but I'm afraid it's out of the question. As a Governor of the BBC I'm expressly forbidden to broadcast.'

Apologizing for my ignorance, I admitted that in the circumstances, it put paid to my new plan.

'Don't say that, it sounds an excellent idea – I'll talk to someone about it.' I thanked him sincerely. I had a feeling he would do what he said.

Some weeks later it was agreed to give me my head. The programme and I were handed over, lock, stock and barrel to the Talks Department under George Barnes, Head of the Spoken Word. (I always thought that the most idiotic title ever dreamed up. How, was it imagined, did other radio departments communicate? There was no Head of the Unspoken Word, of course.)

In an attempt to get away from the mundane questionnaire, hitherto scripted for interviewers by roving journalists, I pressed for the billing of the new 'Close Up' series to read: 'Leslie Mitchell, in conversation with . . .'This gave me the opportunity to react to what was said in a normally intelligent manner, rather than probing for information in pretended ignorance. During the war everything had to be scripted. There was no possibility of continuing my television practice of ad-libbing from headlines, but I had learned the advantage of dispensing with a scriptwriter. So I decided to enlist the services of a high-speed parliamentary reporter. These were secretaries of considerable intelligence and experienced in verbatim shorthand.

With the reporter present I could interview my personalities in the certainty that we would be faithfully recorded word for word. On receiving the rough script, I would tidy it up for length and content, then send it back to my victim. Almost inevitably there would be an urgent telephone call. 'I say, Mitchell, I've just read the script. It isn't even good grammar. I'm sure I don't talk like that!' It took time, but having explained that I wanted people to speak as they normally did, *not* read from an alien script, they agreed to try it out. And they *did* sound spontaneous.

My plan failed only once when I invited the novelist, Rose Macaulay, to appear in 'Close Up'. As usual I first went to see her to settle the subject of our discussion. I had in mind 'The Effect of the War on Women'. We had an interesting preliminary conversation and I tried to arrange a meeting with her and my invaluable high-speed reporter.

'Oh no, Mr Mitchell, I'd be no good at all. It would come out very badly. But I've listened to your programme quite often. Why don't you just write me a script?' *So* – against all my instincts – I produced a script, hopefully trying to remember her phrases or turns of speech.

The broadcast was very successful. Miss Macaulay wrote me afterwards: 'Several people I've met thought we were being spontaneous. Little do they know . . . Of course, if it had been, my part at least would have been full of 'ers and hums and going round in circles. My aunt's cook (who was thrilled to hear your voice) said: "Miss Rose got the best of the argument" – I expect your aunt's cook thought *you* did!' That *I* should write for Rose Macaulay!

The new series was successful enough to achieve Number Two in the Forces Network, a high rating in the listening charts of those days. Early on in the series, however, I met George Barnes face to face in one of the endless BBC corridors. 'Leslie,' said he, 'this "Close Up" programme of yours has put me in a very embarrassing situation. I find the Talks Department now has a popular programme on its hands. That is something we have always striven desperately to avoid.' Although he said it pleasantly enough, there was a ring of truth in what he said. To him 'popular' programme implied a large and unintelligent audience.

This attitude always infuriated me since it presumed that the job of serious broadcasting was to preach only to the converted. I still believe the aim of public discussion should be to interest as many people as possible – not by talking down to them, but by saying what there is to say in an interesting and informative manner. Adults usually object to being lectured, and although part of the BBC's charter calls upon it to 'educate, instruct and inform', theirs is no captive audience. The majority of adults resent being talked down to and their resentment takes the form of switching to another programme or turning off altogether.

Obviously, in the pursuit of mass information, instruction or education, the first necessity is to arouse the interest of an audience – then to hold it. This can be and has often been done: examples taken at random are Julian Huxley on biology, Sir Thomas Beecham and Sir Malcolm Sargent on music, Professor Bronowski on science, Sir Brian Horrocks on military strategy, Sir Kenneth Clark on art, and Sir Mortimer Wheeler on archaeology. But where in England can we find the equivalent of America's Ed Murrow, who for years held a vast audience with his intelligent interpretations of the political, economic and social questions of the day. And Alastair Cooke had to leave England to attain his present eminence. Americans welcome the common touch, and pay for excellence in any form.

The fact is that in England, 'personality', with its attendant publicity, is too often regarded as a cheapening disadvantage which detracts from the worth of both speaker and subject. Sir Winston Churchill was one obvious exception, but he too was regarded with deep suspicion in his formative years. The extrovert has always been disliked by the quasi-intellectuals of England.

In my own case, I had started work with the BBC as an announcer, and announcers were forbidden to express personal opinions or to project themselves in any way. Fortunately, the fact that my own personality began to emerge through my work was suffered benignly, since I was known to have been an actor – and in the BBC actors were generally regarded as unintelligent oddities. In fact, dear Valerie Hobson received a letter from a head woman of the Talks Department enclosing (in error) a list of possible speakers for a future programme. Mentioning a number of well-known people, it ended: '. . . of course, there *are* actors and actresses, but they are not intelligent'. Who's talking . . .?

I remember in particular an interview with the film star, Leslie Howard. My secretary failed to turn up, so I went alone to see him at Denham Studios. We had met before on a number of occasions and liked each other. There were no difficulties. I took my notes, then made my way home to Harefield. The 'Close Up' interview was to take place at the BBC on the following Sunday. The Friday before I was attacked by fearful pains which proved to be due to stones in the kidney, and was told by my doctor there was no possibility of undertaking either the journey to London or the interview. I vigorously rejected his advice, since there happened to be nobody who could replace me in the schedule. He finally agreed that I could go with my wife if she would carry a hypodermic syringe containing a necessary painkiller. Phyl somewhat nervously assented after some elementary demonstrations of how to make an injection.

Came the day and George Barnes decided to join us. At the BBC studio below ground was an adjacent waiting-room from which speakers could be observed through glass panels. I went through to see Leslie Howard and have a short preparatory talk. Phyl sat with his girl-friend in the waiting-room, and tidily set out the prepared hypodermic syringe on the table beside her, watching me anxiously the while. Suddenly George made his entrance. Looking quickly around, he smiled a strange smile and gave her a prodigious wink. Phyl, who had not yet met him, was rather disturbed. She pulled her skirts further over her knees – had she been showing too much leg? – and waited.

But the *interview* itself was a success. Talking about it later, George said, 'I liked the programme – excellent. I hadn't realized you stage-people were so open about things.'

'What things?' I asked.

'Well, drugs and so on – I presume the hypodermic belonged to one of the girls?'

It was reactions of this kind which made me realize what a blot I had made in my BBC copybook by having been an actor.

As my confidence grew, so I tried again to extend the range of the 'Close Up' programme. It occurred to me that a large percentage of the electorate had never had a chance to vote since the establishment of a coalition government during the war. With the end of the war in sight, it was obvious that there would be an election and a very large number of potential voters would be completely ignorant of the aims and objects of the individual political parties. With this in mind, I approached George Barnes for permission to question representatives from each party.

Until then it had been my job to devise the subjects, and find the speakers. My new idea was received with grave doubt; but eventually it was decided that *they* would choose the political speakers for me. Their choice fell on Arthur Greenwood for Labour, Wilfred Roberts for the Liberals, and Sir George Courthope for the Conservatives; Lord Davies also spoke about the aims of the New Commonwealth

Party, and Arthur Gibson on the aims and objects of the TUC.

Being one of the seven and a half millions who had never voted – and felt no great desire to do so – I had no difficulty in treating these discussions with complete impartiality. It quickly transpired that each party wished to be described as 'progressive', and though the word might once have had some significance, it now meant nothing more than a desire to appear far-seeing and up to date.

However it is always dangerous to get involved in politics when you are not directly concerned. I was astounded when Ralph Hall-Caine, son of the great novelist and an old friend, who had long been a Conservative MP, refused to speak to me over a period of years. In his opinion, my presentation of the Tory case had been the least successful of them all. My explanation that I was not responsible for the content or the speaker fell on deaf ears, though we made it up eventually.

Some time later I was approached by Howard Marshall, the famous BBC sports commentator of pre-war years, who was now public relations officer at the Food Ministry. He suggested that my programme might be a useful vehicle in which to discuss with Lord Woolton some of the problems of war-time rationing, as a variation from his official talks as Minister of Food. I duly met the Minister who had troubled to listen to my broadcast the night before and discussed it in some detail – an example of his meticulous efficiency. We talked about the form the broadcast should take, but unfortunately nothing ever came of it. He told me later that he had been informed that the BBC did not consider me of sufficient calibre to interview a Cabinet Minister. I was naturally somewhat annoyed by this criticism.

'Close Up' continued without further incident until the day I was told it was to be taken off the air immediately. The order came from a particularly high-ranking BBC official. I was given absolutely no warning of the decision and, having already arranged a number of programmes in advance, made my own investigations. I learned that my expulsion was due to 'the extreme vulgarity of a remark made by me in "Close Up" the previous week'. Nettled, and extremely puzzled, I attempted to get an explanation from the Head of Talks, but was told he was too busy to see me. By devious means, I discovered that the complaint had been made by a *friend* of the official who had banned me. After further inquiry, it turned out that the programme of which he had complained was not mine at all. The following week I was asked to resume the series.

But once more I ran into trouble with the Corporation. 'Close Up' had been a glorious victory as far as I was concerned, and had received nothing but good reactions from the press and public. Once more the series was brought to a temporary close. George Barnes got in touch with me by phone. We were now on a friendly basis. 'Leslie,' he said, 'we've been happy about the political programmes you've been doing. Would you be prepared to take on a programme about the Empire? You'd have to deal with it discreetly, of course.'

I was deeply interested, and very prepared to be 'discreet', whatever that might mean. I decided to call it 'Red on the Map', and contacted several possible speakers to sound out their availability.

It was now that the BBC Contracts Department rang me up. 'Hello, Leslie,' said the voice. 'I want to have a word with you about your fee – it *is* too high, you know.'

I pointed out that I had been paying an outside secretary and entertaining visitors to lunch in order to get to know them. In fact it often cost me about £3 a week *more* than my fee. Only my Movietone income allowed me to afford it.

'That's not what people are saying,' he answered. 'You must have seen the article in the *Star*.

I hadn't. So my secretary went to find one. It was headed: 'Why the BBC Overspends'!

The writer, without mentioning names, told of a junior member of the Corporation who had jumped in a few years from £5 a week to some thousands a year from the BBC, added to which he was earning regular amounts from a newsreel and work with documentary and propaganda films. This gross overpayment of personnel, etc. I have forgotten the details now, but the victim was certainly intended to be me. I was seething with anger.

I made my way for lunch to the Bolivar – a restaurant and bar of the Langham Hotel opposite Broadcasting House. As I fully expected, the radio critic of the *Star* was there.

'Hello, Leslie,' said he jovially, 'have a drink.' I refused. 'You got something on your mind, you look worried?'

'I am,' I replied. 'What have I ever done to you? We don't even know each other well!'

His face changed. 'Oh Lord, you've seen that article, have you?' I saw he was concerned. 'Actually Leslie, it only appeared in the first edition. I rang the paper immediately and it was out of the later editions.'

So that is why I had missed it. And *he* had not written it? Dark suspicions loomed in my mind. It transpired that he had been ill in bed when he read it, and hurriedly contacted the *Star*. They had taken it out at once. But of course, it would be a breach of professional etiquette to tell me the name of the anonymous author.

Some time earlier, much to my surprise, someone had written an unsuccessful programme series called 'BBC Close-Up.' Could there be some connection? I looked round the bar. At the far end lounged one of the BBC's better-known scriptwriters. I moved over next to him.

'It's appalling, there's so much jealousy and back-biting in the Corp!' I said it to nobody in particular, as I took a drink.

'Why this critical throwaway, Leslie? What's the Corp done now?' he asked.

I took a deep breath. 'Some ass in the Corporation has written an article about me which is not only grossly inaccurate (and that won't please the editor), but has prompted the BBC to discontinue using me. As you know, the BBC strictly forbids its members writing for the press. My solicitor tells me I have a good case for damages.' I watched his face. Was it my imagination or had he paled visibly?

'Do you know who it is?'

'Yes, I think so,' I answered.

'But you wouldn't be such a fool, would you? You'd never work again.'

'No, but apparently I won't anyway! And at least for once I'll be paid quite a lot for nothing!'

It was quite untrue of course that I had approached my solicitor. But at the end of that week, I received an invitation to broadcast at the old fee. I never got any further with the suggested 'Empire' programme. Someone else did it.

Apart from 'Close Up', I was of course working twice weekly for the newsreel, plus any extra special war stories of importance as and when they occurred.

Early war-time newsreels consisted of very unrevealing pictures. Shots of British troops marching through the English countryside hardly made a dramatic story, and were far from indicative of the hectic preparations being made to arm and equip the nation for another Great War. It was a frustrating period for everybody connected with news.

During the early stages of the war, it was often difficult to understand why film censorship was applied so rigidly. The British Expeditionary Force was then taking up its positions in France and Belgium, and obviously pictures might give away their locality, their armaments, or the direction in which they were moving. But the Luftwaffe was already busy observing troop movements in Britain. They were also checking daily on aerodromes and defence works round our coast; so it did seem rather absurd when we were ordered to remove all pictures of coastal barrage balloons, which could be seen from a considerable distance – even from occupied France and Belgium.

The story went that round about this time an exasperated American correspondent in London sent a long cable to his New York office containing technical details of a torpedo in current use by the Royal Navy. Understandably, he was quickly picked up by MI5 and taken for interrogation. He blandly explained that every word in his cable had been copied from the *Encyclopaedia Britannica* and could hardly be called secret information. The authorities were not amused.

It worked both ways of course: one of my first war-time radio interviews was with Ed Murrow, the famous American CBS broadcaster, about news broadcasting. He told me the following story: America had not yet decided to join us, so Ed was reporting – as a civilian – about London during the Blitz. He bravely finished his piece with the sound of a large bomb whistling down and a nearby building collapsing. It was a close thing. Brushing the dust and debris from his clothes, he congratulated himself on getting away with it so luckily, and duly dispatched his recording by plane. The phone rang in his office two days later. 'Ed, that was a great story on the London Blitz. Only one snag. Could you get that bomb sound again? Didn't sound quite real.' Of course, in New York, the war was a long way off.

The difference was soon made clear to *me*. I finished a 'Close Up' at Broadcasting House and went out to look at the night sky. There had been an air-raid warning before the programme started. Now, an hour later, the searchlights were combing the heavens. The anti-aircraft batteries in Hyde Park were belching flames, reflected in the darkness, and the throbbing drone of enemy planes was loud overhead. Falling shrapnel could be heard pittering on the slates of buildings around.

After a look round I decided to have a cup of coffee in the canteen before undertaking the seventeen-mile drive to Harefield. I sat with friends and talked shop. Suddenly the lights went out and there was a tremendous crash which, even two floors down, shook the walls. I automatically started to dive under the table. Then I pulled myself together and started running upstairs. The emergency lighting had not yet taken over and it was pretty dim. Upstairs in the entrance-hall there was a huddled group of people in the gloom.

The commissionaire spotted me. 'Don't go outside, Mr Mitchell. There's nothing we can do. Your car 'as 'ad it, I'm afraid.' *My car!* The car I had worked on and cleaned and looked after ever since my honeymoon? My one and only brand-new car?

I pushed my way past him. There she was, poor love, burning furiously. A great hole in her door. Canvas hood reduced to nothing. Windscreen and windows gone. I leant through the off-side window frame and felt for the fire extinguisher. It was almost red-hot. I looked round and saw the body of a special constable. It was not a pretty sight.

I spent the night with other BBC employees in the basement of a nearby building.

By morning the bodies had been moved and my car had cooled. I went to her and, sitting on the seat springs, slowly began unscrewing the St Christopher badge on the dashboard. Some BBC types came along and stopped to look. 'Good lord, Leslie – this *your* car?'

I sadly confirmed the fact and added, 'It wasn't an amusing evening was it? But I wish I knew who the chap was who kept shouting "It's all right everybody, it's only a bomb and the damn thing's gone off now! Don't panic! Stay just where you are!" I could have killed *him*! He nearly started a panic!'

One of the girls gave me a sharp look. 'But Leslie dear, it was *you*!' I still can't believe it – but that is what the girl said. Two days later, I came out a nasty yellow all over. I had got jaundice.

An unpublished Home Security Report describes the incident:

BBC Land Mine – 8 December 1940

The immediate impact on mind and body of a bomb explosion near at hand should not be belittled. Some 50,000 bombs fell on the capital. Many times that number of ordinary Londoners thereby suffered such an intense shock, even if they were physically unhurt, as comes to few people in the whole length of a normal peace-time life. Here is a report from a man who was probably nearer to the explosion of a large bomb than anyone else who remained conscious and survived to tell the tale.

'Several things happened simultaneously – my head was jerked back due to a heavy blow on the dome and rim of the back of my steel helmet. I do not remember this for, as my head went back, I received a severe blow on my forehead at the root of my nose. The missile bent up the front rim of my steel helmet and knocked it off my head. The explosion made an indescribable noise – something like a colossal growl – and was accompanied by a veritable tornado of air blast. I felt an excruciating pain in my ears and all sounds were replaced by a very loud singing noise (which I was told later was when I lost my hearing and had my eardrums perforated). I felt that consciousness was slipping from me and at that moment I "heard" a clear loud voice shouting "Don't let yourself go! Face up to it and hold on". It rallied me and, summoning all my will power and energy, I succeeded in forcing myself down into a crouching position with my knees on the ground, my feet against the kerb behind me and my hands covering my face. I remember having to move them over my ears because of the pain in them – doubtless due to the blast – it seemed to ease the pain. Then I received another hit on the forehead and felt weaker. The blast seemed to come in successive waves accompanied by vibrations from the ground. I felt as if it were trying to "spin" me and tear me away from the kerb. Then I received a very heavy blow just in front of the right temple – which knocked me down on my left side in the gutter. (Later, in our First Aid Post, they removed what they described as a "piece of bomb" from that wound.) Whilst in the gutter, I clung on the kerb with both hands and with my feet against it. I was again hit in the right chest – (and later found that my double breasted overcoat, my coat, leather comb case and papers had been cut through and a watch in the top right hand pocket of my waistcoat had the back dented in and its works broken). Just as I felt that I could not hold out much longer I realized that the blast pressure was decreasing and a shower of dust, dirt and rubble swept across me. Pieces penetrated my face, some skin was blown off, and something pierced my left thumb nail and my knuckles were cut, causing me involuntarily to let go my hold on the kerb. Instantly, although the blast was dying down, I felt myself being slowly blown across the pavement towards the wall of a building. I tried to hold on – but there was nothing to hold on to. Twice I tried to rise, but seemed *held* down – eventually I staggered to my feet.

'The front of the building was lit by a reddy-yellow light – the saloon car was on fire to the left of me and the flames from it were stretching out towards the building and not upwards. Pieces of brick, masonry and glass seemed to appear on the pavement, making – to me – no sound. A few dark huddled bodies were round about and right in front of me were two soldiers – one, some feet from a breach in the wall of the building, where a fire seemed to be raging, was propped up against the wall with his arms dangling by him, like a rag doll. The other was nearer, about twelve feet from the burning car. He was sitting up with his knees drawn up and supporting himself by his arms. His trousers had been blown off him. I could see his legs were bare and that he was wearing short grey underpants. There appeared to be one or two dark huddled bodies by the wall of the building. I had not the strength to lift any of them. I wondered where the water was coming from, which I felt dripping down my face, and soon discovered that it was blood from my head wounds.

'The effect of the blast on my clothes is possibly of interest. I was wearing bicycle clips round the bottoms of my trousers at the time. After the blast was over, my double-breasted overcoat was slit up the back and torn in several places, but was being held together by the belt. My trousers and underpants were pitted with small cuts about an inch long, but presumably the bicycle clips prevented the draught getting up my trousers and tearing them off.

I managed quickly to find another car, a second-hand MG, to use for my Home Guard, newsreel and BBC commitments. Three weeks after losing the Ford, on 29 December 1940, I came up to London for another 'Close Up' with Bernard Newman, the well-known journalist, at Bush House in the Strand.

When we finished the broadcast we were warned not to leave the building. From the flat roof we saw the sky lit like daylight. To our left St Paul's Cathedral appeared to be engulfed by flames. To our right big fires had sprung up in the direction of Buckingham Palace and Victoria Station. Warehouses in the City and on the South Bank of the river were ablaze in all directions. It really did seem for a few moments that we had lost the war.

The air was filled with smoke and flying ashes. In the distance we could hear the crackle of burning timber and the sounds of falling brickwork. I decided to look for my movie camera which I had stupidly left in my car in a nearby garage. I ran across the street and into the garage. A fireman was standing there, black with grime. 'Your car?' he said. 'There aren't any bleeding cars coming out of 'ere. The lift's gone. The water mains 'ave gone. And I've all but gone myself. Can't get your car, mate! Sorry!'

I slept under the piano in the studio until morning. Fortunately I did get the car back later – intact.

As I mentioned I also used the MG for my Home Guard commitments. With my dud leg I was incapable of marching any distance. One day we had an exercise in which I agreed to play the part of an enemy tank.

I was driving along an apparently empty stretch of road with the windows open, when a large brick came sailing through the window, grazed my head and passed out of the other window. I accelerated sharply round a bend, stopped and picked up a rock. Turning the car round and calling loudly, 'Look out,' I hurled the rock vaguely in the direction of my unseen assailant. I could see nothing and nobody – our section was good at camouflage – but there was an almighty yell and a stream of white-hot language. I had hit the 'enemy' full in the face! I took him back to hospital for treatment, and he appeared to take it in good part – but it shook me.

In the early part of the war I had become a Local Defence Volunteer together with a member of the Movietone staff, Jack Cross, our chief projectionist. He and I were good friends, and he lived quite near to us at Rickmansworth. We joined up together at the time when there were literally no modern weapons to distribute in England. They had all been issued to the Expeditionary Force. In some cases members of the LDV were even issued with pikes from historic armouries.

Came the big day when our first rifles arrived. Jack and I went to headquarters to check the issue. Jack had been through the last war and knew about firearms. As we listened to the instructor explaining their use, there was a loud explosion and a bullet buried itself in the floor about an inch from Jack's foot. He went home and spent the rest of the war in the Fire Service. 'Not for me, Leslie,' he confessed. 'I like to *know* who's trying to kill me.'

Later the LDV became the Home Guard – *now* the butt of comedians. Not then. We took it all seriously. But I found my wretched infirmities were a constant drawback, sometimes giving rise to the suspicion I was 'playing up' or 'laying it on thick', not least among the lads in my section.

We were defending a part of the Grand Union Canal, the official border of the outer London defences. We also manned pill boxes along the canal side. It occurred to me that not only should our defences look over the canal, but we might well be forced to swim across it to get back to our base. So I got together a detachment of volunteers to demonstrate the difficulties of swimming in full uniform, with rifle and tin hat. Not only that, on the far side, the Irish Guards had built an assault course, and I determined we would have a go at that as well.

We assembled on the canal bank, and I went first with a piece of rope which I had attached to the hedge. I got over breathless – wet – but military. 'Come on, chaps. Come on. One at a time. You're all right. Keep going. Hang on to the rope. It's not deep. Come on. . . . Come on.' The first hero went straight to the bottom, tin hat, rifle and all. Only the bubbles escaping to the surface betrayed his where-abouts. I plunged in and helped him to the far side. The third hero tripped in the weed and fell headlong. Another needed rescuing.

At last we gathered at the start of the Guards' assault course. First a swinging bridge; then a tall brick wall; then a rope jump across a crater, and so on, back to HQ at the top of the hill. 'Come on,' I bawled, 'come on, it's not a dance hall – get cracking!' Seeing the last man over the swinging bridge, I started to run after him. There was a blinding pain and I collapsed. When I collected my senses there was no sign of the others. Slowly I returned to the canal and somehow got back.

Our cottage was only half a mile away. My mother-in-law saw me stagger into the garden. 'Darling,' she said, 'this whole business is bloody ridiculous. Get out of that uniform and I'll pour you a brandy.' It was a stiff brandy, and I appeared in civilian clothes with the car about ten minutes later at HQ. 'It's all very well for *you*, chum,' muttered an exhausted figure. It was no good my trying to explain, but from that day on I was forced to wear a spinal jacket.

At Harefield, being in a direct line with the German flying-bomb launchers and London, we did receive many 'overthrows'. In all I believe we had over a hundred and twenty incidents in our area.

On my return home one evening from the newsreel, at that time still in London, Phyl met me excitedly at the door. 'Oh darling,' she said, 'am I glad to see you! I was in the kitchen this evening and an aeroplane flew past – right outside the window! I was frightened to death.' As the cottage stood beside the canal at the bottom of a steep hill, it was obvious she had been mistaken. It was dusk now, but she had heard no sounds of a crash – no bang, no fire, no explosion. I laughed her out of her fright, and we went to bed.

The following morning I was up early. There, in the marshy ground on the other side of the canal, the Royal Engineers and RAF were assembled in force, dissecting – very gingerly – one of the first unexploded flying bombs of the war. Phyl had been right. Now *I* was scared.

An essential safety precaution during the Blitz was to get away from windows. Flying glass killed more civilians than could be counted. I made Phyl and her mother, Constance, promise to throw themselves on the floor if they ever heard the nearby scream of a bomb.

One winter morning I was lying in the permitted war-time amount of bathwater. The sirens had gone, announcing another daylight raid. Then, after the noise of desynchronized engines – sure sign of enemy planes – there was that high-pitched scream, an explosion, and a shockwave through the cottage.

From next door came a more frightening scream. My mother-in-law's room! I dashed in, naked, and stood there in the doorway. Constance had fallen on the cat. It was the cat that screamed – my mother-in-law was no light weight.

Meanwhile strict censorship had become a vital necessity. What with film from the invaded countries and the beginning of the Battle of Britain, the newsreels had more than adequate material on which to draw, and there arose a very real risk of accidentally giving away secret information about troop-movements or new types of armament and aircraft. During the Blitz we had to be careful not to show the extent of damage done by the Luftwaffe. Dispositions of the Fleet could be assessed from pictures of the Navy at sea. The whereabouts of leading commanders or statesmen could be traced by the scenery behind them. Eventually a censor had to sit with our editorial board for the screening of *all* material. Much of it had to be scrapped.

When news came of the sinking of the *Bismarck*, we begged the Admiralty for any kind of film coverage to illustrate the victory since none of our cameramen took part in the action. After some delay we received a story from the Admiralty on 16-mm film, obviously taken by an amateur, but still worth showing as the only record of a historic occasion. We watched it with mounting excitement. Clearly the film had been taken from one of our smaller ships – perhaps a destroyer. The movements of the camera indicated that she was rolling quite considerably in not very rough weather. On the skyline appeared the bulk of a large battleship. This must be the *Bismarck*.

The camera held steadily on her – she was moving in the same direction. After some moments there was a violent explosion in the area of the bridge. There was a flash of flame, then a long plume of smoke. This was the climax of the film. Obviously a newsreel scoop – factual moving pictures of one of the most dramatic events of the war.

Suddenly doubts began to assail me. Having been an enthusiastic user of 16-mm film for years, it seemed to me that the pictures of the *Bismarck* could not have been taken from a greater distance than two miles, judging by the size of the battleship in comparison with the screen. If, as I thought, the film had been taken from a British corvette or a destroyer, she would hardly have held on to a parallel course at such short range without being blown out of the water. Could there have been some mistake? I expressed my doubts to my colleagues. We looked at it again. Eventually they asked the Admiralty to send an expert to check. In due course, an old friend, Commander Anthony Kimmins, arrived. (Having forsaken playwriting and film-directing for the duration, he was back in the Navy.) He, too, was puzzled. So there was another delay while yet another expert was sent for. In the early hours of the morning, the sad truth came out. The battleship was British, and being put out of action by a direct hit. The film was *not* shown. I believe what we were watching was the occasion in which poor Esmond Knight, the actor, lost his sight on the *Prince of Wales*.

Like all newscasters, we were often requested to put out items intended to deceive the enemy. One of the simplest was a story we did (in conjunction with the Food Ministry) with the brilliant fighter pilot, 'Cat's-Eye' Cunningham, a leading ace of the RAF. He was among the first to bring down an enemy plane from one of the newly developed 'night-fighters' – hence his nickname. This was at a time when the Ministry of Food was holding a considerable glut of carrots. The public had to be persuaded to buy them. Children were to be seen eating them on sticks as a substitute for almost unobtainable sweets, and even adults were persuaded that carrots raw, carrots mashed, carrots boiled – but anyway, carrots would do them no end of good. In fact they would also help one to see better in the dark. In the blackout this was a worthwhile incentive in itself. We presented pictures of me with Group-Captain Cunningham cheerfully munching his way through a meal of raw carrots and solemnly stating that his success in night-fighting might well be attributed to this diet. The truth was that the

RAF had incorporated radar in their new night-fighters. It was believed that the enemy had not yet discovered this, but the increasing accuracy of our fire was causing them growing losses.

Throughout the war, I suppose those of us working for the newsreels became more *visually* aware of what was going on in different battle areas than some of the Top Brass whose job it was to concentrate on one theatre of operation or one of the Services. Needless to say the strategy behind it all was *not* revealed to us.

Pictures poured in from every source: from the Americans in the Pacific; the Australians in China and the Forgotten Army in Burma; the Russian front. They came from the fleets of the Atlantic and Mediterranean; from convoys to Russia and fighter and bomber attacks over occupied countries and Germany; and, of course, from the home front during the Blitz. All were covered by teams of cameramen, in and out of uniform, whose job it was to go to the danger-spots and bring back pictures at whatever risk to themselves. Theirs was a thankless job, and no one can really assess their contribution to the morale of the civilian population.

A moving picture makes a deeper impression on the general public than any written dispatches, and much of the spirit of urgency among civilians in offices and factories stemmed from their better understanding of war through the eyes of the newsreels. I believe even the brilliant reports of BBC reporters and war correspondents seldom had quite as much impact, though of course newsreels had to summarize *everything* into twenty minutes per week.

From the earliest days of mankind, and the caves of Lascaux, history has similarly come alive through pictures – the only truly international form of mass communication.

11. Allied Interests

As the grim realities of the Blitz began to recede, my own horizons broadened. It was during the war that I first met a truly remarkable young man, Harry Alan Towers. Before 1939 he had been working for Radio Luxembourg in some minor capacity, but he had since developed into a first-rate scriptwriter and producer of radio programmes. At the time we met, he was only twenty-one and, as a corporal in the RAF playing an extremely active part in the Services' Broadcasting Units. Inside him, I swear, was some atomic pill which produced sufficient energy to run the entire Air Force, let alone their broadcasting unit. Ideas poured from him in an overwhelming stream, and his commercial instinct was so highly developed, he might have become a millionaire without difficulty. In fact, I believe he did have that in mind.

He was writing a series of radio programmes on the film industry and I was MC. We were all enormously impressed by his quick thinking and resourcefulness. Before long, he and I decided to team up as a partnership. Knowing the *Daily Mail* was looking for a promotion scheme, we hit on the idea of producing a number of recorded all-star shows for South East Asia Command – the Forgotten Army. These programmes were to be recorded live from well-known theatres all over the country, and invited audiences would be confined to relatives of men in the Far East. The idea was that the troops would not only hear a first-class radio variety programme, but would feel in closer touch with their relatives and friends at home.

The *Daily Mail* professed interest, but did not see quite how the scheme could be worked out. I suggested they saw my new partner, explaining that his somewhat untidy appearance and obvious youthfulness should not deter them from listening to what he had to say. In due course Harry went to see them, armed with names, facts and figures. In record time, he had overcome all opposition and sold the idea.

Also during the next two years, we worked on radio adaptations of a number of currently successful films, a new series on famous cases from Scotland Yard, and promoted the *Daily Mail* Annual Film Awards. Many of the recorded programmes we devised together were heard in Canada, America and Australia. Later after we had parted company, by a strange quirk of fate Harry found himself another partner – a Canadian radio producer called *Les* Mitchell! This created a confusion both here and abroad which persisted for a long time. In fact, I learned that there was a mistaken impression that I was working with Harry in commercial radio, which of course was forbidden to anybody working for the BBC.

I have already made the point that my freelance activities were often a subject of deep suspicion in the BBC, possibly because of my obvious interest in making a living. This was natural perhaps since my having no private income *did* lead to my accepting almost any job offered me.

In 'Close Up' they had almost allowed me my head – apart from the occasion when they tried to ban me for somebody else's mistake. But another incident demonstrated that my attempts at versatility were still unacceptable.

The 'Brains Trust' was at the height of its popularity under the witty jurisdiction of Donald McCullough, its question master. For some reason, he was unable to take part in several programmes, and I was invited to replace him. I did so diffidently enough, and was pleased to learn that a large number of listeners had written to the BBC in complimentary fashion about my handling of the programme. Shortly afterwards, having shown me some of these letters, Howard Thomas, the producer, asked me whether I would be agreeable to sharing Donald's job, appearing alternately with him, a suggestion to which I happily agreed.

Once more officialdom stepped in. They discovered they had already engaged me for a BBC variety programme with Vic Oliver, and gravely informed me that I could hardly expect to take part in a serious programme as well. It seemed somewhat ridiculous in view of the fact that I had already proved myself acceptable in both functions.

Fortunately I was later asked to join the original 'Brains Trust' team as question master under the auspices of the *Daily Express*. I travelled with them to Navy, Army and Air Force stations all over the country, and came to know the team individually.

Dr Joad was an intriguing speaker, but I was disappointed to find that his reaction to any given subject would vary from audience to audience. On one occasion he would speak vehemently against; at another he would be equally vehemently in favour. In either case, he was misleadingly convincing. I remember how angry he became at one RAF station when I introduced him as 'the Monarch of the Gen'. I believe he got more pleasure from displaying the range of his mind than he ever got from a straightforward exposition of the answer to a question.

Another member of the team, Julian Huxley, was invaluable because of his natural understanding of the public. A brilliant scientist and biologist, he also had the common touch and was able to explain the most abstruse facts and problems to the average man. He was also modest and unassuming. No wonder he became so popular. Lord Winster became a great friend. He was a typical English gentleman of the old school with a strong sense of humour. He was also excellent in debate, whilst Manny Shinwell radiated commonsense. He would take on all comers with spirit and overwhelming self-confidence. He had climbed a long way from his early days as an underpaid dockworker in Glasgow, and he revealed a burning sense of humanity and humour. A heckler would get short shrift from him in debate.

Sir Walter Elliot was a man of almost unreasonable charm. His rich, Scottish accent and his interest in people distinguished him among his distinguished colleagues. He was the perfect diplomat, and a man of real heart. He took Phyl and me round the ruined chamber of the House of Commons shortly after a bomb landed there and set the great Hall on fire. He painted a vivid historical panorama as we walked sadly round.

Later, in 1951, Phyl came with me to Edinburgh for a political meeting at which I was MC. Having introduced Sir Walter as the first speaker, I stole back to the audience and sat next to her. The speaker was waxing eloquent: 'To stand here in Auld Reekie with all these bonny Scottish faces watching me brings a song to my heart . . .' and similar sentiments followed.

Phyl listened. 'Darling,' she whispered, 'for thirteen years I've thought you were joking!' I suppose I am very Scottish.

One of the most remarkable members of the team was Commander Gould. He had the misfortune to have a wife who was an invalid. Over the years he would sit in his library studying encyclopedias and other reference books. His precise knowledge on an apparently endless number of themes was due entirely to his incredible photographic memory. As a subject came under discussion he would mentally flick through the pages of a treatise or encyclopedia, and recite almost verbatim what had been written there. By contrast Commander Campbell was a wonderful foil for the distinguished eggheads with whom he broadcast. His seafaring stories provided light relief to make the serious matters discussed more widely palatable. On the one

occasion the Corporation decided to remove him from the programme, there was a distinct drop in audience ratings and he had to
be put back.

Mavis Tate, wife of a member of the world famous Tate & Lyle
family, was a sensitive and educated woman who had turned to
politics. She had great charm; she and Phyl got on well together,
sharing a common interest in old china and porcelain. We toured
together for some time with the 'Brains Trust' team.

About this time the Allied Forces entered the ghastly deathcamps
of Belsen and Buchenwald. In the House of Commons it was decided
to send MPs to investigate the facts. Names were chosen by ballot.
Mavis Tate was named and resolutely refused to let another MP
replace her. 'It is my business, as an elected representative of this
House, to see and report what I find to my constituents.'

She went in a group of MPs and told us that when they arrived they
were not even sprayed with DDT. The smell was sickening, and the
piles of human bodies of all ages were enlivened by occasional
twitches from apparent corpses. She came back to London and wept
as she talked to us about it. 'I can never, never forget it,' she told us. 'I
haven't slept for nights on end.' Weeks later she committed suicide.

I, too, have never forgotten. When an interviewer asked me what
was the most horrifying film on which I had commented during the
war, I immediately answered, 'Belsen and Buchenwald'. Yet when
we showed the much-edited pictures in London, there was a crowd of
people outside the Empire Cinema with banners proclaiming: 'Don't
be misled! These films are propaganda. They are fakes!'

The stupidity of this reaction revolted me. How could anyone be
persuaded that the people in the film were acting.

When the BBC refused to allow me to continue with the 'Brains
Trust', I broadcast with Vic Oliver in 'Yankee-Doodle-Doo' – a
series of variety shows with an American slant. This was about the
time that large numbers of US troops were arriving in Britain. With
them, need I add, came that ace English–American comedian, Bob
Hope.

In the summer of 1943 they assembled in their thousands at Bristol,
where temporary buildings had been erected for their arrival. The
BBC decided to hand one whole show over to Bob for the simul-
taneous benefit of our welcome allies and the British audiences. He
was working with the USO camp shows, and top American performers and singers travelled everywhere with him to entertain GIs
wherever they might be.

I was included in the show, and we were hastily handed an all-

American script. I was not absolutely sure about some of the lines. 'Bob, what's this about "Solid Jackson"? Who *was* Jackson?' I queried, 'and why is he solid?'

Bob stopped the rehearsal. 'Hey, kids, come listen to this! Here's a guy who doesn't know why Jackson is solid. Les, see how many ways you can say it – come on – give!' By the time I'd finished, they were falling about with laughter, tears rolling down their faces. (Of course, it's a simple Americanism implying 'You're damn right, old boy!')

Bob's company included David Niven, Francis Langford and Tony Romano the singers, with Hal Block, our American gag-writer. We rehearsed from ten till six non-stop, with a short break for lunch provided by the American canteen. Unfamiliar soft drinks, and un-heard-of items appeared on our plates – unheard of, that is, on *our* plates since 1939, four years ago.

And the Hope Circus was a novelty too; four outriders on motor-cycles to clear the way. Three separate cars for the cast and one for Hope, his gag-writer and two secretaries. The leading motorcyclist kept on turning to watch us behind him. Anxious about him (accident-conscious as ever), I said, 'That sergeant is going to hit something unless he's careful.' Bob reassured me, so I relaxed, but as we turned into the entrance of the camp, the man hit the brick supports of the gates and crashed to the ground. He was taken to hospital unconscious.

We did three extra shows that same evening with different audiences each time. It was an eventful day and an historic occasion – the landing in Britain of by far the largest American contingent up till now, to join us in preparation for the coming invasion of occupied France.

The 'Yankee-Doodle-Doo' programmes were re-broadcast in the United States. But the show was too 'English' in concept to be successful there. An earlier popular pre-war programme between Britain and the US had been 'Five Hours Back' – a magazine pro-gramme. Now Robert Foot, the BBC's Director-General, took the idea a stage further and suggested a two-way programme between the USA and London, featuring stars from both countries. So 'Atlantic Spotlight' was born, and gradually built up an audience on both sides of the Atlantic. In this country, NBC's commentator, Ben Grauer, had a fan club, and I, as the British MC, achieved a similar following in the United States. It was of course essential to use a previously censored script, but we had opportunities for quick exchanges of greetings or news between items in rehearsal. Somehow from these snatched moments Ben Grauer and I became firm friends although we had never met.

'Atlantic Spotlight' ran for over three years and made some contribution to Anglo–American understanding. We often included successful plays with members of the English cast playing opposite members of the New York company. On one occasion dear old Cyril Maude, who had, years before, played the name part in a very successful London play called *Grumpy*, played the part again on 'Atlantic Spotlight'. Suddenly the line from New York went dead. The old pro, not a whit put out, continued by ad-libbing. 'I know what you're going to say, dear boy.' Then *his* answer and so on. When the line came alive again, he was back in the play with an answer to a question from New York. Nobody outside the studios can have realized there had been a breakdown.

Another play excerpt performed on our show was from *Arsenic and Old Lace*, which my father-in-law, Firth Shephard, produced in London. 'See a Shephard Show' had become a slogan in the war-time English theatre. On one of the first nights the cast presented him with a plaque, one of his proudest possessions – 'The Firth is our Shephard. We shall not want!' He had a reputation for really looking after the people who worked for him.

I did two programmes on radio with him; one before the war in a series called 'Showmen of England', which also featured C. B. Cochran, Billy Butlin and Bertram Mills. In the second, 'Shephard's Flock', he presented stars from his shows. They included Leslie Henson, Binnie Hale, Richard Hearne (Mr Pastry), Stanley Holloway, Cyril Ritchard, and Sydney Howard – all top names in the theatre of that time.

Phyl at one time read plays for her father, but after she had picked two winners which he rejected, she gave up. One of them was *Edward my Son*, I remember. Firth felt strongly about involving his family or friends in his work, and had a tendency to discard anyone else's ideas about the theatre. He was proved quite right, and he seldom produced a failure until 1947. That was the year he decided to back three shows with his *own* money. It was also the year the winter weather closed in, and all Europe was thick with snow and frost; the year in which heating and lighting had to be cut to a minimum. Theatres were forced to close. Firth personally paid all the artists and the theatres involved. Shortly after, he was taken seriously ill with heart trouble, and never recovered his health. All his accumulated savings had gone after a long and outstanding series of successes.

On 'Atlantic Spotlight' we also had community singing with some of the troops in Normandy joining with the studios in London and New York. This led to one unexpected pleasure in my fanmail – a grateful letter from an Austrian refugee girl from Vienna, now living in England; her father had escaped from a concentration camp and somehow made his way to America. They had been a very musical family, she wrote, and she and her father used to listen to the programme every week, join in the songs together, and write to each other about the contents. They did meet again after the war – following eight years of separation.

My various contacts with Americans in England included working as a British 'voice' at parties thrown by local USAAF airmen at Christmas and on Independence Day. I also interviewed some of the first American GIs to arrive in this country.

For the broadcast I called up American GHQ in Grosvenor Square and asked the senior officer if he could detail a suitable GI, explaining that I wanted a 100 per cent American who was making his first trip outside his native heath. I wanted to publicize the strangeness and the loneliness of these men so far from home, abroad and on the wrong foot. He obliged, and I got Sam V. Cooper from Dallas, Texas.

I talked to Sam like a brother. 'What don't you like about England?' He was determinedly polite. He had obviously read the book of instruction on how to behave in Britain. I was persistent. 'Come on, Sam. You're not enjoying yourself yet, are you?' Finally I broke him down by explaining that people here didn't realize what it felt like to be in an alien country, knowing nobody and sharing the discomforts and dangers of the war.

'Well, Les,' he drawled, 'it does seem crazy that you all drive on the wrong side of the road.' He paused. 'Sorry, sir, I mean the left side of the road.'

'Drop the "sir", Sam. I *want* you to say "the *wrong* side of the road". What else?'

At last he came clean. People were so unfriendly. They never spoke to you. The warm beer was undrinkable. No one offered to show you where they lived. The taxis were lousy, dirty, and not fast enough. The food was terrible, especially brussels sprouts! They didn't eat stuff like that in the States, etc. I put him on the air and explained he was under military orders to repeat exactly what he had said to me.

The General called me the following day. 'I don't know much about your programme, Mr Mitchell,' he said, 'but we're getting complaints from the switchboard here about calls for that soldier I sent you. It's swamping our military effectiveness!'

Sam became a good friend and I took him to see our genuine olde English cottage. He stayed for a weekend on leave. But the time came when he was moved on.

'Where are you going, Sam?' I asked.

'Well that's a military secret, Les. But I'm sure sorry to go.'

Six months later I had a telephone call. It was Sam. Could I join him for lunch nearby. I could and I did. Sam was nursing a heavily bandaged arm in a sling.

'Hey what's *that*, Sam? You been in action?'

'Oh shucks, it's nothing, Les, just nothing.'

I persisted.

'Well, it was like this, Les. We've been training in Ireland and an Irish guy insulted the British. So I hit him, and I busted my arm.' Dear Sam; a *real* Texan.

Phyl and I met various other American soldiers of all ranks and enjoyed helping them to relax while they were on leave. One particularly memorable occasion came in 1944 when I compèred the first BBC broadcast of the famous Glenn Miller Band. Major Miller (as he was then) gave the concert in Bedford. His famous drummer, Ray McKinley, told me afterwards, 'Les, you know that break I had in the show?' (It had been a fabulously long break demonstrating his mastery as a drummer.) 'That Mayor lady came up to me and said, "Bravo, Mr McKinley. It was just like a thunderstorm." Just wait till I tell my folks back home!'

It was only shortly after this broadcast, on 15 December, that Glen Miller, like Gustav Hamel so many years before, disappeared without trace over the Channel in a single-engined plane.

Shortly before Glen Miller's disappearance hit the headlines, the London newspapers were reporting another important event – the disbandment of the Home Guard, as the war in Europe was drawing to a close. Three of the biggest London newspapers got together and organized a 'stand-down' concert at the Albert Hall on Sunday 3 December 1944. It was a star-studded occasion and some six thousand Home Guards made up the invited audience.

I had not expected to be among them as I was spending the day at a special stand-down parade with my own 13th Battalion Middlesex Regiment at Rickmansworth. Just before I left Movietone for home the night before, I was handed a note. 'Lord Rothermere has asked especially for you as MC for the show at the Albert Hall!' Lord Rothermere was one of my bosses as owner of the *Daily Mail* which, with Twentieth Century Fox, owned 50 per cent of the Movietone newsreel. I was horrorstruck at the thought of doing a job unrehearsed at the vast Albert Hall, but there was no alternative. I bought a gag-book at the village bookshop, stuffed it in my pocket and presented myself for the final parade. In the book I found only one gag which seemed relevant. It was a four-point story about a German soldier who reported sick and went through successive hospital doors to find himself back in the street again. Fortunately I got big laughs that night when he went through the first *and* the second doors, so cheerfully abandoned the last two to unstinted applause.

But the show *was* first rate and the vast audience in receptive mood so everything went like clockwork. George Robey and Violet Loraine sang 'If you were the only girl in the world', a sentimental revival of the song they had sung many years before in the *Bing Boys* – a favourite musical of the First World War – which had been sung and whistled by many of the audience when they had been youngsters in Kitchener's Army.

Tommy Trinder was at his best, every joke provoking yells of laughter. Gert and Daisy (great war-time favourites) had one particularly nice line: 'The boys in Burma are so *proud* of their dads'. The audience, of course, was full of 'their dads', who appreciated the compliment and showed it. Vera Lynn, the Forces' sweetheart, received an ovation which should have surprised even her, used as she was to great welcomes. And dear Cicely Courtneidge won another ovation for a splendid recitation about the Home Guard – 'There are two ways into England'.

But now I was to find a way out.

In 1945 Sam Slate, an American war correspondent in London, called on me to work with him for the US Army in the South of France. My knowledge of the country and my ability to make myself understood there were undoubtedly behind the invitation.

I managed to get permission from Movietone (like most people I had not had a real break since 1939), and quickly got the necessary permits and passport. I wore my Home Guard uniform with a beret, but was rather embarrassed by the shoulder badges initialled WC which were intended to convey my status as a war correspondent. It never missed with the Americans, particularly in their Paris headquarters where 'BBC' had been posted on the lavatory door. The rude jokes and meaningful nods and winks were only circumvented by pointing out that they were also the initials of Winston Churchill, and eventually by procuring new badges with 'War Correspondent' in *small* lettering.

We flew to Marseilles. Sam Slate and I the only civilians on board. It was an uncomfortable trip in a war-time Dakota with no seats. Cold too. We got over the Alps and tried to find Marseilles, but it was shrouded in mist. The American pilot sent back a personal message by word of mouth. 'Tell the English guy, they've told us to go on to Toulouse. There's no visibility down here, but I think we can make it.

Does he have any objection?'

I replied, 'I'm a Scotsman, not an Englishman, and it'll sure hurt you as much as it'll hurt me if we crash.' He put the nose down, cut off the engines and we drifted in shroud-like silence. There was a loud bang – we must have bounced fifty feet – then another bang and the sound of the undercarriage wheels on the rough surface. We had made it.

I was paying my own out-of-pocket expenses, and had arranged with the authorities that my money would be sent to me in France. Naturally in the prevailing conditions there, just after the liberation, there was utter confusion, but no money. I had to borrow from GIs and officers on a daily basis. In Nice I called on the Consulate there to explain my difficulty. 'Good god,' said the Consular official, 'you're jolly lucky to expect £100 – more than *I* get for expenses. Afraid I'm not here to keep Home Guards in comfort.' I resisted the desire to kick him. It would really only have hurt my leg.

But my odd get-up did get one splendid reaction. I was introduced into a briefing session held by General Ratay in charge of the Marseilles assembly base. A splendid Mexican with fierce moustaches, he spotted me at once and called for an introduction. Then he slowly gave me the most impressive salute I had ever been given. Apparently he was convinced I was Monty making a flying visit.

I was put under the wing of a Lt–Col. Finlay who sent me out with the US Military Police that evening. 'Les,' he explained, 'you should see it. It's quite an experience.'

It certainly was. Sitting with the driver of a van, I was taken to the 'red light' district. Apparently the 'Snowdrops', as the police were called (on account of their white helmets), already had prepared lists of addresses. They went into the bordels and came out with GIs in every state of undress. Many of them were far from sober, some of them growing lumps where truncheons had hit them; but all of them had been found off limits. I felt really sorry for the transgressors.

We ended up in Paris, and at last my money arrived. I was able to pay all my loans back. There *were* signs of relief when I paid them. After all, none of my creditors knew anything about me.

So now I decided to show them the city. I invited six of them to come on a night out with me. First to Harry's Bar. There were a lot of women about looking coquettishly in our direction as we entered. My guests did not like the beer or the wines of France. It had to be either champagne or cognac (which were easy to pronounce). Before long the effects began to show. 'Hey, Les,' shouted one, 'you speak the language. Tell this mademoiselle I think she's beautiful and I'd like to *parlez* some more with her!'

I explained to her that the gallant American soldier found her very attractive and much regretted his inability to tell her so. In due course he came over to me. 'How much do you think she'll want?' I had no idea, never having travelled this particular course, but suggested a sum. He took some money out, then handed the wallet to me. 'Keep it, Les, till I get back to the hotel. I don't want to get rolled.'

The rest of us went to a cabaret – the Bal Tabarin – and were given a ringside table. Some girls with a little English came and sat on our laps. Each ordered champagne. I had never before, nor have I since, tasted such flat, unenjoyable bottles. I began to wonder if they had been poisoned by the retreating Huns. One fascinating sign of the German occupation was that all the Latin-type girls had dyed their hair blonde to suit the occupying forces, but were midway back to restoring their crowning glory to the darker colour natural to them. Poor dears, they never quite caught up with the changing fortunes of war.

Eventually our party ended at 3 a.m. I expressed the determination to return to the hotel. Said a youngster of twenty-one, who had stuck to me doggedly through the long evening, 'I'm like you, Les – I'm sophisticated too. We've *done everything*. *We* got over *women*.' Ruminating on this profundity, we returned to the hotel.

I was sitting, lone at the breakfast table later that morning, when there arrived one of my party guests. He looked a little wan and tired, I thought.

'Hello, Jim, how did you get on?' I asked.

'Well, I took this kid home – the kid you translated for. She was a real *nice* kid. Poor, but proud you could say. She had an invalid brother and he had to have money for doctors, you see? Her father had been killed in the war, so she had to look after her mother, and she's still very young – and pretty innocent too, I would say. Well, I'm a family man and I suddenly thought: Gosh you're a bum, Jim! What are you trying to do with this simple kid? I got dressed, gave her a kiss and bailed out. Her mother was at the foot of the stairs. She seemed to be asking for money, but I got to the front door and ran like hell.'

'It's like Insurance. *They* only pay out when somebody's lost something – get what I mean?'

This trip to France took place some months after our life at Harefield had been tragically disrupted. One Sunday early in 1945 I was working downstairs in the cottage when I heard a loud tapping on the stairs outside. At first I took no notice, thinking it might be Phyl or her mother hammering a nail. Then I remembered Phyl had gone up to the village. The knocking started again. I continued writing. Then once again that noise, only louder.

I went cautiously up the stairs. Constance was standing at the top
with a shoe in her hand. She pointed to her mouth. Her jaw had
slipped and she was unable to speak. Gently I led her to her room and
made her lie on the bed while I phoned the doctor. I thought it might
be a mild stroke, and she was obviously very scared. The doctor came
at last and confirmed my suspicion. Poor Constance, just as her hopes
of returning to Cannes looked like being fulfilled – this!

I arranged for Phyl to take her to Brighton for a complete rest. But
it just did not work. At last the doctors sent her to University College
Hospital where the surgeons diagnosed a tumour on the brain. Only
one of them offered to operate; the others warned us it was a chancy
business, and might very well leave her paralysed or mentally
affected. I contacted Firth Shephard to ask him what decision he
would make. It was too great a responsibility for us.

Very unhappily he accepted the majority decision. Phyl and I spent
every hour we could spare with her mother and after a deeply distres-
sing three months, Connie died in hospital. It was an overwhelming
blow for Phyl as she and her mother had been drawn even closer by
the war and my frequent absences elsewhere. For me it was a tragic
loss as we enjoyed such a happy personal relationship, and shared a
common love and regard for Phyl.

It is difficult to recall the 'feel' of the end of the war. You could meet old
friends again, travel about the country without a tin hat or a gas mask
round your neck. You could buy *some* food, *some* drink and *some* petrol
without being entirely dependent on coupons. The VIs and V2s had
stopped. The daily threat of death and destruction had been removed –
the blackout, too. Most civilians were still a little punchdrunk.

We offered to buy the cottage, but Commander and Mrs Colles
decided to live there in retirement, to enjoy a much-needed rest. So we
moved to a flat in London and began to contact old chums.

One evening Alexander Shaw, the documentary film producer, his
wife Nutkin, the novelist, and Eric Portman, the actor, were with us. As
we talked, trying to catch up with lost time together, there was suddenly a violent crash and a shrill whining clatter from the hall outside. I
think we all paled. Conversation stopped abruptly.

Recovering after a second or two, Alex cautiously opened the door,
and I followed him. It was *not* an unexploded bomb. The catgut which
wound the spring of our ancient carriage clock had broken and the
spring had suddenly unwound itself, breaking the surrounding glass.
We all needed another drink. The war had not been good for people's
nerves – even the stay-at-homes!

12. A New World

Early in 1946 a chance to visit the United States came at last. There were difficulties since the GIs and other American VIPs returning home had priority. However with the help of Twentieth Century Fox I managed to book a flight to New York. It was my idea to make contact with American friends, particularly Ben Grauer.

I also wanted permission from Twentieth Century Fox in New York to visit their studios there and in Hollywood, with a view to collecting 'trailer' and other film material for use in BBC Television which was to re-open at Alexandra Palace in June of that year. This would be for a continuation of the programme I had been doing on radio throughout the war – 'Film Time'. It would be an expensive trip, but the war was over, so damn the expense.

One of the nicer reactions of young Americans during the war was 'Gee, Les, you ought to be an American.' While I realized this was intended as the highest compliment, they were usually mystified when I explained I was proud of being British and did not want to change. Nevertheless the link between us was their sense of freedom. They would all work at a variety of jobs in a variety of places to unearth their latent talents. They would work between terms of school or university to keep themselves by their own efforts. And best of all, in general they were not mean minded. If they saw someone's success, they tried to emulate the example, not inquire miserably, 'Why should *he* do so well?' The Americans exuded 'get up and go'. I found it very exhilarating after the heavy hand of bureaucracy in England. That, of course, had been magnified by the demands of war.

Now I had a chance to find out more about the land of opportunity. Phyl had always encouraged me to take the plunge, so in March 1946 I launched myself towards the USA.

Unfortunately the weather in the South of England had 'come down', and visibility was practically nil. At the last moment Pan Am diverted its passengers by train to Prestwick, in Scotland. I lodged myself in a carriage and found to my surprise and pleasure that one of my neighbours was Edith Evans. We greeted each other happily. She, it appeared, was travelling on her own too, by a different airline.

We were all impressed by the food-boxes provided for her at the last moment. Each contained an apple, ham sandwiches, fruit tartlets and a wing of chicken wrapped in a lettuce leaf. Phyl had given me two oranges and cut me sandwiches of tongue and cheese with a small flask of brandy and six Mars Bars. But it was to be a long night so we generously shared with our companions, all six of them. Edith was a little smug about the fact that Binkie Beaumont, the impresario, always looked after her so well wherever he sent her. I decided to talk to Pan American about that later.

At about 1 a.m. the door slid open and a ticket inspector appeared. He punched our tickets – one, two, three, four. Then came a pregnant silence. He was looking at Edith's ticket. 'I'm sorry,' he said. 'I'll have to ask you two ladies to go to the end of the train.' He indicated Dame Edith and a GI bride going to America for the first time.

Consternation. 'Why? – What for? – What do you mean?'

Dame Edith's voice took on the wondrous tone she was to use as Oscar Wilde's Lady Bracknell in *The Importance of Being Ernest*.

'In a *rear* compartment?' she exhaled in blank astonishment.

'Yes, lady – you can't sit in a first-class compartment with a third-class ticket. There's a third-class compartment reserved for your party at the end of the train.'

Much spluttering from Edith. 'American Export' had arranged everything; hers was a very expensive fare to America and back; was it likely that she would be given a third-class ticket for a footling little journey to Scotland? But she *had* been. The inspector was not impressed.

I gallantly offered to rise from my sleep and search for American Export's representative. . . . I banged my way through an apparently never-ending series of corridors and doors, lurching and staggering my way to the end of the train. The last communicating door was locked. When ultimately I got back the inspector had vanished. But not for long. He returned and stood his ground until Edith, breathing fire, had paid £2 excess, and the GI bride likewise. Officialdom was satisfied. We of the Pan American contingent breathed happy sighs of relief and went to sleep again.

In the early morning hours, Edith, recovered from her discomfiture, bet me five shillings that she would arrive in New York first, and gave me her telephone number so that I could check. I took her on, satisfied that *I* was travelling with the great American Pan Am reputation to back me. We took off from Prestwick at approximately the same time, but when my plane landed at Shannon I found Edith already enjoying lunch. I joined her – I had forgotten what real butter and cream tasted like.

Owing to bad-weather reports, the two pilots had to decide whether to fly via Goose Bay or by Gander airports. *We* went by Gander and 'American Export' took the alternative route. I sat with Richard Bender who had recently produced *Dear Ruth* for Gilbert Miller in London. About 2.30 a.m. Mrs Whateley-Smith, the air-hostess, came and talked to me. She knew about me, having married and lived in England during the war, and gave me an introduction to a friend – 'the youngest admiral in the US Navy'. 'Go see him, he's *nice* and *verry* pro-British.' She also introduced me to the captain of the aircraft who invited me forward to the cockpit.

It was a moving moment. There, ahead of us in the beautiful soft half-light of dawn, the Northern Lights were reflected on the grey cotton wool spread all round us. A really lovely sight. I was among the *first* civilians to fly the Atlantic since Lindbergh and Alcock and Brown had explored the possibility between the wars. This was discovering America the *new* way. Through the brains and intelligence of man the impossible was becoming possible. One day it might be possible to travel to the moon and explore other planets in the universe. I had been involved in modern scientific exploration: radio and television were just breaking the surface. They would soon develop further than anyone had yet imagined. And what of the power of the tides? What of the earth's magnetism? What of second sight? Are ghosts really a figment of the imagination or do they exist? My imagination was excited.

At 5.30, approaching New York, I was invited forward again. Down below, the city was bright with light. The criss-crossed ribbons of the avenues, traffic islands shining out unashamedly to the sky. The grey Hudson river wrapped like a cloak round Manhattan Island. As we circled round for the landing at La Guardia Airport, beacons winked out from the mist and we pointed slowly their way, to land safely at last. It was 6 a.m.

The American taxi was a disappointment. The smart gleaming road-sters of the Hollywood films were even more brokendown than some of ours at home. On my taxi one door was unusable – the handle had broken and it was tied in by rope. The engine was more powerful than the average London taxi so we went faster, and the streets being wider, there was no necessity for the narrow turning circle of those at home.

A second disappointment was the brokendown appearance of the outlying precincts. I did not remember seeing *them* in Hollywood films either. But gradually, as we approached the city centre, the full impact could be felt. From Beekman Tower – my hotel on 49th Street (No. 3, *Mitchell* Place, by the way) – I looked out from the twenty-ninth floor and absorbed the alien scene. All the skyscrapers were different shapes and different *colours*. The colours struck you at once because all the movies one had seen then were black and white: colour had a softening influence on the hard, sharp contours of the buildings.

I had a bath and shaved in someone else's deserted room. Mine would not be available till the afternoon. The phone bell rang. I had been traced by Edith Evans. After asking if I was comfortably settled in, she added, 'By the way, you owe me five shillings. I've been here for hours!'

I accepted defeat, and she inquired what plans I had made. I explained there had, as yet, been no time. 'Then I should very much like you to meet some dear friends of mine,' she said. 'They're giving a party for me next week and you shall be my escort.' I was very touched by this. She really had a heart of gold, and it was an unexpected kindness. I arranged to pick her up and take her to the party in due course.

On going downstairs to check with reception, I found a note from Ben Grauer. 'Welcome to New York, Leslie,' it read. 'My apartment is 1 West 67th Street. My coloured maid Bessie will look after you. Move in till I get back from three weeks in Mexico – if you don't, we'll never do another show together. Regards. Ben.' I learned from BBC Headquarters in the Rockefeller Center that Ben, having had pneumonia, had been ordered away for three weeks, which accounted for his apartment being free. They strongly advised me to accept his offer, which I willingly did.

I settled in, with the aid of Bessie. Bessie Young was a love. She had hunted New York for anything English – English muffins, English cakes, English tea, English beer, English crackers (the edible kind); I was overwhelmed. 'Bessie, dear,' I told her, 'if you believe that any of these things taste like what we have at home, you're crazy. You just give me what Mr Grauer has for breakfast, and I'll tell you if anything's wrong.' She gave me a beaming smile, and we started a lifelong friendship.

Sam Slate was back in New York with the BBC after his overseas service, and introduced me to his wife, Ella Parr, and their daughter. We all got on very well together. One day, when Sam had a cold, he sent his wife off with me to show me the city. 'Have you ever seen Grant's Tomb?' she asked.

'No, but I'm willing,' I answered. So we went. A fine monument and an enduring part of American history. I thanked her for showing it to me, but had to confess that my ignorance of American history left me uncertain about which side Grant was on in the Civil War.

'Wa-ll, Les,' said Ella Parr, 'you all know the man you have jerst been dealing with in Europe?'

'Hitler?' I guessed.

'Yeah! – He and Grant are blood-brothers!' Yes, she *did* come from the deep South. . . .

The party for Edith Evans was given by two close friends of hers. Jim Smith was a successful businessman. His wife Pat was famous as an actress, having quite recently won ecstatic praise for her performance as Birdie in the film of Lillian Hellman's *The Little Foxes*. Her stage name was Pat Collinge. She was Irish–American with enormous charm and a gentle sense of humour, and I fell for her at once. Through the Smiths' kindness and hospitality I met many well-known figures connected with radio, films and the theatre in New York and I never forgot my debt to Dame Edith for that introduction.

Among the guests were Tony Miner, a producer in CBS Television, and Frank Chase, the producer of a currently successful radio show, 'Leave it to the Girls'. I was given flattering references by Edith Evans, who went out of her way to publicize and introduce me. She also promised to telephone Phyl on her return to London the following week.

I was to discover quite a number of colleagues from my acting days. Colin Keith Johnstone had gone to New York to play Stanhope in *Journey's End* and decided to settle there. Maurice Evans, who had played Raleigh in the London production, was now New York's leading Shakespearean actor, whilst Melville Cooper – Trotter, and George Zucco – Osborne, were happily settled in the American scene. Of course, the play had been a world-wide success and many actors appeared in it, but it was great to meet some of the 'originals' after the long oblivion of war. It is always fun to meet old stage colleagues.

About this time Winston Churchill was in New York following his famous Fulton speech in Missouri. His theme there had been that Russia needed watching, and only if the United States and English-speaking Commonwealth populations remained together in unity would the future threat of a trial of strength be averted. To the newly welded population of the USA this should have been self-evident. But they were suspicious. Most Americans had come from Europe in past generations to escape political and religious persecution. They believed they didn't need Europe. They had been called there, on two occasions now, to fight major wars, and they had won. Enough was enough. They had their own lives to live.

So it was that I watched angrily while unruly communist elements of the CIO paraded with banners and shouted anti-Churchill slogans: 'We gave you our sons. What more do you want?' – 'Go home Churchill. No World War III.' – 'Get out of America'. He drove through them all in an open car to City Hall, where he was to be presented with a gold medal and the Freedom of the City of New York by Governor Grover Whalen.

I had a pass for the occasion and joined the Movietone crew. 'Well, this is the first time I ever heard *this* man booed,' I said to the cameraman.

'Les,' came the answer, 'he's the biggest bastard of them all. I'd be happy to see him shot.' Restraining my disgust, I merely pointed out that that was what he was there for, photographically speaking. He did not smile. On my way back I was glad to see the double row of armed police stationed round Churchill's hotel.

I had had another example of anti-British reaction earlier. The general manager of Kodak in England had given me an introduction to the head of Kodak in America, a General Curtis. The general was not in New York when I called him, but I was invited to meet a deputy. My main object was to borrow a ciné Kodak for the duration of my visit, as my own would have been overweight on the plane, and to establish friendly relations on the American side.

I went to see the man at Kodak, a typical well-dressed American. He received me coldly. As I sat down, he started talking. 'I understand you need to borrow a camera? It seems to be a major part of the English economy, this borrowing from the United States.'

Thinking this might be a clumsy American joke, I countered with the explanation for my request.

'More convenient?' said he. 'Here in the United States over the past few years we have been deprived of meat and essentials like gasoline, we have been forced into shortages of every kind to spare you British "inconvenience"! Among other things we have been made short of is cameras!'

I got up to go. 'I haven't finished yet,' he said

'No, but *I* have,' I answered, and walked out.

I only learned later that he had given the same treatment to Howard Thomas of Pathé who was also in New York with the same introductions. When we met over a drink, Howard explained the reason. The deputy was a *German* American and had been a member of the Bund. He had been interned until just before we arrived.

One does not always realize that many first-generation Americans are still the sons of their fathers. But I learned one thing. Some Americans might not like you because you are British. But if they like you personally, there are no more generous and welcoming people in the world.

I was still in New York when Ben Grauer arrived back from Mexico. I was waiting for him with Bessie. He came inside the door with a welcoming smile. Then he stopped and stared. 'My God,' he said, 'I thought you were a *little* guy!' And I had thought he was a *big* man. We were both wrong.

I moved back to Beekman Tower, but Ben and I met nearly every day and got on famously. His charm kept him supplied with plenty of good-looking girl-friends, who understood that he was not the marrying type. But they were happy to come around and attend to his wants if and when required. I found one of them busy sorting out his files. 'No, my goodness no, I'm not Ben's *secretary*! He just pays me whenever he wants his office cleared!' His warm charm and personal interest in people and things contributed much to his success. Nobody had anything but good to say about him, and he made it his job to know everybody.

I went the rounds with Ben. To Sardi's – the restaurant famous for its theatrical clientele – where I met Sinatra, still at the start of his career, very much aware of the screaming bobby-soxers who made up a large part of his audiences then. He was apparently interesting himself in the serious social purpose of giving the younger generation a better chance. At Toots Shor's – another famous restaurant – I met Fred Allen, the comedian, a classic example of the straight-faced wit. He would fire off devastating jokes with absolutely no change of expression, and never missed a trick. Ray Milland, who had recently made a great reputation with his film *Lost Weekend* in which he portrayed a congenital drunk, was working overtime explaining that, really, he was *sober* most of the time, and *not* too far gone to work. Remembering my experience in South Africa when *I* appeared drunk on the stage, I had sympathy for him.

The William Morris Agency, who had been advised of my arrival, were unhelpful. I was later told by a friend of Ben's that they would not show interest unless I was staying considerably longer in the USA. There would be no time to make it worth their while. But I *was* asked whether I would rather be paid in cars or refrigerators. The answer was in the negative.

Fletcher Markle, a Canadian Air Force friend, was now back in Toronto and cabled me to join him there for a few days, expenses paid, to do a radio show. I was delighted at the chance to meet his wife and his son to whom I had been appointed godfather by proxy.

As I phoned I asked the operator, 'Could I have a Toronto number please?'

Quick as a flash came the retort. '*Save* the "please".' In New York you don't do favours. If you are being paid to do a job, you do it. You do not expect thanks. Anyway I got the long-distance call immediately and arranged to fly to Canada the following week.

Now Harry Alan Towers cabled that he would be joining me in New York and was flying on to Toronto. It was a quite unexpected development, but I made arrangements for his arrival and booked him a room in my hotel. He arrived and immediately asked me to introduce him to my friends and acquaintances. After a party, a particular friend in the film business phoned me back. 'Swell party, Les. But that young character you introduced tried to tell me he was the London representative for our studios. But *I* am! Is he crazy or something?' I explained he was crazy like a fox, and used his youth as a cover-over. When I tackled him with the story he just laughed and said there must have been a misunderstanding. But it was Harry who went to Hollywood. Not me. Another misunderstanding maybe?

Toronto and Canada was another new experience. My first reaction was to the sudden appearance of Union Jacks – a rare sight in the USA – and the comparative modesty of the architecture after the overblown grandeur of the skyscrapers of New York. Here was a land fabulously rich in potential, but not, as yet, so spendthrift. It was something of a relief to come down to man-sized proportions again.

Fletcher Markle met me at the airport. Marriage had left its mark. He had altered: a new-style moustache drooping at the corners, a more serious adult expression. Where now was the thrusting keen young writer who in twenty-four hours had written a first-rate film on London's VI bomb attacks? He did seem to have slowed up. His wife Blanche I met for the first time and we liked each other. Stephen, my godson, was cultivating his vocal chords to good effect, but somewhat to the detriment of Fletcher's work.

When we had settled down, Fletcher explained he had arranged a series of parties for me. Most of his friends in Toronto were connected with radio. He was regarded as the young Orson Welles of Canada and had written a number of highly successful series. Currently he was writing for 'Stage 46', a series of one-hour shows called 'Who do you think you are?' in which a little man dreams he is living heroic lives in the style of famous writers.

I met Bernard Braden and his wife, Barbara Kelly, the leading theatrical stars in Toronto. Canada, like South Africa, and Australia, was largely dependent on radio for its entertainment. Live theatre was confined to the main cities and the players were mostly members of companies from England. Television was to solve problems of distance later; but not in 1946.

I met John Drainey, another very well-known Canadian radio actor, and we all had a great party together. During the evening I was told that a Mr Harding had been inquiring after me. Try as I could, there was no recollection of anyone of that name, and I admitted it. Apparently this Mr Harding was standing in for the BBC's Canadian representative, Gladstone Murray, whom I had been hoping to meet. He had flown to New York on business. Gladstone Murray had been widely tipped as Sir John Reith's successor, but had unexpectedly been transferred to Canada. There had been many idle rumours about this development, but I never heard a likely explanation.

At a later party given by the Draineys I met Harding. He was standing by the door as I entered, and we were hastily introduced. The face was vaguely familiar, but not one I had ever known personally. The body was rocking slightly. 'I gather you've never heard of me, *Mr* Mitchell,' he said, stressing the 'Mr' rather aggressively. 'You must be one of the least welcome visitors to these shores. In this country we reserve our greetings for people with manners,' he added, and sat rather suddenly on a nearby stool.

'You must be Harding,' I said, 'and you're tight. If you can remember, where did we ever meet before?'

'At Pathé News,' he said. 'Have a drink?' He meant Movietone News, of course, and slowly, if reluctantly, I recalled our meeting.

The occasion was a visit by the BBC to Movietone's recording studios in Soho Square. Michael Standing had arranged to visit us for a radio programme describing how newsreels are made. They arrived and carried out interviews with the editor, the sound engineer, and other members of the staff; and then came to me in my sound-proofed booth with the plate-glass window looking out on to the screen. Finally Michael (whom I knew well) introduced me there and left me as the film started. But he absentmindedly took with him his BBC microphone, by which we were all being recorded, and left only his stopwatch. The programme came to an untidy end; we had to re-record my conversation with Michael and that part of my commentary for the screen. It was then that I had been introduced to his assistant-producer, Mr Harding – Gilbert Harding!

When he returned to England, we *all* got to know him. In fact, he and I did become friends in the end. There were many good stories about Gilbert, but one I remember him telling me was about the early days of his conversion to Catholicism.

He had been invited to attend an important gathering in Edinburgh to meet some of the leading figures in the Catholic world. He attended several dinners and banquets as a clever, noteworthy young convert. After the distinguished guests had returned to Italy and elsewhere, a British Cardinal took him for a walk on the Pentland Hills. They walked together in silence for some time before the Cardinal spoke.

'Mr Harding, you have been a welcome guest at our meetings, but I wonder if you are aware of the impression you gave our guests?'

'Why, no, Your Grace. I hope I have not offended anyone,' queried Gilbert.

'I thought it was not your intention,' said the Cardinal, 'but the guests were all of the opinion that *you* were their host!'

Gilbert certainly knew how to hold the stage.

Back at the BBC offices in Rockefeller Center worked Stephen Fry, son of the famous cricketer, C. B. Fry, whom I had met during the war. Stephen had offered to introduce me around on behalf of the BBC. I was duly grateful.

The press was interested in my background. More especially about BBC Television as *nobody* could believe there had been a daily *public* service anywhere in the world. I visited TV studios in New York where NBC and CBS were still involved in the experimental stages. Only at NBC one of the engineers told me excitedly that he had seen me on a TV screen before the war. That was not unheard of. The TV signal was known to bounce from the ionosphere in all directions – but only as a freak, dependent on sunspots and other conditions.

One of the Twentieth Century Fox executives told me, 'Well, you *may* have had television in England. But if it shows its snoot above the sidewalks in this country, we'll smash it back into the ground!' Of course, he represented Hollywood and the film industry.

Meanwhile Ben invited me to join him at a United Nations session. I was provided with the necessary badge and police permit. The hall, the Council Chamber at Hunter College, was well arranged. At the centre a curved table with names of the countries represented. A table below for translators and secretaries. Running round three sides of the room was a glass-fronted balcony, divided into booths for radio, press and television. This was the first time I had seen the new image-orthicon TV camera at work. It was a revelation. In the dimness of the Council Chamber, with normal lighting, it produced pictures comparable to those we had only achieved in England with special high lighting.

We had always known that colour television required more lines than those we used for black-and-white. But the manufacturers (mistakenly in my opinion) were introducing new sets for the re-opening at Alexandra Palace based on the BBC's pre-war standards. This would mean a new set would have to be bought if and when colour was developed. I had received a request from Maurice Gorham, BBC's new Television Director, to tell him of anything of interest I might see while I was in the United States. Although I was no longer a member of the Corporation, I wrote a full report on the image-orthicon camera, which was, after all, the result of considerable research undertaken while we were engrossed in the war. I added details of CBS colour.

The letter I received later said, 'We (the engineers and I) were much amused by your letter. Your suggestions were unfortunately impractical. Thanks all the same.' I have since discovered that an attempt had been made by the BBC to buy the new cameras. But at that time they were not produced in any quantity even in America. My friends at Marconi in England were amused themselves when I told them the story. It was *their* camera design, but they had not yet got any themselves.

Years later, in 1954, I had an invitation to produce Marconi's first colour television demonstration in England. Dr Leslie Jesty, their chief designer, and Wing-Commander George Kelsey, their sales manager, encouraged me to demonstrate its virtues. So I chose all the natural vari-coloured fruits and added two girls – one fair, the other brunette. They *all* looked good enough to eat. But the BBC representatives decided the pictures were not 'compatible' without explaining quite why.

Television was still my favourite topic. As an ex-actor I had been fully aware of the much wider personal impact created by TV than by film or theatre performances. Viewers became more personally involved in what they saw on their small screens. In pre-war days, of course, there had been all the fascination of seeing a brand-new concept of teaching and entertainment unfolding in front of you. Most of our fanmail was intelligently constructive, not confined to autograph hunters or stage-struck misses. It aroused a thoughtful interest from people who foresaw its growth. And, of course, many offshoots of the medium were brought to light by the war – radar and infra-red photography for a start, and later, the satellites which circle the skies today.

I was to find on my return to England that since the film industry refused to help them, BBC Television would not give publicity to films. All my efforts to produce a topical cinema feature were wasted. Movietone's general manager, Sir Gordon Craig, had bet me £10 that television would never come to anything. I took him on, but he died before I could prove my point.

Wedding guests: my mother, Philip Leaver, Phyl's mother,
Aimée Locke and Phyl's father, Firth Shephard

We made it! 2 June 1938

Above: A happy family scene outside our home at Harefield:
Phyl, her mother and myself, with Charlie
Inset: Members of the London Defence Volunteers and the
Women's Voluntary Services (Phyl and myself) in 1940

Another 'Journey's End'! My car outside the BBC, also in 1940

At work during and after the war
Above left: With Major Glen Miller during his first British broadcast
Above right: With 'Professor' Joad on my first 'Brain's Trust'
Below: With Anthony Eden for the first TV General Election broadcast, 1951

I just *had* to include these two photographs:
Above: Talking to HM King George VI at the Royal Film Performance, 1950

Below: Sharing a joke with the Duke of Edinburgh at Lime Grove Studios, 1953.
HM The Queen is talking to Bill Fraser, the Scottish comedian

Above: Acting as stooges. Miriam Karlin and I fail to see
a Terry-Thomas joke

Below: 1957, TV comes of age. With Jasmine Bligh and Ted Langley
(BBC senior cameraman) with pre- and postwar cameras

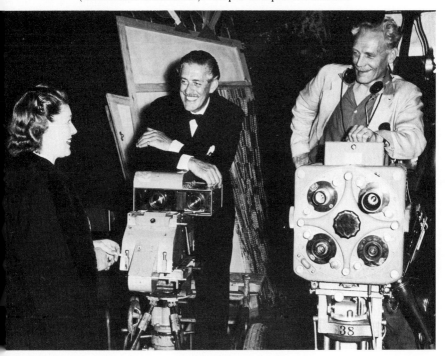

Above: Interviewing speed king Donald Campbell for
'Visitor of the Day' on Associated Rediffusion

Below: English wit with French charm – relaxing
with A. P. Herbert and Yvonne Arnaud

Above: Two firsts: William Tainton, Baird's
original live model, with first regular TV announcer

Below: Receiving the Baird Award from Mrs John
Logie Baird, 1964

Off to a new start! With Inge, my Great Dane

13. Unprintable Negative

It seemed that the effort and expense of my visit to the USA had been wasted. Television would *not*, as I had believed, grow stupendously immediately after the war. I even heard a leading BBC representative explain on radio that 'the Corporation was not interested in the sale of television sets!' This might well be so literally speaking, but it overlooked the fact that TV would remain an amusing novelty until its audience increased in size.

Faint hearts and doubters surrounded post-war TV development in Britain, just as Hollywood was opposed to this natural competitor. Audiences were unable or unwilling to pay money for TV sets. They had become, once more, satisfied with radio. Sport promoters and theatre moguls foresaw a drastic reduction of box-office profits if their entertainments were to be watched from a home base.

I returned to my past involvements with Movietone and what radio and television scraps were thrown to me.

Joan Gilbert, who had been Cecil Madden's personal secretary before the war, had since made a big radio reputation. She was now appointed the BBC Television organizer and interviewer for 'Picture Page'. It was suggested that she should invite me to work with her on the programme. Nothing loth, I accepted the new situation with pleasure. Joan and I had known each other since our early days at St George's Hall.

It soon became obvious that she was not to be allowed the freedom enjoyed by the pre-war 'Picture Page'. Most well-known personalities were now reserved for the Talks Department and we were offered the leavings. Looking at Cecil Madden's pre-war list of names for the programme, it was obvious that conflicting ideas were boiling up in the new departmental echelons. Once again the old situation of 'lectures to the uninformed' had reared its ugly head. A clique of young intelligentsia was to be taught how to put over serious subjects to a growing audience. On one occasion, rather surprisingly, I *was* engaged to partake in one of their programmes. At the last moment, the head of department informed me that they had after all engaged someone else. She was astounded when I insisted on my contract being paid.

This official attitude stemmed, I think, from a long-outworn belief that *all* educated people had *some* private income and *somewhere* to live. But gone were the 1920s and the last carefree years of peace and plenty. The strident notes of a new world had yet to be heard.

At the re-opening of TV at Alexandra Palace in June 1946, I made my reappearance with the words, 'As I was saying when we were so rudely interrupted . . .', so marking an interval of over six and a half years since the war-time closedown.

I had renewed my association with Harry Alan Towers and re-joined the radio programme 'Film Time'. Harry and I, through the *Daily Mail,* instituted the National Film Awards of 1946 and the first post-war 'Ball and Parade of Fashion' at the Albert Hall.

Meanwhile I tried hard to interest film-makers in the value of TV as a publicity medium. It could work both ways: with excerpts from forthcoming films and their stars, the BBC would get good material and top names for nothing, the film industry would get wide promotion for a minimal price. I wrote letters on this theme to most of the British film producers, including Sir Alexander Korda.

To my surprise he replied immediately asking me to see him at his new London Film Productions office at 146 Piccadilly. He was charm itself. I went straight into the subject of my letter, but he stopped me. 'Yes, that is a good idea we can discuss later, Mr Mitchell. There is something else I would like to discuss with you. How would you like to be my new Director of Publicity?'

Frankly I was stupefied. The idea had never occurred to me. I had never been concerned with that side of films, other than making trailers for Michael Powell and Emeric Pressburger when they produced *Colonel Blimp* during the war. I expressed my doubts to Korda.

'No, I am well informed about you. You have experience in production; you are well-known in stage and film circles; you have good contacts with the press. – You will be ideal.' He gave me a week to think it over.

I went straightaway to see John Myers – his original pre-war publicity director, and brilliant at his job, who was now with the Rank Organization. He seemed to have no doubts. 'Take it, Leslie. Take it at all costs. Only Alex could have thought of it. Of course, he's dead right, you'd be ideal.'

Still unsure, I asked him for a description of Korda as a boss.

'Wonderful,' said he. 'Sensitive, understanding, brilliant. Just treat him like a woman: with affection and admiration!'

'What part of his anatomy do I have to kiss?' I queried.

'Oh, he's not like that at all. He likes people who stand up to him. You'll get on well together.'

Frankly I could not see the possibility of so good an opportunity elsewhere. I went back to see Korda.

'You can have what money you want,' he said, 'and we sail for New York next week.' I hastily explained that I was still under contract to several organizations – Movietone, the *Daily Mail*, and BBC TV and Radio. It would be at least three weeks before I could make myself available. He was obviously disconcerted; however, after a brief telephone conversation, he accepted the delay. So the die was cast.

One of the first necessities was to find a completely new staff. The temporary publicity representative had been with Korda on two previous occasions and had been twice fired, or so I was told. But Korda stressed that he should be included in my set-up, so I gave him a rise and made him my assistant. In that way he could be a useful aide, and I would quickly find out if he was not. The only other existing members of my department were Clarissa Churchill and a Miss Lloyd Thomas, both of whom were writing for the glossy papers. Clarissa was to become Lady Eden, the wife of Sir Anthony, a few years later.

By dint of probing and discussing my needs with the film world, I soon found a number of experienced and reliable people to fill the empty posts. What I was not told was that Korda, having relied on raising considerable sums for his future films, had been forced to lower his sights. He had been in America most of the war years and had little understanding of the changes that war had wrought on England. He found it hard to believe that coal was still rationed; that colour-printing had to be carried out in Italy; or that petrol was still being rationed. Labour, too, was not instantly available. Everything cost more and took longer than he remembered. So it was that the plans I had ready for him on his return from the USA had to be deferred.

The offices at Shepperton were still being rebuilt for London Films, and it was there that I had to keep my staff. Above all, we needed top-ranking stills cameramen. A friend called me up. 'Leslie,' he said, 'Bill Batchelor and Ted Reed, the two best cameramen in England, are coming to the end of their contracts with Rank. I thought I would let you know.' Thanking my stars, I contacted them and offered them the jobs at Shepperton. At first they were unsure about it, but Korda saw them personally and quickly persuaded them to accept. He was a super-salesman.

I felt mean about this because my friend John Myers had been their boss, but somehow I *had* to become harder headed and harder hearted. I was in a tough business. So I rang John and asked him to lunch at the Savoy where I apologetically explained what I had done. He looked steadily at me. 'The trouble is I'm never sure whether you're serious; but if you really mean it, I must warn you we signed them up again last week, and you've got a nasty court case on your hands.' The meal ended, and we both made a hasty return to our respective offices. Fortunately I had made no mistake.

For my second trip to the States I insisted on taking Phyl. Her good sense and charm would, I knew, stand me in good stead. I left with an introduction from Korda to our New York office staff, and a personal introduction to Spyros Skouras, the powerful head of Twentieth Century Fox. We sailed in the *Queen Elizabeth* on Friday, 13 February 1947. It happened to be Phyl's lucky number (and her birthday), so I took a chance it would turn out fortunate for us both.

At this time the *Queen Elizabeth* had not yet been fitted with stabilizers. When she was in heavy seas, she would lie on her side, like a huge whale, while passengers and crockery flew through the air in all directions. I myself saw one passenger turn a complete backward somersault in his chair. He got up ruefully rubbing his head, replaced the chair facing the opposite direction, only to go through exactly the same gymnastics as the great ship completed her 150° arc.

It was difficult not to be affected by the movement. Fortunately I am a good sailor and Phyl too stood up to it well. But came a moment during a particularly rough passage when we were sitting near the huge bar in the smoking-room. Suddenly from the serving door there appeared a steward carrying a large trayful of drinks, in professional style, on the palm of one hand and close to his head.

As he came in, the ship was reaching its critical angle and he leaned further and further back to retain his balance. Convinced he was going to fall headlong into the glasses on the tray, I sprang from my chair to help him. I remember passing him at high speed and choosing to protect myself with my *good* arm. Then all was quiet. I came round to see the agonized face of Phyl bending over me; beside her was the worried face of none other than General Curtis of Kodak. I hastily made the introduction, anxious for Phyl to have someone at hand if I was to pass out again. Finally I was collected on a stretcher and laid gently on my bunk.

Unfortunately it was impossible to X-ray me so they kept me to my bunk till we reached New York. As we berthed there was the usual collection of press-men and photographers. Anyone with a snappy turned-down brim and an alert look was greeted by, 'Mr

Lessley Mitchell?'

'Nope,' came the reply.

Eventually a funereal procession appeared on the gangway, carry-ing a stretcher. On it lay Korda's new publicity chief.

'Mr Lessley Mitchell?' they inquired with disbelief.

'Yes,' I whispered faintly.

Later they told me I had broken two ribs and my left collar-bone, but there was no time to do more than get myself strapped up. There was work to do. We had received a cable aboard ship from Pat Collinge and her husband Jim Smith, insisting we should dine with them on our first night in New York. I made it with Phyl's help and we had a great evening in spite of my aches and pains.

We had been met by representatives of the New York office of London Films. And they quickly gave me a list of press and film meetings which they expected me to attend. Foremost was one with Sir Carol Reed and Cary Grant, but as I had received a message from Korda *not* to discuss any future plans for his British output, I played it down with everybody, explaining that I had come to learn my job from acknowledged American experts. I noticed there was a slightly hostile approach from the New York staff, but put this down to their desire to know me better before making themselves too helpful.

There was also the normal American suspicion of a European interloper. As an American girl once asked me in a New York taxi, 'Is it true all you British are queers?' Conscious that I had behaved *too* well during an enjoyable evening, I threw myself on her, and slowly released her while she could still breathe. After repairing her make-up she looked at me. 'I take it *all* back,' she said. 'But you just *have* to speak up for yourself in the United States.'

When I contacted the great Spyros Skouras, he invited Phyl and me to lunch at his home in Mamaroneck, just outside New York. We duly arrived and received a warm welcome from his wife and family. Also present were several interesting people I had met the year before with Ben Grauer.

The Skourases had adopted a young and mischievous Greek boy who joined us for lunch. He disappeared while we were all talking, so I presumed he had sneaked away somewhere. I noticed as the meal progressed that the ladies appeared to be somewhat ill at ease, even a little flushed, and could think of no explanation. Suddenly there was a suppressed scream from the lady opposite. Spyros knew at once what was going on. In a voice of thunder he yelled under the table, 'Come out, you disgraceful boy. Come out at once, and I will make you a good lesson.'

The child crawled out, grinning like a Botticelli angel. 'I'm sorry, Papa,' he said. He had been untying the ladies' stockings from their suspender belts.

After lunch our host invited me to tell him what I was doing for Korda. I explained that after the war-time years as commentator with Movietone (which was part of his Twentieth Century Fox empire), I had been offered the job of Publicity Director for London Films. He checked with his film directory that I had been working for him indirectly for the past eight years. Then he made me an offer. 'You want to learn about publicity? I'll tell the boys. You will be shown everything.' Getting on to his HQ he told them to give me full cooperation during my visit. It was the luckiest moment of my journey.

We were invited to stay for dinner and afterwards went to the cinema, built in his attic, to see the latest Twentieth Century Fox film about to be released. We were finally sent in his car back to New York and our hotel. From now on everything went well. When we arrived in Hollywood there was no London Films car to meet us, but there *was* one from Twentieth Century Fox.

I was really puzzled by the seeming ineptitude of arrangements made for me by Korda's New York office, but I discovered on my return to England that they had been confidentially warned that I had plans to make changes in the staff. So naturally they did not take to me kindly. This information was strictly untrue as I had no jurisdiction over anything but the London scene, and not much over that so far.

Throughout our trip in Hollywood it was the influence of Spyros Skouras that opened doors for me. I was invited to a number of publicity departments belonging to different film companies. It was depressing to find how British film advertising and publicity material was wasted here. In most cases it was firmly junked, and a brand-new campaign evolved.

I was amused to find stills of a costume drama had been skilfully altered by removing the lace of the low-cut dresses and ruffles to give an impression of near-nudity, the results being transferred to advertising posters. Apparently in the unsophisticated areas of the Middle West, men in period costume would be regarded as 'fancy-pants' or 'cissies' and received with cat-calls and howls of laughter. This was the *New* World, they wanted no part of the Old. Nor did they pretend to understand it.

A searing demonstration of that trans-Atlantic separation occurred while I was with Phyl visiting one of the big department stores in Hollywood. A Jewish woman rushed over to greet our hostess. 'My dear,' she said, 'we're so *excited*, we just got our names in the papers. Two cousins of ours were sent to those gas ovens. Isn't that something?' Phyl was so upset she had to move away and stare out of the window.

One of the publicity men I met had been to England as a guest of Admiral Carpendale, a BBC governor. Evidently the gallant Admiral lived in the depths of the English countryside in an old Elizabethan house. My acquaintance had been upset by the fact that he was compelled to use the chamber pot during the night and a pretty young servant girl had removed and emptied it. 'Here,' he said solemnly, 'that would be looked after by coloured folk – and I couldn't stand for that business of everyone calling me "sir", and touching their – ' he hesitated, ' – forelock, do you call it?'

'That's not very common nowadays,' I said. 'When *was* this?' Apparently it had been in the late twenties. But I told him, 'I don't quite get your worry about being called sir. Here everybody says sir – Yes, sir; No, sir; You bet, sir!'

'Ah,' he said with a knowing look, '*we* don't mean it.'

On one occasion Carol Reed invited us for dinner at Romanov's – one of the top Hollywood restaurants. The proprietor claimed that though there were many R*omano*vs (the family name of the late Tsar), he was the only *Rom*anov. The restaurant was full of celebrities and, our party having settled down at our table, Carol looked round and suddenly stiffened in his chair. Romanov himself was coming over to greet us. 'Leslie,' hissed Carol under his breath, 'turn this way and keep talking, I don't want the little man to see me.' I did as he asked, only turning momentarily to say 'Good evening' before Romanov left us.

Later Carol explained the mystery. When he left King's School, he was unable to find a job, so his older brother, who was in New York, told him to travel steerage to America where he would be waiting to meet him. It was a rough journey and when the ship arrived, there was no brother in sight. The crowd of emigrants was directed to Ellis Island – Carol included. There he was in a strange land, stranded, with no way of communicating with his brother or the outside world. Lonely and scared in this crowd of foreign strangers, he made friends with an elderly man who took him in hand. 'Now not to worry, young man. We'll soon have you out of here. It is all a mistake. Your brother misunderstood the date. Stick with me and all will become right.' Carol stuck with him, and they shared meals together. Eventually his brother was able to contact the Ellis Island officials, and they were reunited. The strange comforter had been *Rom*anov himself. But Carol's innate shyness stopped him from making himself so publicly conspicuous.

Ben Lyon and his wife Bebe Daniels went out of their way to be
helpful. He too had just taken on a new job as Casting Director for
Fox. We went to several of their parties and met a number of famous
stars.

Later when I was being shown round one of the giant Hollywood
stages we came to a caravan used as a dressing-room whilst a film was
being shot. As we passed, a very pretty woman looked out. 'You must
be Mr Leslie Mitchell,' she said. 'You are over here on behalf of Alex
Korda, aren't you? Do come in.' My guide went off on other business,
promising to return shortly and continue my tour.

The lady I now recognized as one of Hollywood's better-known
stars, a very beautiful South American girl I had admired in a number
of pictures. 'Do make yourself at home, Leslie. You don't mind if I call
you Leslie?' she said. I didn't. I lodged myself on the floor beside her
make-up table while she sat gracefully in the chair.

'Is Alex going to do *Salome*, Leslie?' she said casually. Conscious of
instructions not to discuss Korda's future plans with anybody, I
hedged. 'It's been discussed, as you obviously know. But nothing has
been decided yet.'

The lady stood up and slowly began to disrobe. 'Tell Alex you've
seen me, Leslie. I would give anything to play Salome. . . . See, my
figure is still young. A firm bust, small waist, good legs – do you not
agree?' Sweating slightly, I felt compelled to accept her statistics and
agreed wholeheartedly with her estimate. Quickly she threw her
dressing-gown round her. 'Tell Alex, you have seen me *personally*,
Leslie. I hope we shall meet again.' I was dismissed.

I arrived at the bar a little late to meet my publicity colleagues *and*
Phyl who had been waiting for me. When I explained that I had had a
personal interview with the glamorous lady in her caravan, the men
all burst out laughing like hyenas.

Personalities apart, it was obvious that the film world in Britain had
to expand its aims. While Hollywood expended vast sums on promotion and advertising for its films, it could recoup that expense from
box-office receipts in the USA alone. The profits would come from
exhibitors *outside* America, including England. British films on the
contrary could hardly expect to recoup their expenditure in Europe
alone. The difference clearly lay in the size of the populations involved
and therefore the size of the cinema audiences in each case.

As I saw it, my major aim was to save expenditure on production
costs by at least meeting the demands of American publicity in
advance and taking their type of stills – leg art and cheesecake – while
the film was in production. This would save paying for two separate

publicity campaigns. We could also further stimulate America's interest by cabling hot news to Hollywood columnists who were widely syndicated throughout their country. These became basic thoughts before I prepared to return to London.

At this moment Korda sent me a cable. 'Arrange to return by air; your cabin essential for stars needed in London.' I contacted Cunard's offices in New York. They could not help. They had arranged a later booking on *Queen Elizabeth* on account of my accident, but the booking was for me and my wife personally and could not be transferred. There was a long waiting list and they were not prepared to alter their arrangements. After I explained the situation to the New York office, they cabled London.

By reply came a longer cable. 'Paulette Goddard tells me that you are bringing with you her personal presents to me in the form of lots of cigars. Stop. They are even more welcome than yourself. Stop. If you have not enough money for duty Codrington will await you with sufficient. Regards. Alexander Korda.'

Phyl and I had already promised to take a few parcels for friends of Americans we had met, but we could hardly have expected the avalanche that descended on us when we embarked. Phyl was forced to stack the cigars – literally hundreds of them – in the small bathroom to allow us room in our cabin. They were all wrapped – bunches of twenty boxes at a time – in stout brown paper firmly bound around with cord. When we sailed, it was necessary to unstack them each morning to get to the bath.

The sea, this time, was kinder and once more we sat at the captain's table. This was to be his last Atlantic crossing after long years at sea, so it was a special compliment. As we came to the last day of the voyage Phyl and I went for a long stroll on deck. It was a fine day and the great ship made no movement.

No movement? I looked over the side. The ship was stationary! *Too* stationary. I looked astern. The giant propellers were thrashing the water *towards* me! Still no movement. 'Phyl darling,' I said. 'You won't believe it, but we're aground.'

She turned on me like a tigress. 'Don't dare say such a stupid thing. You and your imagination. You could start a panic talking like that.' She dragged me down to our cabin. I looked out of the porthole. We had completely stopped. Engines and all.

I took poor Phyl, still unconvinced, on deck again. An hour later the first tugs began to arrive. By the end of the day we counted thirteen tugs straining at their cables without effect. Press photographers in aeroplanes were taking pictures of the huge hulk wallowing in the tide. Frantic cables were sent out. The bars had been closed as we were in home waters, and a certain amount of bad feeling grew among thirsty passengers demanding refreshment. But gradually rules were relaxed for the emergency and we all retired to bed.

The following morning our steward arrived early in the cabin. 'Very sorry, sir,' he said. 'All hand-luggage has to be taken off to lighten the ship. The tugs are coming alongside to take off passengers'. With agonized feelings I watched Korda's priceless cigars thrown overboard to land each time with a dull thud on the deck of the tug below. In due course Phyl and I joined the cigars, with less impact, by the ship's ladder, and we moved off to our berth in Southampton.

Movietone was there to greet us and take pictures, but my face failed to register any great happiness at being home again. The Korda representative was there to pay duty on the battered boxes, so I left the explanation to him. A week later the tobacco tax went up!

Some weeks later I was sent to the Brussels Film Festival. Sir David Cunynghame, who was on the board of London Films, called me to his office. 'You'd better go over and find out what's happening,' he said. 'There seem to be rumours of strife and misunderstandings in Brussels. See if you can clear it up.' I flew over and almost at once bumped into John Myers and Anthony Downing who were there representing the Rank outfit.

Realizing I had a tough assignment, John explained the situation in Brussels. He had been in touch with the London Films representative who obviously had no experience whatsoever in film publicity. John had even felt compelled to help him by giving up poster sites around Brussels which had been reserved for Rank. Paulette Goddard, one of our leading stars, had failed to attend a dinner held in her honour. Some press representatives complained they had been treated with discourtesy. In fact there was a move among the press in Brussels to overlook the Korda group. I at once made it my business to apologize to all concerned and smooth ruffled feelings.

The following day there was another official dinner in honour of Miss Goddard. Used to the promotional gimmicks of the Hollywood scene, she was obviously not impressed by the toned-down version that war-torn Brussels could provide. About two-thirds of the way through dinner she got up from the table, accompanied by her two companions, and left without a word. After a decent interval I went to find them, but they had left the building. On my return, I made an abject apology for their absence and explained that our star was suffering from a violent migraine headache and had been forced to retire. No one believed a word of it, but the burghers of Brussels did show appreciation for my handling of the situation.

The party over I drove round the restaurants of the city. At the third attempt I was successful in finding the three women sitting in a crowded dining-room. 'Mr Mitchell,' said Miss Goddard, 'how clever of you to find us. What happened?' I explained that I had informed our hosts that she had a migraine. 'Well, it's your business to see I'm entertained and looked after. So far you haven't come up with *one* good idea. I'm bored with these civic parties. I want to see some night life. Come on, take us some place.' I explained patiently that there was *no* night life in Brussels. After six years of enemy occupation the Belgians were still suffering every shortage. They had not yet recovered from the effects of all-out war. The lady snorted her disbelief. 'Well, maybe I'll be able to show *you* the town,' said she. 'All you have to do is make a few inquiries.' With that the three women got up and left.

Fortunately we had been joined by Michael Wilding, a Korda star of great charm whom I had known for many years. I begged him to stay with me for the rest of the evening and, with his usual good humour, he agreed. After paying the bill we went out to the entrance-hall. The women had ordered a taxi. 'Just follow us,' they said. We obediently got into a second taxi.

We drove round the city, stopping at various points, while the leaders discussed whether they would investigate the rather sleazy bars and cafés. Finally we arrived at what appeared to be a private house. The girls got out and walked in, while I paid off their taxi. The door opened again. It was one of the girls. 'Oh Leslie, will you go in and deal for us? There's been some mistake.' She was obviously upset, so reminding Michael of his promise to stay with me, I went inside as our star made a hurried exit. There was the sound of our taxi leaving. Michael and I were alone together. . . . It was a brothel! To placate the irate Madame I offered to buy some champagne for the girls; the two of us drank with a gaggle of somewhat *déshabillée* girls till the champagne was finished. Then I paid the rather exorbitant corkage, and we departed for the hotel with astonished farewells ringing in our ears.

On my return to London I was summoned to see Sir David Cunynghame again. He congratulated me on having successfully dealt with the Brussels incident, but was obviously a little uneasy about something. At last he came to it. 'There have been rather extraordinary rumours about one aspect of your visit, Leslie,' he said.

I had been expecting this. 'Oh, you mean my evening in the *bordel*?'

'Then it's true?' he said, looking astounded.

'Yes, but I wouldn't want to publicize it, I had with me one of the main stars of our current film – Michael Wilding. There was no harm in it. Just a nasty little trick by another of our stars. It didn't work out.'

'My god, Leslie,' he said, 'you *are* learning fast.'

Some days later I joined Korda in the theatre to see some of the early rushes for the current production. He sat beside me and, without turning his head, said in a low voice, 'Leslie, you have the goodwill of everybody, but where are the results?'

I countered by explaining that I had been working hard both here and in America. The results would be forthcoming the moment I had a department to help me put my ideas into operation.

'If you do not provide results, I am sorry, but reluctantly we must part company!' He pressed the button to start the day's rushes, and we watched till they were run through.

'Sir Alexander,' I said, 'we must have advance publicity for this film. Can you not let me have any of the discarded takes or stills to release, otherwise it will be too late?'

This time he turned to me. 'You have not listened to a bloody word I have spoken,' he said. Patiently I recounted verbatim what he had just said to me; then I walked away.

Alexander Shaw was waiting in my office to lunch with me. He gave me a quick look. 'Are you all right?' he asked. 'You look ghastly.' I sat at my desk for a moment. I reflected that I hadn't the physical or mental stamina for a job so obviously dependent on the whims of my employer, genius or not. I recovered myself; Alex and I had a relaxed luncheon. I had suddenly become aware that I might have been engaged as a publicity stunt by Korda for Korda, not for his film output.

But he had one more time-bomb for me. He had decided we were *not* to set up our own publicity department for London Films after all. Instead he asked me to visit the main advertising agencies to discuss the possibility of *their* taking over the account.

At J. Walter Thompson's, a leading agency, I met a personable character by the name of Ingram Fraser who seemed particularly interested and asked to be taken to Shepperton to assess the situation there. I took him round personally and introduced our skeleton staff. On the way home he volunteered the information that Korda had promised him the job I now held when they had met in America during the war. I was not reassured by his tact. Nor would I have given him the job which Sir Alexander gave him when they met again. He was to become my assistant.

Now Korda decided, at last, to give me my head. 'I want you personally to take over the publicity for an excellent film, Leslie. *A Man about the House*, with Kieron Moore. You will do a good job? It is a Ted Black picture, and you will keep *my* name out of it.' I had already approached Tony Wysard about posters for this film. He too had been threatened by Korda with replacement, but took it in his stride; they had worked together before. Tony came up with an excellent 'teaser' poster – showing the young Kieron Moore, as the Italian hero, stripped to the waist. There was no lettering to indicate the name of the film, or the actor.

One headache was cured for me by Aspro. They decided to vacate many of their main advertisement hoardings at this precise moment. I managed to plaster the most visually effective points in London with Kieron Moore's torso. Public interest was aroused and the film opened to first-rate reviews. Kieron was a success from the first showing, and Margaret Johnston joined him with Dulcie Gray in the starry firmament.

My next test was responsibility for the smooth running of the annual meeting of the Cinema Exhibitors' Association, which was to be held in Eastbourne. Happily the film chosen for the occasion was *A Man about the House*, and a number of stars were to be present.

It was quite an impressive gathering and included many leading film personalities. Chief among them Sir Aubrey Smith – still young in heart as ever; Michael Wilding, Kieron Moore, Glynis Johns, Dulcie Gray, Margaret Johnston and Diana Wynyard. With the aid of British Lion's staff, the arrangements went without a hitch, and I congratulated them and myself, knowing that our responsibility ended when we had delivered our stars to the theatre. I watched the last limousine draw up and discharge its burden.

Then I joined Phyl in the foyer with a light heart. As the daughter of a man of the theatre, she had been brought up to smell disaster. She was looking distraught. 'Darling,' she said quietly, 'you *must* go upstairs. It's urgent!' I explained that my responsibilities were now over; we could both relax. 'Go, darling, you must go,' she urged.

I went to the back of the dress circle to find a gaggle of enraged film stars. There were no seats for them; all the reserved seats were occupied. Apparently the theatre manager had engaged extra staff to assist with the seating arrangements for this star-studded occasion. As the first cinema exhibitors arrived, they were told that all dress-circle seats were reserved for VIPs. So up they went and sat in them. I introduced Sir Aubrey Smith from the stage while desperate re-arrangements and apologies were made to all concerned. Eventually order was restored, the film began and Sir Aubrey, Phyl and I watched it standing at the back of the dress circle. I loved that man.

Some weeks later I joined Korda in the studio. 'I'll be leaving for New York tomorrow,' he said, 'and I require a half-hour and a one-hour radio treatment of *Anna Karenina*. I want them before I leave, in the morning.'

This was getting laughable. I raced home and telephoned what was required to a BBC radio producer, Gordon Crier, and a scriptwriter whom I knew. I told them I was prepared to pay well if they would join me in an all-night script session. We sat, the three of us, through the night with iced water, coffee and sandwiches to sustain us. Two secretaries sat with us and in turn typed the pages as we completed them. By 8 a.m. I had two radio scripts, bound and printed, to take to the great man.

Back at the studios, I approached him and held out the large envelope. 'Here are the two radio scripts you wanted, Sir Alexander.' With astonishing strength, without opening the envelope, he slowly tore the scripts to pieces. 'This is not what I want,' he said. Nor I.

I decided that the time had come to call it a day and made my departure with a sigh of relief. One reaction came from the man who was responsible for the finance and distribution of London Films, Sir Arthur Jarratt. He wrote me this letter:

British Lion
Film Corporation Limited
76-78 Wardour Street
London W1

9 October 1947

Leslie Mitchell Esq.
146 Piccadilly
W I

My dear Leslie Mitchell,

In reply to your letter of the 8th October, let me at once say that the advertising and publicity campaign for *A Man About the House* was, in my opinion, one of the best advertising campaigns I have ever seen for any film, in fact two newspapers commented on how good it was, and I am delighted to read of the broadcasts you have arranged for this picture.

The campaign and the reception Kieron Moore has received from the film critics has definitely shown Kieron Moore as a star and I am sure that this, alone, must give you enormous satisfaction as it has me.

I hope that you will be successful – as I know you will be – in whatever you undertake and eventually decide to do, and trust that from time to time we will meet, and I shall always be delighted to see you at any time you find yourself free.

Yours sincerely,
Arthur Jarratt.

Some three months after I left London Films, Phyl and I lent our flat for a party to an American friend who invited his London acquaintances. It was a good party, and I was surprised to see Captain Tom Hussey arrive, one of Korda's closest friends, both socially and business-wise.

He came over to talk to me. 'Nice to see you again, Leslie. Unhappy business your resignation. Could we have a quiet word somewhere?'

I took him into my office. We sat there with our drinks. Hussey turned to me. 'Of course you know the new publicity man is going?' I didn't, but expressed no surprise. 'I think I can tell you that Alex is not at all happy with the publicity department. He's going off to the States again tomorrow, but he'd have you back at your own price, if you phoned and asked him.'

'Here's my card,' I said, 'with the telephone number. I would be interested to hear from him.' Tom Hussey looked at me keenly. 'You can't be like that. Not with Alex!' But I was.

Five years later, having long since recovered my nerve and my reputation, I was invited by Paramount to attend the première of *Gilbert and Sullivan* and interview the VIPs as they arrived. I was also asked if there would be any difficulty about my interviewing Sir Alexander Korda whose film it was. The occasion celebrated his twenty-first anniversary in British films, so I naturally accepted. After all this, for me, was a professional engagement.

And the event held other attractions for me. In 1936 I had appeared on TV's first intermediate film system, which had been abandoned. Now here it was again, in a new, improved version. The Cintel cameras in the foyer were to film the celebrities as they arrived, and Paramount's Kinescope system projected the pictures onto the full-size cinema screen in the auditorium. The interval between the actual takes of the camera and their showing could be extended. The occasion was another historic development in television as well as a tribute to one of the world's greatest film-makers.

The audience at the Plaza cinema included celebrities from all walks of life. Mr and Mrs Gaitskell, Mr and Mrs Selwyn Lloyd, Sam Goldwyn, Sir Carol Reed, James Mason, Sir Arthur Bliss, Sir Malcolm Sargent, Margot Fonteyn, Wendy Toye – the list was endless. I interviewed many of them. Among those I spoke to were Ronald Neame and Ann Todd. They moved into the theatre, and a few moments later Ann came running back to me. 'Leslie,' she gasped, 'I've just seen us both doing our interview again – in there!' Many people did not realize that cinema projection of television had arrived.

The bells rang to announce the opening of the film, and at last –

with still no sign of the guest of honour – I abandoned my post.

The film over, the first person to greet me was Korda himself. 'That was good, Leslie. Thank you very much. I did not come for the interview after all. I trust you, of course, implicitly, but I am not such a good actor.' Holding my arm, he propelled me to where Phyl was patiently waiting. 'Ah, Mrs Mitchell,' he said, 'it would give me great pleasure if you would bring this man to a party I am giving on the stage of the Savoy Theatre. You will please come as my special guests.' We went, and enjoyed every moment, but I was glad not to be working for him.

Looking back I am sad that I met Korda so late in his career. I had always admired his genius, from his own favourite, *The Private Life of the Gannets*, which he made with Julian Huxley in 1935, through *The Private Life of Henry VIII* and *Rembrandt*, to *The Conquest of the Air*, which he never completed but on which I spoke the commentary just before the war. Twelve reels of it – and most of the leading actors of the time, in a history of flight from Icarus to Handley-Page. It was eventually sold to a cameraman, I believe, when London Films left Denham.

He was a remarkable character and undoubtedly a genius in his time, but that brilliance was slowly fading. The financial strains and hazards of post-war Britain had been his undoing.

14. Freelance Again

I was heartened to find that I had not been dropped from BBC or newsreel work. If anything, my recent involvement in the film world proved an unexpected booster.

Almost as soon as I left London Films I was invited by BBC Television to act as a commentator at the wedding of Princess Elizabeth and the Duke of Edinburgh. I was stationed outside Buckingham Palace. The television pictures were admirable and I enjoyed my first big royal occasion more than I expected, though I was understandably nervous beforehand. That night as the crowds broke up I made my way to Soho Square to speak the newsreel commentary for Movietone. I was relieved to find that I had not lost my touch, and the critics were kind.

I also acted as MC for a weekly series of programmes on radio – 'Alhambra of the Air', into which I had previously slotted stars from London Film Productions.

But my health *had* been affected. I was nervously exhausted and out of sorts, so finally Phyl persuaded me to do something about it. Early in 1948 my doctor sent me to see a top Harley Street dental surgeon in the belief that I was being poisoned by some legacy of my accident. He took endless pictures of my shattered jaw, and sent me home. The following night my GP came round to see me. 'You go into the Clinic tomorrow, Leslie. I've booked a room for you. The surgeon has to remove quite a bit of your jaw. It never cleared up after your smash-up. It means a week or two in the Clinic, I'm afraid, but it must be done.' I cancelled all appointments for three weeks and applied myself to getting well.

I think the surgeon must have climbed into my mouth personally with a pick-axe. I came to after the operation with a face like a pumpkin and still bleeding like a pig. Soon the door opened and a charming girl came in. 'Oh, you poor thing,' she said. 'Mummy's had the same operation and she told me to give you this.'

''oes she 'ook 'ike this?'' I mouthed faintly.

'Oh she's worse; the doctor did her *after* you,' she said cheerfully.

'This' was a bottle of champagne. Nothing loath I made her pour some into a toothmug and after drinking it, went to sleep again.

The following day I returned her mother's compliment. The third day we agreed to play cards together, to while away the painful tedium. We sat concentrating on our cards; our faces were still very swollen and painful so conversation was kept to a minimum. About 10.30 p.m. the door was opened suddenly. It was the floor sister. 'Mr Mitchell,' she said in a scandalized voice. 'You *must* know male patients are not allowed in the ladies' rooms at night!'

I had had enough pushing around. 'Do you suppose we could do *anything* enjoyable in *our* state?' I demanded. Off she went and spent the night writing a report about our goings-on. Only my doctor was amused.

The operation was successful from a medical point of view, but I had to work hard at learning to talk normally. Microphones are all too revealing when there's the slightest impediment in one's diction, and I had a painful and dreary few months ahead while I rehearsed daily with my tape-machine to overcome the effects of the addition to my jaw. Perseverance won. At the end of April I acted as a TV commentator for the Silver Wedding of King George VI and Queen Elizabeth.

Financially I was in poor straits again, however. Mrs Locke, to whom I owed so much in my early days, had fallen on hard times. She had been accustomed to every luxury while W. J. was alive. Unfortunately his books were not reprinted during the war, and most of his film rights had been used or explored. His books were now becoming 'dated': he had written most of them between 1914 and 1930. Now in the forties they seemed, sadly, whimsical and over-sentimental. Even the dialogue had dated – phrases like 'I say, how topping', and 'what a ripping idea', were now used mainly by comedians in variety. Edwardian concepts of women and purity had altered radically too.

In fact there had been no income worth speaking of from his books, and Aimée was now very hard up. In the early part of the war I had approached a number of her friends for loans of whatever sums they could afford, as a standing account for her upkeep. The money was to be repaid from any film rights that might be sold. I raised some £3000, and made my own contributions as and when possible.

But now my mother, too, had to be financed. She had sailed once more for America, at the earliest opportunity after the war. From New York she had gone to Baltimore to stay with friends and decided to settle there in an apartment. Suddenly, with the devaluation of the pound and the clampdown on British assets abroad, she was forced to make her return since I was prevented from sending her even the small allowance on which she had been living.

Typically, she sent me a cable. 'Must bring minimum of furniture with me. Please cover.' I hastily insured her belongings for £1500 and arranged to meet her ship at Liverpool. She had only two trunks and a large suitcase, but explained that the remainder would be delivered to the flat I had found for her in Ebury Street. I put her up temporarily in a Sloane Square hotel. Fortunately she liked the flat and quickly summed up its possibilities – a double bedroom, a large sitting-room, kitchen and bathroom.

Two days later her furniture arrived. The removal men had a word with me first. 'Hope you're insured, guv'nor. Got a bit of trouble 'ere.' Slowly four or five of them carried out a Bechstein baby grand piano. I *thought* they carried it with extreme caution. Then at the top of the stairs to the entrance, they tipped their load. A tidal wave of salt water swept down the steps and the driveway. 'Must have been carried on deck, sir. That's all *we* can think!' Mum's the word!

My mother's furniture and belongings were, of course, under-insured, but before long she had a new piano and various replace-ments for antique chairs and tables she had brought with her. The explanation was that the ship she had sailed in was not large, but the storms she encountered were.

On top of all this, Aimée Locke decided she must move from the little house we had found for her. Knowing her almost uncontrollable habit of spending too much money, I arranged with her landlord, Sir Everard Duncombe – a most understanding man – to refuse to release her from the leasehold. I had explained to him that the cost of moving her to a new abode was quite beyond our means and hers. He generously delayed his own plan to take back the house and make use of it for a relative. We each promised to keep the arrangement secret.

Aimée invited Phyl and me to the little house for a weekend. Before lunch I discovered her in the kitchen preparing a large ham cooked in champagne. 'Darling,' I protested, 'you don't have to be so extrava-gant for us. We're family. Remember?'

She looked up briefly. 'I will *die* before I stop offering my guests the best. Whoever they may be.'

Sadly, God was to take her up on that boast.

Weeks later she discovered that it was I who had been providing her income with her friends' assistance. She went out straightaway and took a job as chef in a country house. Her reputation as a cook and a hostess was easy to establish; her 'table' had been famous in the past. Her employers gave a celebration dinner-party for their special friends, and she provided a positively Lucullan meal. But they found that she fully expected someone else to do the washing-up. And when they came to inspecting their store cupboard, *all* their carefully hoarded post-war delicacies had been exhausted. The larder was bare.

A few days later poor Aimée was taken ill with jaundice and admitted to hospital.

There she underwent a gall-bladder operation. I went to visit her and found she still had not forgiven me for concealing the origins of her income.

When she died, we found she had, typically, quarrelled with her solicitors and rewritten her will. She made me sole executor, and left 'a choice of her furniture' to a niece. The lady took counsel's opinion and found that it meant, in legal terms, *everything* so long as one item was left.

The solicitors had a field day, but I was forced in the end to leave two of the major debtors unpaid. Fortunately they were both rich enough to 'forgive' repayment. I was left the rights of the Locke books, and still have dreams of one day reviving some of the stories. W. J. Locke remains a considerable story-teller.

At the end of 1948 Firth Shephard suffered a severe heart attack. Phyl went with him to Cornwall where he was sent to recuperate. He returned to London somewhat improved in health if not in spirits. He had seen the fruits of a lifetime's work disappear by a trick of fate. He died on 3 January 1949. The fates were certainly in malignant mood.

I had also become increasingly despondent about 'Picture Page' which, owing to the pressures being put upon it, was losing much of its spontaneity and interest. One of my main tasks seemed to be inter-viewing obsessed model-makers who brought replicas of Canterbury Cathedral they had constructed from used matches.

The redeeming favourites, as always, were animals. On one occa-sion Joan Gilbert suddenly said, 'Well, I really *must* go over now to introduce our next visitor – a baby bear. I won't ask Leslie to join me. He doesn't like animals.' Irritated by this quite untrue comment, I walked round to the keeper, who had with him a tin of honey. I motioned to him what I proposed to do, and joined Joan in vision. The bear turned round and feverishly started licking my hands. Joan was thunderstruck till she observed the trick I had played on her.

On another occasion, which I now confess publicly for the first time, I took advantage of Joan's good nature. I was having an excellent lunch at the expense of a journalist who, as I knew, worked for a well-known advertising company. We were sitting happily together while I wondered why he had invited me. Came the coffee and he offered me a cigarette, which he lit for me. 'Haven't you got a lighter, Leslie?' he asked.

'No, I'm afraid not,' I answered – meaning I had left mine at home. Over the table he pushed a small parcel. It contained a brand-new cigarette lighter. 'I thought you might use it on "Picture Page" when anyone is smoking, old boy,' he smiled.

I was suddenly angry. Did he really imagine I would advertise his — lighter and risk my career, all for the sake of a free meal? (Advertising was strictly forbidden on the BBC in those days.)

Going back to the office, my temper cooled and I became amused at an idea I had. In my letter of thanks, I apologized for not having accepted his offer with a good grace and suggested another way to publicize his product.

The following week Joan went to the camera and held up a new table lighter. 'Aren't people kind?' she said. 'This has been sent to me by two viewers with this letter: "Dear Miss Gilbert, we have both long been fans of you and Mr Leslie Mitchell in 'Picture Page'. Noticing that you now have a brand-new setting for the show, please accept the enclosed lighter for the use of your distinguished visitors. Two fervent admirers".' As she held the gift in close-up for the third time, I stealthily crept out of the studio. Fortunately there were no repercussions.

Out of the blue came a welcome relief from the humourless interviews I was being saddled with. Terry-Thomas burst upon the scene in 'How do You View', a series of light-hearted sketches, produced fortnightly, which included an interview spot. In this spot Terry adopted a new zany character for every performance. They were only funny if the interviewer appeared to be seriously interested in this character and quite unaware that he was being idiotically funny. I was engaged as the interviewer and the spot was enormously successful except with those who believed I did not realize what I was doing.

Among them was the Head of Television. He spoke rather sharply to me. 'Either you want to become a well-known commentator or you wish to return to the Charing Cross Road.' I couldn't help replying that Movietone was being shown in English-speaking countries all over the world. Television was still in its infancy.

In 1950 I was asked to be MC for the Royal Film Performance. The film was *The Mudlark*, starring Irene Dunne and Alec Guinness, with young Andrew Ray – son of Ted Ray, the comedian. Apart from being responsible for the commentary on the show, I appeared with Terry-Thomas in his now-famous interview sketch, in which he impersonated the gong-basher who preceded all Rank films as their trade-mark. It involved a long and straight-faced introduction from me, in which I built up this internationally famous figure of the British film world. 'Few of our most successful films could have been exhibited without his professional help,' etc. Terry would trail on with a large drumstick in his hand, and clad in ill-fitting long woollen underwear. He explained in a rich cockney accent, 'I just 'appened to pick up this ideear, when I come upon a bloke bashing a gong in the 'all of a boarding-'ouse I was visiting. Course, I've 'ad to *extend* it a bit!' Behind him hung a giant bronze gong at least twelve feet across.

The script, beautifully written by Sid Colin, was a gem, and Terry used it with enormous success in Europe and America. But the joy was in the way the audience was always taken in by the mock seriousness of the introduction – and on this particular occasion even the royal family was momentarily taken in.

Later as we stood in line to be presented, J. Arthur Rank was about to name me when the King interjected, 'Oh, I know this one very well, Mr Rank; we all watch television.' He went on to ask me about a most unfortunate appearance of mine on TV just shortly before. Without warning I had been faced with two opposing cricket teams. Knowing nothing about cricket (dare I admit it?) I had to ask who was who, and what was what, which embarrassed them no less than me. His Majesty laughed, and added seriously, 'D–d–don't you get t–tired of interviewing all these people?'

'Not so tired, sir, as *they* must be of being interviewed by me,' I replied. For a moment his blue eyes stared at me, and I thought I had offended him. Then as he overcame his stammer, he laughed heartily and moved along the waiting line of artists.

I also travelled with the film stars to a replica of the Royal Show at Cardiff. Here I met Gloria Swanson for the first time. She had just made a wonderful comeback in *Sunset Boulevard* after several years' absence from the screen. But she was nervous as a kitten. 'Gosh I'm so scared,' she said, 'I don't know what they want me to do.'

I reassured her. 'It's a simple personal appearance in the entrance to the theatre. I'll be there – you have *nothing* to worry about. I'll ask you a few questions and when you stop talking, I'll ask you another. But don't worry, Miss Swanson. I'm one of your greatest fans and I've been interviewing people for years. Just relax.' Rather dubiously she agreed to do just that.

Came the night – the foyer crowded with screaming fans – and Gloria Swanson's Rolls-Royce drew up. As she was recognized, the crowd grew even more hysterical. 'Gloria,' they shouted. 'It's Gloria.'

I went to meet her and conduct her to the BBC microphone. 'Miss Swanson,' I said, with my famous leer, 'looking at you in the hard light of these arc-lamps it seems almost impossible to believe that you're the daughter of a young mother.'

'I'm the daughter of a *what*?' she urged. After a pregnant pause we both started laughing uncontrollably. I was glad to be no longer working as a publicist.

Gradually I began to suspect that the BBC pundits were becoming anxious to replace me in various jobs which had become associated with my name. There was a tendency for programme chiefs to say, 'Yes, there's Mitchell. Isn't there anybody else?' – particularly those of them who wanted to put friends of theirs in my place. Not surprising really – I had lasted for nearly fifteen years, and it happens to everybody in the public eye.

But I could not *afford* to give up. I had to think up new ideas. I arranged productions for a series of exhibitions and publicity shows with industrial and commercial companies. I toured the country with the 'Brains Trust', 'Twenty Questions' and similar panel shows. Finally at the end of 1950 a decision was made for me. I was removed once more to the Clinic.

This time it appeared to be heart trouble, and I was treated for angina as well as a complication of my old spinal damage. During three weeks' incarceration I was kept under intensive care and my life was saved, I believe, by the vigilant attention of a Nurse Brass, who was working temporarily in the London Clinic, prior to becoming matron at a well-known hospital in North London. With each recurrent bout of pain she seemed to be there day or night to give me an injection and ease the agony. She had the gifts of a natural healer and the training of a first-class nurse. I was and still am deeply grateful to her.

As I had to remain immovable in bed, I allowed my beard to grow. When the time came to leave the Clinic I was wheeled in to see my specialist. He explained that he was satisfied I could now go home, provided I took life very easily for the next few months. When I inquired why it was difficult to walk, he told me to see a back specialist; so far as my heart was concerned, he had done all that was possible.

I persevered during the next week or two; it was the Christmas season. Gradually, as walking became easier, I decided to walk all the way to the hairdresser to have my beard removed. On the way I ran into George Campey of the *Evening Standard* who had written a number of favourable comments on my career in the past.

He stopped dead and looked at me in amazement. 'Leslie Mitchell
– is it?' I confessed from my overgrowth that it was in fact me. 'God,'
he said, 'I nearly didn't recognize you. Come and have a drink.' While
I was drinking, he went to the phone, and before long a press photographer arrived and took close-up pictures of me and my beard. I had
not thought about it at the time, but that was the end of my career in
an advertisement for razor-blades.

I was soon back at work again with the Film Awards and personal
appearances, including a lengthy interview and photograph montage
for the *Sketch* which ominously portrayed me at the bottom of a ladder,
rather than at the top.

In June 1951 I once again accepted the task of running the 'Stage of
Fame' for the Annual *Sunday Pictorial* Film Garden Party, held at
Morden Hall Park. Some 27,000 fans turned up for this big event. All
available British stars were involved, as were many visiting celebrities.

On one occasion the fans became unruly and rushed the stage to get
autographs from us all. There was nearly a disaster as the trestles on
which the stage was mounted began to give way under the weight.
Fortunately I managed to manoeuvre the frightened stars to ground
level, where we were once more overwhelmed, but with less danger of
serious injury.

The strain of interviewing some thirty or forty top stars without
rehearsal was considerable; but the 'Stage of Fame' was a leading
attraction and one *had* to be indefatigable. I carefully arranged that I
should take three weeks' holiday as soon as the show was over.

On my return from basking in the sun, I was approached to compère
'The Big Show' – an American radio show intended to demonstrate
that television was not necessarily superior to steam radio.

It had a high-powered international cast, including Tallulah
Bankhead, Michael Howard, Jack Buchanan, Vera Lynn, Fred
Allen, George Sanders and Beatrice Lillie.

NBC engineers rigged up microphones as and where they wanted
them, while BBC engineers followed suit. The London Palladium
was packed, but the broadcast met with a mixed press reception.
Since it was being broadcast to a mere two million British listeners as
against some fifteen million Americans (for the recorded version), it
had, not surprisingly, been designed with an American bias.

Much to the British engineers' amusement, the tapes were flown
back to America and arrived without a sound on them. They had been
stored too near the engines and automatically demagnetized. A BBC
copy had to be flown hastily to the States as a replacement.

This was about the time that BBC television programmes were extended to the North. On 12 October 1951, the Holme Moss transmitter was opened, so extending Britain's television audience by many thousands of viewers. The occasion was marked by a gala variety show relayed from London's Lime Grove Studios, called 'Hallo up There', the aim being to introduce to northerners as many outstanding television personalities as possible. I was involved in two programmes that evening – 'Picture Page' with Joan Gilbert, and 'How do You View' with Terry-Thomas.

Quite out of the blue, two days later, came a telephone call to my office. 'Mr Leslie Mitchell,' the voice said, 'Mr Anthony Eden would like a word with you.'

Bracing myself for some unexpected practical joker I took it in my stride. 'By all means, put him through,' I said. But the voice was immediately recognizable. Pleasantly and confidentially he explained to me that he was due to appear on television to put forward the Conservative Party's plans for the forthcoming General Election. Would I be interested in appearing with him as interviewer?

My first reaction was gratification that I had been singled out for the occasion by someone of Anthony Eden's political stature.Then I explained my predicament. I had been approached previously by a Cabinet Minister to act as interviewer, but the BBC had intervened. I did not want to find the same difficulty arising in the present situation.

The deputy leader of the Conservative Party was definite about this. 'My dear Mitchell, I understand you are no longer a member of the Corporation, so they have no right to prevent you accepting. This is a political broadcast in which Central Office decides who shall take part, and we would like *you*.'

I looked to my defences. 'I am afraid this may be the most expensive broadcast I have ever made.' Eden was obviously confused by this. 'Well, I don't know whether Central Office could afford a very high fee.'

'Oh, not expensive to you, sir,' I said, 'expensive to *me*. Perhaps I could discuss this with you at some other time.'

'Then you *will* do it?' he said.

'Gladly,' I answered. It would have been ridiculous to refuse.

Anthony Eden told me later that a BBC official had advised him not to pick me as I was not knowledgeable about the political scene. To which he answered that I obviously had a large following which was why he wanted me – to increase his own audience.

We arranged to meet at Warwick Castle where he was staying with his nephew, Lord Warwick, while he prepared an election speech for

Edinburgh. I decided to play safe by getting two tape-recorders and engaging the services of my trusted old friend, S. E. Reynolds, to double-check on details of the presentation. Reynolds was currently producing television shows for the BBC and was therefore completely up to date on latest production methods. I was not going to risk falling down in that connection – I had not produced anything since pre-war days. But it was a simple two-camera job and S. E. agreed the treatment with me before sending it to the Corporation.

We arrived at about midday and I started setting up the tape-machines. I quickly discovered an unexpected snag. The voltage at Warwick Castle was insufficient for the machine. Frantic appeals for help to the Castle electrician brought the reply that he would get it right by 2.30, leaving us with no alternative but to record after lunch.

During lunch I had the first opportunity to talk with my 'victim' personally. He had, of course, all the charm and good looks for which he was famous, but I got the impression that he was a tired man. Time, with its heavy responsibilities, had taken a toll. But he was interesting, and interested in everything that went on around him. We had a pleasant and refreshing encounter, and he returned to preparing his Edinburgh speech.

At 2.15 I invited Mr Eden to re-join us. My first question hit the mark.

'That's a very good question. But first I'd like to talk about another aspect.' He explained that he thought it was more effective to start with another point.

The second and third question he answered fully and effectively. Came question number four. 'Ah,' said he, 'I thought you'd bring *that* up. But in fact my answer to that will arise as a result of the answer to *another* question.' Painstakingly I tried several more questions. But he was still worrying about his unfinished work in the study, and his attention was wandering.

'I know,' he said, with that charming smile,'obviously you have all the right questions. Suppose I record the main points of my speech? Then you can interpolate your questions back in London. How would that be?' I expressed doubts, but agreed to try, although I was pretty certain it would be futile. The method would kill all spontaneity – the broadcast would never come to life.

The following day I set about replaying Eden's speech time after time, cutting it at the end of a phrase and adding a question which would fit neatly into his next sentence. Armed with sandwiches and coffee I laboured through the day, but there was no way of enlivening it – it was dead as mutton. I eventually gave up my efforts at 3 a.m. the

following morning. At 7 a.m. I telephoned the Central Office representative, Mark Chapman Walker. 'Sorry to wake you so early,' I
said, 'but this is urgent. The Eden broadcast tonight cannot be
arranged this way. It won't work and it would be better without me.'
The unfortunate man came post haste to my house and listened to my
tapes. He could not fail to agree with me. It was totally ineffective.

My own suggestion, made seriously, was that he should issue a
statement that I had broken my leg in an accident and Eden should
make a solo appearance, while I lay low. There was not much time to
spare. Eden was due in London on the overnight sleeper from Edinburgh. It was a worried PRO who went to meet him.

He phoned me at 11 o'clock. 'Could you re-shape the interview
with Anthony if he came to see you at *your* house'

'Yes, fine. I'll expect him in about an hour.'

Phyl got up and dressed in spite of a bad migraine, while my
secretary and I reassembled the tape-machines and microphones.

At midday Eden appeared. He looked rested and fresh. 'I gather I
was not much good,' he said. 'What do you want me to do?'

Having heard rumours of his quick temper, I was overwhelmed by
this approach. Quickly I explained that all I required was a record-
ing-session with him to establish the timing and the *order* of my
questions which I had reframed.

Phyl made her appearance. Eden, taking one look at her, held her
hand. 'My dear girl,' he said, 'you've got a terrible migraine, haven't
you? I can recognize the signs, I have them myself. Please go and lie
down. You shouldn't have got up.'

Phyl obediently did as she was asked. There was nothing we could
do to help her. Privately I thought what hell it must be for someone in
Eden's position to suffer migraines.

He was in great good humour and stayed with me for well over the
promised hour. I had been able to re-order our discussion successfully, and played it back to him to prove it.

The broadcast was to be from Alexandra Palace at 8 p.m. The date
was Tuesday 16 October 1951. I arrived some half-hour in advance.

George Barnes was there to greet me. 'My dear Leslie,' he said, 'the
parts you play!'

When Eden arrived we were conducted to the studio for a camera
and lighting rehearsal. Over the loudspeaker came the voice of the
producer. Having welcomed us both and indicated where we should
be seated, her attention turned to me. 'Isn't it amusing, Mr Mitchell,
to think that you introduced me on television only a few years ago,
and now here I am to tell *you* what to do.' It was the voice of Grace
Wyndham Goldie. Mrs Goldie had been a regular contributor to the

Listener and the *Radio Times*, and later joined the Television Talks Department as a producer. She had the reputation of being somewhat left of left. It was not a reassuring thought.

I countered sharply. 'I hope there's no misunderstanding, Mrs Goldie. The production details for this broadcast have been laid down elsewhere. Like all political appearances it has been prearranged by Party Headquarters.'

Mrs Goldie was not to be diverted. 'I'm afraid it's been some time since you were involved in production, Mr Mitchell. We've had to make changes for purely technical reasons.'

Eden looked across at me with evident concern. Although I had checked with S. E. Reynolds to obviate such an incident, for a moment I too was worried.

The cameraman nearest to our table leant down from his raised position. 'Don't worry, Leslie,' he muttered. 'They've only changed the numbers on the cameras!'

A wave of relief came over me. 'It's nothing, Mr Eden,' I said smoothly. 'You turn left for your final speech, instead of right!' A few minutes later we were on the air.

There was no real sign of trouble. Just one remark from Mrs Goldie before I left. 'I had no idea you had political ambitions.'

I denied the implication. 'I haven't any,' I said, 'I just want to be good at my job.'

That evening I joined Anthony Eden at his house in Mayfair for dinner. We sat back afterwards and talked about the broadcast. Eden naturally wanted my opinion. I was convinced that he had gone over well. A sincere and knowledgeable man, he had spent many years as Foreign Secretary and understudy to Churchill. His charm and expertise could hardly fail to make the broadcast attractive and convincing. The most worrying criticism was that we 'sounded too posh'. But at least, without adopting a cockney or regional accent we could be more widely understood, and that was essential.

At last before I left that evening, Eden turned to me again. 'I gather you fear that our broadcast together will affect your career. Do you mean you'll be fired by the BBC?'

'No,' I replied, 'but I think my contracts may not be renewed. And it is, after all, a monopoly.'

He thought for a moment. 'But that's grossly unfair, isn't it? You haven't quarrelled with them about anything?'

'No, I haven't, sir, but I do believe that broadcasting should constantly reflect all points of view and from different angles. It should not veer from side to side like a rudderless ship. Reith, though he had his faults, was one man who had a levelling influence. But a broadcaster can now be excommunicated from his job by the fads or fancies of anyone. What then of freedom of speech?' Eden was interested in our discussion, and we parted company in satisfied accord.

The broadcast was generally found acceptable and successful. There were the expected criticisms from papers of the left, especially as we had over-run our time, but *The Times* wrote on 18 October 1951:

NEW TECHNIQUE IN TELEVISION
Questions for Mr Eden
(from our Radio Correspondent)

With political television in its very infancy, the second General Election broadcast on Tuesday by Mr Eden provided an interesting contrast in style with that displayed by Lord Samuel on the previous evening.

Mr Eden was questioned by Mr Leslie Mitchell and the discussion, which was both enlightening and sincere, had a spontaneity embellished with mannerisms well suited to television. While Lord Samuel preferred, without shame, to read his address, the Conservative speaker aimed to create an intimate atmosphere; indeed the viewers sat beside these two men while they reviewed the problems facing the nation and the world. Towards the end of the discussion Mr Eden turned to his much greater audience across the fireside and summed up the Conservative Party's policy.

Political television may still be in the experimental stage, but this broadcast showed that it can be made a success . . .

It was a historic first-time television interview with a Cabinet Minister on the eve of a general election.

Once again I was invited to compère the Royal Film Performance, sadly this time without His Majesty due to his indisposition. I briefly interviewed the stars as they arrived in the foyer of the Odeon cinema. At the end of the film I also took part in the stage show and read a telegram of good wishes sent to the King and his reply regretting his absence.

There were two replica performances; at Newcastle and, on the following day, in Birmingham. The film was *Where No Vultures Fly* starring Dinah Sheridan, Anthony Steel and Harold Warrender, all of whom I knew well and had introduced on TV.

On my return to London I was involved once more with Terry Thomas in his 'How do You View' series. I was host with Jerry Desmonde for the BBC Christmas party, but with the New Year my anticipated withdrawal from the programmes came about.

I was described as being 'too lah-di-dah' for northern viewers, and was also involved with Gilbert Harding in an unsuccessful show called 'False Evidence'. Gilbert was a judge, Franklin Engleman and I were counsel. I arranged with Franklin beforehand that we should raise objections to everything Gilbert said. This was a mere precaution against allowing him to take over the programme from both of us. To my horror, Gilbert relapsed into silence each time we raised an objection. Gone was the sound and the fury of 'Harding *in Excelsis*'. All efforts to rouse him failed. He was quite unrecognizably meek and ineffective.

After three programmes had failed we all sat together in a restaurant. I decided to find out what was wrong. 'Aren't you feeling well, Gilbert,' I asked. 'You seem so down in the show.'

'I'm glad you brought it up, Leslie. I thought I'd done something to *offend* you both!'

He brightened up considerably when I explained we were trying to get him to retaliate. But it was too late to save the show. Gilbert was always at his best when solo and centre stage.

By early 1952 my absence from TV was becoming a source of comment in the media. Robert Robinson of the *Daily Despatch* wrote:

TV is not so chock-a-block full of talent that it can afford to neglect a personality of Mr Mitchell's talent. . . . Is it his own wish that his TV commitments be few and far between? If it is, he does himself a grave disservice. He is a great favourite. . . .

There were also letters from the North lamenting my absence from the screen. But laments do not pay bills.

In June I once more introduced film and theatrical celebrities on big-screen television in a cinema. I produced fashion shows, opened fêtes, addressed viewers' societies on television production and accidentally found myself in my birthplace introducing 'The Edinburgh Festival Magazine'.

Out of the blue I was invited to lunch with Oliver Poole, a leading Conservative, at Bucks Club in London, a club I had never before visited. I was delighted to accept. My host asked me whether I would be interested in joining the publicity team at the Conservative Central Office. Looking back on my disastrous year with Korda I decided that I was not sufficiently trained or ambitious enough to fight my way through the cut and thrust of politics. I rejected the idea gracefully, explaining that I was not really a political animal. I thought my host looked faintly relieved!

Some time later came a roundabout suggestion from Fleet Street that I might be invited to become a film and television critic. This too was obviously out of the question since it meant criticizing the people with whom I had worked for so many years. Anything derogatory I said would sound like sour grapes.

So it was that when I was invited to visit Cecil McGivern at the BBC in 1953 I went with some interest. He it was who had informed me when he became Head of Television that he naturally was not engaging me, since there were many people who actually *needed* a job. He'd gone on to explain that as I was married to the daughter of a very successful theatre impresario who had now died, I was obviously too well off to bother about work. When I had explained that my father-in-law died owing £17,000, and left nothing to my wife, that I worked very hard to run my second-hand car and my small mews flat, he had remained unconvinced. So now what?

I arrived and was ushered into Cecil's office. He was friendly and conciliatory. 'We've just realized that you've worked very little for us recently,' he said, offering me a drink, 'and after all you were in TV before any of us.' Unmoved, I accepted the description. 'We must do something about it,' he said cheerfully. 'What sort of thing would you like – a weekly show of your own? – fortnightly – ?' His voice trailed away.

'Weekly would be nice,' I said. 'It would pay more bills.'

'You think you have enemies in the Corporation, don't you? Who, for example?'

I was not to be drawn.

And when he started telling me I had been omitted from the TV programmes by sheer mischance, I explained that I had warned Anthony Eden about my fate in 1951.

'You did *what*?' he inquired. And that was the end of that armistice.

15. A Case of Utter Rediffusion

Following my fruitless meeting with Cecil McGivern I realized I could no longer depend on work from the BBC. The only method of keeping up was to commercialize my reputation. Over the next two years I took every job offered me. I was to be found opening shops, introducing new kitchen-ware, writing for newspapers, producing flower shows, fashion shows and, of course, advertising lighters.

I was also involved in a series of 'Brains Trusts' for the Conservative Party, acting as question master. In towns around the country teams were made up of leading Conservatives and local people of distinction. 'Brains Trusts' were becoming increasingly popular in this country, and I enjoyed my part in them very much. But the indiscipline of British crowds was just beginning to take shape. On one occasion I noticed in the audience a noisy element of youngsters, obviously waiting the chance to create trouble.

It came when a local MP got on his feet to answer a question. Boos and shouts of raucous laughter greeted him. I called for order. Even more noise and ruder shouts of abuse. I stood up, and, with the aid of the microphone, easily topped the noise they were making. The shouting stopped.

'Thank you,' I said, 'we are here for an intelligent discussion, but if you want a *row* – *we* can make it. Now shut up, or get out.' As I sat down there was an astounded silence as the trouble-makers edged their way out. Then a long burst of applause from the remainder of the audience. That was the power of television in those days. I'd been 'on the telly'. It certainly would not work today.

I appeared once more with Terry-Thomas before the royal family. The occasion was HM the Queen and Prince Philip's visit to Lime Grove Studios in October 1953. George Barnes had now taken over the increasingly important job of Director of Television. He was knighted by Her Majesty during the evening.

Terry-Thomas on this occasion played the part of a not-very-bright Beefeater at the Tower of London. The royal couple were obviously greatly amused by his zany impression. Afterwards the Duke told me he had enjoyed the interview. 'But this is a bit out of your line, isn't it?' he said. I explained that I enjoyed the Variety.

Since those days, of course, rules have been relaxed. More people are finding they *have* to spread their talents, if only to pay their taxes.

During this time the parliamentarians were already discussing whether or not there should be an alternative system to the BBC in television. I was called on by a number of friends and acquaintances in both Houses to discuss the problem. Before long I came into the open with a letter printed in the *TV News* of 27 November 1953, with the opposite view expressed by Christopher Mayhew.

I can do no better than include the full text of both statements.

Leslie Mitchell says – **'YES' to Commercial TV**

As an ex-member of the permanent staff of the BBC as well as one of the pioneers of television, I have had, perhaps, as much chance as anybody to study the subject on both sides of the Atlantic and both sides of the screen. But, having also worked from the age of seventeen in the competitive world of stage, film, radio and television as stage manager, producer, actor and commentator, I may be biased in the matter of competition, since my world has been one in which other people's efforts and talent have been competitive to my own.

Television is automatically the greatest advertisement available to anyone, and in my opinion too many television personalities are forced to regard their appearances as useful stop-gaps between other more lucrative or important jobs.

Advertising and television in fact are inseparable. The shape of a whisky bottle, the cover of a match-box, the action of a lighter, the outline of a well-known car – all these and many other objects cannot fail to bring to mind the names of the makers concerned.

I do not believe for a moment that the popularity of a product is a sign of shoddiness. In television even education and instruction must be popular to succeed. With the switch in the 'off' position, teachers are at a disadvantage.

No one will gainsay that the BBC, confined to the terms of its Charter, has done a remarkably good job, but it has no monopoly of integrity or talent, and surely competition can do no worse than spur it to greater effort. Certain it is that the BBC will remain.

As I understand it, all that is suggested is that for the first time viewers will have an opportunity to watch television programmes which originate from a source other than the BBC. Advertising will be under control. It can be left to the present *sponsors* – the people – to decide what they want to see. The public is entitled to the television it deserves.

'Not On Your Life' – *says Christopher Mayhew*

Commercial TV? Not on your life, as far as I am concerned! I've watched it; performed on it; had a play produced on it; and loathe it. The fundamental snag is the division of motive behind it. The apparent aim is to give pleasure; the real aim is to sell toothpaste. Often, the two things don't match up, and viewers suffer.

They say you soon get used to the advertisements. Believe me, you don't. I've watched them for hours in the USA. They are specially designed so that you *don't* get used to them – so that you just can't help noticing them. No matter how tactful or tasteful, they are infuriating.

'Anyway, you would get the programmes free' – so the commercialisers tell us. Nonsense. We would pay for commercial TV just as certainly as we now pay for BBC TV. Advertisements may pay for the programmes; but we pay for the advertisements. Every time, that is, we buy a TV-advertised beer or shampoo or mouthwash, we shall be paying for commercialized TV.

People who say, 'Commercial TV could afford to give you . . .' are really saying, 'Commercial TV could make you pay. . . .' 'But,' they say, 'the BBC is a dangerous monopoly.' What is meant by monopoly in this sense? The BBC provides platforms for opinions, not opinions themselves. It no more monopolizes broadcast opinions than the Postmaster-General monopolizes telephone conversations. Provided its governors are chosen fairly and openly – as they always have been – and provided it is constantly exposed to public examination – as it is – the BBC presents no danger to our liberties whatever.

Don't think I'm satisfied with our present TV service – I'm not. In my home, we want more and better programmes, and at least one alternative choice; and we want them quickly. But this is an argument for letting the BBC expand – not for commercialization.

Sir George Barnes invited Phyl and me to dinner. 'You're a performer, Leslie, aren't you? I mean you're not interested in politics and things like that?' I accepted the description. 'I mean, do you know a lot of politicians?' he said cunningly.

'Oh yes, I've met quite a few,' I said.

'But they're not close friends, are they?' he persisted. I had to explain that in my private life I had few *close* friends. Who has in our business? That was the end of the inquiry.

But I did attend a number of dinners in the House of Commons to which I was invited as a knowledgeable outsider. That in itself was a comfort since so many important decisions had been made by committees which did *not* include anyone with personal knowledge of the medium. Some of them had never even watched television. I was, naturally, merely invited to give my opinion on various aspects over the dinner-tables. I had no power to implement my beliefs. But I was received kindly by MPs on both sides of the House, and I was helped by recurrent inquiries in the press about my considerably reduced number of appearances on the small screen.

On one notable occasion a well-known Conservative MP got to his feet during one of these discussions and said, 'I know something about

television. I've just had it put into my house. In the nursery. Only
recently I looked through the half-open doors and saw my children,
silhouetted against the lovely gardens and lawns outside, pointing
their little toes and taking part in a television dancing lesson.' He
beamed with pleasure at the recollection. 'Now, if the BBC can
provide sensitive, charming occasions like that in the home, why in
the name of heaven should we be invited to adopt the vulgar insensi-
tive approach of advertisers and what they will provide?'

As he finished I got to my feet. 'Sir, I must point out that television
is intended for adults too.' When we broke up for the evening, he
refused to speak to me or shake my hand. But he was one of the first
MPs to appear on ITV.

Among friends who had encouraged me to come out into the open
with my beliefs was Stuart McClean, the Managing Director of the
Daily Mail, with which I had long been indirectly associated through
British Movietone News. He encouraged me to believe that I would
get support from the *Mail* if I were to be helpful in my campaign for an
alternative television network.

Of course, one of the obvious difficulties would be finding sufficient
trained staff in this country. The BBC in my opinion was and still is
overstaffed on the executive side, but they could hardly spare very
many from their programme and production staffs.

This point was well made before the war, at a meeting of heads of
departments, when the Director of Drama was pleading for increased
spending power. 'The rising interest in our play programmes points
to the growing importance of. . . . ' The Variety Chief spoke about the
increasingly popular demand for music hall and begged for more and
better slots for his programmes. The Head of Talks was insistent that
books and lectures were helping the masses appreciate the arts and
sciences in a far wider sense.

Then a little man at the end of the boardroom stood up and banged
the table furiously with his fist. 'Gentlemen,' he roared, 'to hear you
talk, one might think that the BBC existed for no other reason than
broadcasting!' I think he was Head of Catering. Even the BBC
marches on its stomach!

On 1 July 1954 the debate on the Television Bill was concluded in the
House of Lords. The second reading was carried by 130 votes to 64.
Commercial television was born, but not without a fight, as was
shown in the letter columns of *The Times*.

Predictably, Lord Reith strongly condemned the Bill as 'ill-
considered and ill-conceived'. The Archbishop of Canterbury considered it 'A bad Bill still' – and added that 'almost every organization

concerned with religion, education, and social welfare regarded it also as a bad Bill'. Lord Hailsham attacked it. 'The vice of Commercial Television. . . .' Those were some of the headlines in the report on Parliament in *The Times* of the following day.

By August it was announced that Sir Kenneth Clark, as he then was, would be the first chairman of the Independent Television Authority set up under the new Television Act. In due course I was invited to go and see a Captain Brownrigg who had been appointed Chief of Staff for England's first independent television company – Associated-Rediffusion. This was an exciting moment for me. Perhaps I could find a permanent job in this new company, using my knowledge and experience with less opposition.

The gallant Captain made me confused at our first meeting. 'I don't know what you expect, Mitchell. The new company's studios are not exactly paved with gold. What do you want here?' I countered by explaining that I had been sent for by *him*. What had *he* to offer? 'It's not going to be like the BBC you know. We're approaching television in a completely different way.' I expressed interest.

'Well for example – take Wimbledon, or Lord's; you commentator chaps do give the impression it's a difficult business. We'll show you arriving in shirt and trousers, mopping your face. "Phew, it's hot," you'll say. "Here are the results." Something on those sort of lines. You *know*.' I was not so far impressed. But I made it clear that in any case I would not want to be an announcer.

'Ah, you want to get behind a desk, do you? I suppose you're after more money. Is that it?'

I thought it best to clarify my position and made it clear that I did not want to *lose* money by joining commercial television.

'What are you getting now?' he asked.

I told him accurately because I had recently visited my accountants. In fact, I had earned far more from my last year than I had earned from my BBC days.

He looked at me in disbelief. 'My god, Mitchell, that's more than I'm getting,' he said. I didn't believe *him* either, but offered to show him my accountants' statements, if he doubted me.

He ended by explaining that he was going to run Associated-Rediffusion like a ship. We parted on reasonably good terms, and he told me to wait till I heard from him again. It sounded as though they were not leaning over backwards to engage me, so I carried on elsewhere, still hoping for an alternative TV station to open.

Some days later I was rung up by an old acquaintance from Twentieth Century Fox pre-war days. It was Bill Gillett. Bill had been with television in America and wanted to talk to me about his new job as Programme Director of Associated-Rediffusion. We invited him to bring his wife to dinner.

He had not changed much; he still had the 'get up and go' personality that I remembered. He was bubbling over with ideas, and had followed my career with attention. Discussing the short time (less than a year) in which he had to put the new station on the air, he asked for any names I could recommend to him, and we spent hours recalling old times and new personalities. Before he left, he said to Phyl, 'Mrs Mitchell, I want this man of yours to join me in the new company. Try and persuade him; he'd be a tower of strength.'

Gratified at having the invitation given me, however indirectly, I discussed it with Phyl late into the night. Phyl pointed out that she was far more worried about my hectic present life, running all over the country to make my living (I had twice been forced to rest up by doctor's order), and at least if I joined Associated-Rediffusion, it would provide a more regular job with ascertainable holidays.

I for my part was becoming increasingly worried about Phyl's migraines. The attacks were recurring more frequently, and it was about this time that she collapsed unconscious (fortunately when I was at home) and was taken immediately to a nursing home. I remember going with her in the ambulance. Her eyes opened suddenly. 'Don't cry, darling,' she whispered. 'I'll be all right in a day or two!'

But in fact, even with the help of three leading specialists, it took three weeks before she completely recovered consciousness. Our friends were marvellous and went to visit her daily when I was working elsewhere. But it became more and more obvious that something drastic would have to be done.

So in due course, when I was again sent for by Captain Brownrigg, I had more or less made up my mind. He offered me a job as Head of Talks Features, a more or less meaningless title, but suggesting the side of television which most interested me. The money was not exciting, but as Phyl had said, it was regular. And Bill Gillett begged me to accept it, at least until we had set the ball rolling, when he would give my contract more attention. For the moment I was offered a reasonable retainer while we set about engaging staff.

It was left to me to find the announcers. I spent some twelve weeks interviewing people and putting them through tests for looks and talent, particularly quickness of thought. I was liable to say, 'Yes. Very nice, thank you. But at this moment a large monkey has made its appearance beside your chair. It's quite tame. Do something.' The unfortunate young man or woman had to immediately react to reassure the invisible monkey and audience, and won points for charm, humour, diction and general bearing. Having faced an incredible number of unforeseeable incidents in my own career, I *knew* just how valuable a quick mind could be.

The new building in Kingsway which we were to occupy was in fact the old Air Ministry building – Adastral House – degutted and almost entirely rebuilt. Work went on day and night to build studios and new office accommodation. The furniture was moved in even before the builders had finished. Secretaries were made an extra allowance for cleaning bills as their clothes were grey with grime every evening. Desks and typewriters, inkwells, everything was smothered by thick grey cement dust. The heavy machine-gun tattoo of pneumatic drills made normal speech almost impossible.

Most of our business interviews were carried out over lunch or in other theatres. It was an exhausting preparation for a difficult challenge. We had to produce 260 days of television yearly, in competition with the twenty-year-old experience of the BBC staff. Sixty-eight per cent of our staff had to be trained from scratch; the remainder had previous experience with the BBC.

Bill Gillett, who was English, had spent some eight years in the USA during which he had produced some of America's most popular television shows. To meet criticism in advance he publicly declared, 'My aim is to bring back with me the best ideas in American competitive TV and leave the worst behind.'

Certainly without his influence and optimism I doubt very much whether we could have survived those hectic months of preparation. Among the most difficult factors was the growing worry about expenditure. The Rediffusion end of the investment in ITV was less apprehensive than Associated Newspapers. Stuart McClean, whenever we met, would ask, 'How is it going, Leslie?' And I would tell him of constantly recurring setbacks.

One day I was rung up by the Rediffusion's press officer. 'Leslie,' he said, 'I think you ought to know that I have been instructed by the Captain to ring round the press and ask them to stop referring to you as "Mr Television". He points out that if there *is* such a title, it rightfully belongs to him.' I took the point. But I had earned it first with the BBC.

Later, in a discussion with an associate from the early days of BBC Television – Cecil Lewis – I said, 'My chief worry about our General Manager is that he still has no idea what television is about.'

Cecil loyally spoke up. 'I'd like to see how you would go about it if you were suddenly put in charge of an aircraft-carrier!'

'The suggestion is so insanely impossible, you make my point for me,' I retorted. We both started laughing and got on with our work.

I ought to make the point that it was *not* disloyalty on my part. I was worried about amateur intrusions into the delicate business of dealing with highly trained and intelligent people who were, in turn, responsible for making the new station's output acceptable and interesting.

As only one instance of the difficulties: I had at last chosen six of the most promising announcers from my numerous auditions, only to find that two men I had never seen had been already appointed without reference to me. Bill Gillett was worried too, but showed no signs. As he put it, 'So long as we can get the damn thing on the air, we can start rethinking your job and the establishment. For god's sake accept it for the moment. We *need* professionals.' I got myself dug in again and concentrated on everything I was given to do.

I discovered that, in the studio which had been prepared for my Talks Department, the ceilings were so low that overhead lighting could never be used as it would shine into the camera lenses. There was no fan-extractor system, and the presence of sound engineers, lighting men, camera dollies and cameramen, plus the speakers, announcers and make-up girls, could transform the space into a modern Black Hole of Calcutta within minutes. Work had to restart on admitting air and sanity to the operation.

Another disappointment, and a serious one, was the loss of my secretary, Anna Lett, who I had promised to take with me. Miss Lett had worked with the BBC as a TV production assistant and was not only charming to look at, but highly intelligent and knowledgeable about the medium. Once again the Captain put me down. Having agreed to interview her, he offered her a maximum of ten guineas per week. She naturally refused, and moved to ATV in due course as a full-time producer. Later, she became Mrs Christopher Chataway.

Somehow, on 22 September 1955, through the dust and debris emerged the first commercial television programme to be seen in Britain.

One reporter the following morning described my introduction. 'The screen blinks into life at 7.14 with Leslie Mitchell announcing "This is London" – rather as if he was operating a Freedom Radio from an occupied city. . .' All very amusing for him. But I *was* introducing a rival organization. As the BBC's Director-General, Major-General Sir Ian Jacob had plaintively inquired, 'Independent Television? – independent of what?' The answer being, of course, 'Independent of the BBC.' An opportunity to expand and experiment in new directions. With *other* intelligences.

But all the hard work of those months was to be undermined. Early in 1956 Bill Gillett resigned. He wrote to me: '. . . In leaving the

Company I feel I must tell you how much I appreciate the tremendous effort that you have personally put into getting us on the air . . . and helping us to become the top-rated service in England.' His loss was a tremendous blow. One of my main supporters gone, and an unsatisfactory contract into the bargain. Gillett's successor was John McMillan, who had at one time been a BBC Radio executive.

Once more the continuous strain and long hours were taking their toll. My back was again behaving ominously. One journalist described me as 'Urbane Leslie – who looks like a St Bernard who has been to the right schools.' The St Bernard bit was, presumably, due to my failing face muscles.

In fact after the first few months of ITV, my doctor insisted on putting me in a nursing home for a complete rest over a long weekend. While I was there, Phyl was told that my mother had been taken seriously ill with thrombosis.

She died early in January 1956 and, true to form, held the centre of the stage to the last. She never knew that her in-laws had discontinued the annual 'retainer' on which she depended. Her life had not been easy in spite of her beauty and many talents. I was indeed devoted to her and was saddened by her last words to me in hospital. 'Sonny,' she whispered, 'Phyl was quite right. You are my only champion!'

Towards the end of 1956 I had a polite signal from Captain Brownrigg. (All internal memoranda had now become signals.) It was an inquiry about my availability the following summer to travel to Masham in Yorkshire and open a fête for Lord Swinton. Lord Swinton was a director of our parent company, Rediffusion, as well as being a very distinguished figure in his own right. I accepted with interest, not having had a previous chance to meet him.

Before I set off, Captain Brownrigg spoke to me confidentially. 'Don't on any account ask for a fee! Your actuality expenses will be paid here.'

Peter Willes, manager of our Light Entertainment Department, joined me, and we drove north to Swinton Castle the day before the fête. Peter had been a close friend of the Swintons' son, who was killed during the war. We were cordially received and spent an agreeable evening walking in the grounds and observing the bustling activities of groups preparing stalls for the fête in the gathering dusk.

At dinner Lord Swinton grew confidential. 'You know, Mitchell, I would never have thought of you as an "opener". Someone suggested you after I'd tried a chap called – chap with a rather ridiculous name, er – er – oh, yes – I remember – Mr Sooty.'

'Oh, you mean Sooty, the television puppet,' I urged helpfully.

'Yes, that's right. Don't know much about these things.'

At that time Sooty had become a TV star, and Harry Corbett, who manipulated this attractive glove puppet on BBC Children's Programmes, had devised this forerunner to Basil Brush.

'Do you know how much this Sooty-feller wanted?' continued His Lordship. 'One hundred pounds!' This was a reasonable fee at the time, but a ludicrous extortion in the eyes of people with no stage connections. Like the patient who complained about his dentist's bill – 'To extracting tooth: £5.' The dentist forwarded another bill. 'To learning how to extract tooth: £4 10s. – To extraction 10s.'

The day of the fête provided an ideal summer's afternoon. The lawns and paddocks gradually filled with visitors and the stalls came to life as customers gathered round. Children, perched precariously on ponies, trotted past with energetic young women grimly holding the leading-reins and stumbling over the grass. There was a brass band, and every shade of colour to satisfy the senses. A living picture by Frith it seemed. Enchanting.

Came the opening ceremony and I stood on a dais and made the opening speech. There was a gathering of some two thousand, they estimated afterwards. Much to my surprise I was also presented with a splendid memento of the occasion by Lady Swinton – an early Victorian, silver bosun's whistle. I took this to be an acknowledgement of my distant association with Captain Brownrigg and made grateful reference to a thoughtful choice.

Peter and I were invited to stay another night while we all relaxed. Again at dinner Lord Swinton turned to me. 'You work for this chap Brownrigg, don't you? What do you think of him?' I replied cautiously that he had the reputation of being a brilliant administrator. Swinton appeared not to hear.

'Extraordinary fellow,' he continued, drawing on his cigar. 'Been in command all his life and never earned the affection of anybody!' I was astounded by this revelation since there were in Associated Rediffusion a number of ex-naval men who worked with us and appeared to have great respect for the Captain.

I turned the subject. 'I was very grateful for the gift you made me, Lord Swinton. It's very decorative and a pleasant reminder of a happy weekend here in Yorkshire.'

'I was hoping you would learn to blow the thing and pipe Brownrigg overboard,' he said fiercely. I made no promises, but blew myself overboard shortly afterwards. I *still* cherish the bosun's whistle.

From the beginnings of A-R transmissions I appeared fairly regularly

as interviewer and chairman of discussion programmes. I had started
by engaging Colonel Christopher de Lisle as my assistant. During the
war he had been in Intelligence, which made him an obvious choice as
an interviewer, and I set about teaching him the tricks of the trade. He
very soon became proficient and was also of considerable help in
running the departmental side.

Among the programmes I instigated was 'Visitor of the Day' which
involved a different personality daily. This was in the nature of a
lucky dip, as we never billed the visitor in advance. It became
successful largely due to the innate curiosity of viewers. Another
programme, 'Points of View', attempted to follow the established
television pattern of argument and debate such as the 'Brains Trust'
and 'What's my Line?'

For my first 'Visitor of the Day' programme I made a bold bid to
secure Lord Reith on account of his historic association with broadcasting and television. We had remained good friends outside as well
as inside the Corporation. His reply was not unexpected, but it is
worth putting on record.

33 Hill Street
London W1

20 July 1955

Leslie Mitchell Esq.
Associated-Rediffusion Limited
Television House
Kingsway WC2

Dear Leslie Mitchell

Well, well.

Of course I remember you, and with entire goodwill – which doesn't apply to
many.

Do you realise what you're asking?

I have never broadcast – did you not know that?

And what do you expect me to say?

I agree with you that it would be worthwhile to hear, . . . etc. It certainly
would.

And what I would say would probably surprise you and most people; and it
would shock them too.

But do you really think I would come in – like anyone off the street?

I'm quite a modest individual really, but this would be a considerable scoop,
wouldn't it?

Perhaps at 5000 guineas I might.

Yours ever,
J. C. W. Reith.

Amongst those who *did* accept were such notabilities as Air Chief
Marshal Sir Philip Joubert, Lord Harewood, Dame Laura Knight
and Lord Lovat.

'Points of View' was a serious discussion programme which got off
to a good start. Maurice Wiggin in the *Sunday Times* wrote on 13
November 1955:

Close observers will have noticed the change in Mr Leslie Mitchell since he
left the BBC. He now speaks with a mind of his own, kindling discussion with
thoughtful remarks instead of trying to damp it down with squirts of the old
bromide – and seltzer. Such programmes as 'Points of View' are as responsible
and as well informed as anything on the air.

ITV had not yet established itself owing to the shortage of TV sets
which could receive Channel 9, the commercial station; the planners
had arranged the programme for a late hour when the TV audience
normally decreases. A further blow came when it was decided to cut
the length of the programme by half, to fifteen minutes only. This
gave little opportunity for distinguished people to establish a considered opinion on important subjects.

As it happened, the first shortened version of 'Points of View' went
on the air on 7 December 1955; the subject for discussion was 'Who's
Boss – Workman or Employer?' – as topical today as it was then. The
eminent panel consisted of the Rt Hon. Col. Walter Elliot, MP; the Rt
Hon. Emanuel Shinwell, MP; Anthony Greenwood, MP; and Ted
Leather, MP. This caused another comment in the *Sunday Times* on 11
December 1955: '. . . Men of the calibre of Mr Walter Elliot and Mr
Emanuel Shinwell should not be asked to try to do justice to impor-
tant topics on such terms.' Nevertheless it was the forerunner of the
discussion programmes which are now common to the media.

I was of course training my staff of announcers to take over other
duties for which they showed talent. Most of them have succeeded in
keeping their names in front of the public through the intervening
years, many of them in stations outside the London area.

But the papers – ably led by those of them which had failed to
secure a place in the new TV service – were inclined to be hyper-
critical. Several of them decided to concentrate on my ageing appearance. (I was now over fifty and my face had lasted twenty years in
front of the camera.) I found this form of attack more disheartening
than criticism of my work, since there was literally nothing I could do
about it.

There was an occasion while Rediffusion was being launched when
I was host to no less than four Fleet Street editors. Our business

over, I told them, 'It may not be good manners, but as you should know, I am first and foremost an opportunist. Might I make a personal plea? In recent months some of the critics have concentrated on my appearance. Could I ask you to get them back to criticizing my performance?' I then listed my disfigurements – my plastic-surgery triumph of a face, my changed jaw-line, the damage to one eye and my steel brace.

They looked dumbfounded. 'Why did we never hear about this?' they said.

'Well it's not exactly good publicity, gentlemen, is it?'

My dragged appearance ceased to be a common joke almost overnight.

By the end of 1957 the *Daily Mail* had pulled out of Associated-Rediffusion and was turning its attention to another station as an investment, Southern Television, due to go on the air by the summer of 1958. I took the precaution of writing to Stuart McClean about the possibilities of a job in Southern Television before I had even made up my mind about my future.

It was made up for me by Captain Brownrigg, who had taken a dislike to my chief assistant, Chris de Lisle, and fired him. I decided I would not renew my contract with A-R when it expired early in 1958. Meanwhile I was put in charge of presentation.

This was an interesting assignment since it made me responsible for the linking together of signals from all sources which would become increasingly important as more and more stations came into being. Fortunately I took over a first-rate team in the department and concentrated on keeping them happily and usefully employed.

In due course I sent in my 'signal' to the Captain informing him of my desire not to renew my contract. There was no reply. I informed everybody else involved. Stuart McClean suggested I should ask for an *ex-gratia* payment into the bargain. 'You really deserve it, Leslie,' he said. The company didn't think so, so I left it at that.

Before leaving I went to visit the fourth floor, the quarter-deck. Brownrigg looked at me across the desk with an air of distaste. 'Yes, I got your signal, Mitchell. In other circumstances you would be accused of mutiny. I had no intention of replying to it.'

'I am sorry you feel like that, sir,' I said. 'As you know, I was myself intended for the Navy, and might well have served under you. But we are both shore based, and there is no such thing as mutiny to a civilian.'

His face reddened. 'I shall make it my business to see you never work again, Mitchell.'

'You mean *here*, sir, I presume?'

'No, I mean anywhere,' he said, and he *really* meant it.

The news of my resignation was in the evening papers even before I recovered my temper.

'What an extraordinary chap you are, Leslie,' said one interviewer. 'What happened? Just when everything looks so successful.'

(How to get back at the GM for his farewell threat?) At last I answered, 'I'm afraid it's entirely my fault. I was engaged personally by Captain Brownrigg and I thought he said he was going to run the place like a ship. Apparently he didn't say ship at all!'

I was sorry indeed to leave my staff at Television House, Kingsway, but I cherish the farewell gifts they presented to me, and the song composed and played for me at our final meeting.

Before you read it, I should explain that I had been stung by a Portuguese man o' war while on holiday in Majorca. The final verse is an imaginative forecast of my future.

FAREWELL TO L. M. CALYPSO

Mr Mitchell he been with us quite a while (Top man come, top man, he go)
Started with a carpet and Christian de Lisle (O, top man he go)

But our Mr Mitchell no seafaring man
He stay off the fourth floor when he can
The only time Leslie put out to sea
Him eaten alive by a Portugee

Him never the same since he meet dat squid
Wrote stronger letters than the fourth floor did
But Mr Mitchell he knows the tricks of the trade
He can paper his home with the tapes he has made
So Leslie have much cause for celebration
Him get out quick before centralization

Now Leslie's new job needs much precision
Him frogman for under-water television
So very good luck in his strange new station (top man come, top man he go)
From everyone here in Presentation (O, top man he go)

Six years after my resignation it was decided to replace the station identification signal which I had devised for the company.

Nicknamed 'Mitch', after me, it was a circular clockface supported by a rampant unicorn, representing the City, and a rampant lion, representing pride of race.

I received a replica specially made for me, without hands. Across the clockface was inscribed:

To L.M.
From Presentation
1956-8
A TIMELESS MITCH

Of course they were all younger than me!

16. The Return of the Prodigal

August 1957 saw the twenty-first birthday of British television, and though I had not yet left Associated-Rediffusion, I was permitted to join in the BBC's celebrations. A large TV studio had been mounted at the BBC's Radio Show at Earls Court, and I was engaged to explain how a production was built up for transmission. The theatre was on permanent show to successive audiences.

The TV cameramen and studio staff manoeuvred their way about the stage in rehearsal while I explained their separate functions. At one moment the technicians broke for lunch, and I took my place on a travelling camera to explain how it worked. The news spread quickly to the canteen and the crew were soon back in their places, munching their unfinished meal. But I had had a lifetime's training in being adaptable. You are the servant of the people who pay for you. Otherwise the Romans' 'bread and circuses' would have ceased to be, and there would be no jobs. Certainly not in the entertainment world. We all depend ultimately on the support of an audience.

However, such incidents were signs of the mounting power of the unions. The growing expression, 'I'm as good as you are,' can best be countered, as I once heard it. 'Who on earth tried to convince you that you are not?' said a lady. 'But can you not be yourself with a little more charm?'

Now that I was a freelance again, I was not only finding myself back on BBC programmes, but, rather surprisingly, also appearing for Rediffusion and other commercial stations. The critics in general were remarkably kind and went out of their way to welcome me back.

I even continued to open fêtes on demand – until Phyl put her foot down in the summer of 1958. 'Do you know that you're going to be working at fêtes every weekend till September?' she asked. I was anxious to be seen again, but this was ridiculous – so I took no more garden-party commitments. People are inclined to think opening a fête is all fun, quite failing to realize that you have to look well turned out, you have to kiss babies and smile happily at complete strangers, spend money and remember names, travel to and from the venue and sign innumerable autographs, when you might be quietly relaxing at home.

I was however working on several projects of my own at this time. I had long been friendly with Sir Tom O'Brien, the general secretary of NATKE (the National Association of Theatrical and Kiné Employees), the union organizing workers in the entertainment industry. He approached me to join him in his application for a new Scottish television station – his idea being that I would make a good programme director. With my long experience of stage, film, radio and television I was inclined to agree with him, and the application was duly forwarded to the Independent Television Authority in July 1960. Regrettably it failed.

Meanwhile I had visited a studio in Kensington which we had used for Associated-Rediffusion rehearsals and programmes in the very early stages. To my astonishment it was still directly connected by cable to the main network. Having noticed that advertising material was being rehearsed and transmitted by the main companies from their own studios, I had the idea of using the Kensington studios as a separate source from which advertisements could be transmitted live or on videotape by the existing cable connections. It would obviously be an advantage for all concerned, leaving essential studio space for the programme contractors, and increased opportunity and time for rehearsal of live advertisements elsewhere.

With the aid of George Kelsey of Marconi, who was actively interested and helpful about the provision of videotape cameras and equipment, the studio owner Eric Humphries and I set about interesting the main advertising agencies. I must have approached more than forty of them. A number showed considerable interest.

I now approached Sir Tom O'Brien and his colleague George Elvin at ACTT (Association of Cinematograph Television and Allied Technicians) to make certain there would be no objection by the unions to the use of taped material. This was definitely agreed. Elvin assured me that they approved the use of tape since it made for more employment of ACTT workers.

Thus armed, I approached a director of one of the main programme companies to ask his advice. 'Very good idea, Leslie,' he said. But I must warn you that if you succeed, the companies will do everything they know to undercut you.' On top of this I learned from Howard Thomas, now managing director of ABC Television, that ACTT had made a decision that the unions would permit only *one* transmission of each videotape advertisement, thereby nullifying the principal reason for using this method.

In reply to my protest, Elvin wrote later lamenting the fact that I had not appreciated the decision 'clearly stated in a minute agreed by his General Council on 3 *August* 1960'. My ignorance was not surprising, since our interview had taken place on 23 *May* in that year. Oh well, there went another good idea! The effort had been a prodigious waste of time and energy – and now of course *all* stations use videotape in quantity.

In the middle of these battles I was heartened by being invited to work for Southern Television. Having appeared with Elizabeth Allan in Basil Dean's film *Nine to Six,* I now had the pleasure of joining her on television in her popular 'Swop Shop' programme from Southampton, and renewed my association with her husband, Bill O'Bryen, who had been Korda's casting director. The show continued with sustained success for six months; this took me away from Phyl for one day a week, but I drove each way by car, and managed usually to get home late at night.

Of course I could not afford to stop working, but at least I was able to be more discriminating in what I undertook.

In 1961 the BBC celebrated the twenty-fifth anniversary of television. The Prime Minister, Mr Harold Macmillan, was guest of honour for the birthday dinner at Grocers Hall in the City. His speech was broadcast live following a programme which looked back on the achievements of BBC Television, the narrators being Richard Dimbleby and myself. There was also, coinciding with this event, a double-paged feature in the *Times Supplement.*

I was too caught up at Broadcasting House to hear the speeches, but a dear friend of mine, Major Henry Dunsmure, late of the Scots Guards, wrote a note of congratulations about the Prime Minister's reference to me and the comments in *The Times* which I quote once more from sheer conceit.

Leslie Mitchell . . . was the 31-year-old radio announcer and ex-actor who virtually fashioned the art of the television announcer. With *no* precedents to go on he not only mastered the unheard of technique of talking in front of a camera without a script but, with ever-increasing skill, evolved a pattern for the television interview. . . .

I suppose some would say I had 'arrived'.

But Phyl was still suffering increasing attacks of migraine. Finally the doctors sent her to have an X-ray of the skull, always a frightening business – they have to inject you with iodine beforehand. At the same time she was booked for another neurological investigation, the idea

being to put her through the lesser of the two ordeals first. Unfortunately owing to some misunderstanding she was treated in the
wrong order and when I visited her, she was lying stiff with fright
under the impression there was worse to come. She made me promise
I would never let her undergo similar examinations again.

I do not know how Phyl managed through the years to look so
beautiful, so charming, and be so amusing in between times. Everybody said of her that she always looked fresh and well-groomed, even
when she was cooking for a party of eight people and serving at table.
I was very proud of her. And she defended me like a tigress if anybody
spoke critically of me. Certainly I was a very lucky man and tried to
show I realized it. When we *did* get away on holiday, we had everything of the best. Food, climate and scenery. Together we visited
France, Belgium, Italy, Spain and Majorca, New York and Hollywood. She made friends wherever we went; although she was reserved
and diffident, her sense of humour overrode her shyness and made her
a wonderful companion.

It occurred to me by 1961 that, since the doctors could not come up
with any cure, perhaps the answer might be to move out of London
and find a country cottage where Phyl could relax more easily. By
sheer good luck, during that summer I found one – not too far from
London, at Cookham. Now was my chance to make up to my beloved
wife for the long days and weeks we had been separated by my
overwork. A chance for her to unwind, away from all the pressures
which had built up around us throughout our twenty-two years of
marriage.

The new house had a potentially interesting garden of about one
and a half acres and was set within easy walking distance of the
village shops and a short drive from Maidenhead. We built an
extension to the kitchen and a small dining-room while we were
moving in. Phyl was knowledgeable about furnishing and house-
keeping so it served to keep her busy enough indoors while I set
about transforming the garden. I spent a lot of time at home to
please and help her. Fortunately after a snowy winter, our first
summer was warm and sunny, so we could relax together in the
garden with Flute, our Siamese cat.

I bought myself a large mowing-machine with a seat, and a rotary
tiller. Within two years we had a sizeable croquet lawn, a rose garden
and a large lily bed, as well as a number of young trees all producing
pleasure for the eyes, nose and ears. What more soothing sound is
there in summer than the soft whirr of cutters revolving through the
growing grass?

My luckiest acquisition with the new house was a dear Mrs Palmer who became our daily help in every way. She was kind, intelligent, loyal and business-like. She looked after Phyl like a mother and was always ready to keep an eye on her when I was away for any reason.

By the grace of God, Gerald Sanger of Movietone invited me to re-join them as commentator at Denham, only a short drive across country. As well as doing the twice-weekly newsreels, I was also commentating for newsreels put out by the Central Office of Information which were distributed to all corners of the world.

In my spare hours I became more and more contented with our new abode. I like to think Phyl too grew to like it, though at first she had felt separated from her many friends in London. As she explained, 'Gardening is such a messy business, and you have to wait such a time for results. I love *instant* flowers.' But she was pleased with the netted soft fruits I cultivated for her.

We were also lucky in having a number of good friends living in the vicinity. In fact Nicky and Eric Robinson lent us their cottage at Snag's End near Henley before we moved in. Eric and I had never lost contact since the first days of television, and as for Nicky, she is universally regarded as a poppet.

Giulio Trapani had sold Ye Olde Bell at Hurley after the war and literally 'went back to Sorrento' where we visited him. But he quickly discovered he was not the retiring type and hastened back to the district to become the proprietor of the famous Skindles Hotel at Maidenhead. I have known him since the twenties, and we have remained good friends ever since; he always gave us a special welcome and we had many happy parties there. Eileen and John Snagge were not far away, and there were also Nutkin and Alexander Shaw, who have always lived in that part of the world. And we soon made more friends in the immediate neighbourhood.

Sadly Lord Vansittart died in 1957, but his beautiful widow, Sarita, was still at Denham Place. We got to know them well during the war when we lived at Harefield. I had interviewed Van for Movietone, and he had also been a guest on my 'Points of View' programme for Associated-Rediffusion in 1956. I have kept the letter he wrote me afterwards in which he expressed concern at the 'far too great a burden' I was carrying. He went on to say: 'Your working hours are far too great for any human frame. You are an exceedingly young fifty, but even of that youth too much advantage can be taken. The present pressure is altogether excessive. I just don't understand a management which jeopardizes its star. As a policy it is incomprehensible.'

I was devoted to Van, as everyone called him. He had met with unreasonable opposition to his undoubted ability and commonsense.

Only now, forty years later, has it been recognized that his advice to the Government in pre-war days should have been followed. So much for the thirty-year rule, which draws a convenient veil over important political mistakes.

In 1963 I suffered a further health set-back and having read that both President de Gaulle and Mr Harold Macmillan had recently called on the services of a well-known British surgeon to carry out a certain operation, decided to play safe and engage his services for myself. Mr Badenoch later confessed, 'Having read your medical history I looked at the scars on your body and decided to create with the new operation a balanced picture of an anchor.' He succeeded admirably. I only pray that another surgeon will not decide some day to draw a crown on one of the few open spaces left.

When I had recuperated I was called upon by John Oxley, programme chief of Westward Television to make an hour-long programme of my life, to be called 'A Long View'. This meant considerable research, in the course of which I hired a photographer to take pictures of the house at Clewer from which I had made such an unhappy exit some forty years earlier. But the house and garden were deserted. Looking through the windows, I saw flowering weeds had forced their way through the parquet flooring; paint and wallpaper was peeling from the walls. The garden balustrade to the river was broken and the wrought-iron gates were hanging precariously on one hinge. Of the charming and elegant gardens of the past little remained. I abandoned my quest.

Now nothing remains. It lies partly under a new road.

I was interviewed by John Pett of Westward about the script. He later took a prominent part in the programme. Eventually it was decided to make more of my *working* life and the story of television. I was able to contribute some of my own film material to add to that shot by the television teams. This was one of the first major documentaries to be undertaken by Westward.

Phyl accompanied me to Plymouth for the final rehearsals and even appeared in a short sequence with me. But she was far from well and they were careful not to ask too much of her. We were given a visitors' book signed by the entire production team and an autograph book to use in the future. They were a grand lot and made our work a pleasure. And I was also allowed to buy a copy of the programme, which I still have.

Unfortunately it was never shown in London as the big shots of the West End then had no intention of accepting material from a new and growing regional station. They naturally preferred making and selling their own programmes. It *was* shown however by Grampian, TWW, Tyne Tees and Ulster, who received it with praise. It was described as a 'Top Documentary from the West'.

But there was no pleasure for me in that. Shortly before, having been told by the doctors to try and persuade Phyl to go out more often, we were dining at my club with a close friend and his daughter. Phyl had been fighting a headache and suddenly I noticed she was having difficulty with her hands. She turned to me and asked, 'Darling, could you cut my meat for me, please?' Looking anxiously at her I realized she was in desperate trouble.

Picking her up in my arms I carried her from the table out of the crowded dining-room. Her last words were, 'Careful, darling. Do be careful of your back.' A fellow-member, a well-known doctor, attended to her and sent for an ambulance to take her to the West-minster Hospital. I followed in the car, but at midnight I was advised to return home to get some sleep.

The night became a confused nightmare. I drove home to the empty cottage and put out food for Flute just before the telephone bell rang. It was the hospital asking me to return. The end was near. I found Phyl still breathing with the aid of a machine. I kissed her forehead and thought I detected an effort to open her eyes – maybe it was my imagination.

Valerie Hobson, Phyl's dearest friend, came to the hospital and took me away. The doctors told us they would phone at once if there was any change. I sat all night at the Profumos' house in a chair downstairs. Valerie sat quietly with me. Jack came down several times to make coffee for us. At last there *was* a telephone call. Phyl was dead. It was 20 January 1965.

I remember very little of the ensuing months; my unhappiness was too deep. I do remember with lasting gratitude how kind everyone was and how hard they tried to help me to forget my loss. Valerie and Jack Profumo, the Shaws, Nicky and Eric Robinson, the staff at Movietone and Westward. But I found it impossible to shake off my misery, and eventually sailed for New York at the invitation of Ben Grauer and on the advice of Valerie and my doctor. I sailed on the giant French liner *France*.

Early on the second day I was attacked by a painful rigor of the back and stomach muscles, and found it difficult to get up and dress. However I did so and made my way to the ship's doctor. There was a long queue of passengers. Twice he passed me on the way to and from his surgery. The third time he said, 'You are in great pain, follow me.' After laying me on the bunk and examining me, he ordered me to return to my cabin and gave me a deep injection. After a short time the pain eased up and I lay more happily on my bunk. I ate very little on the voyage, but was able to get up on the last day but one, after repeated injections.

On arrival in New York harbour I was leaning on the rails, watching the busy scene as the vast ship tied up at the dockside. Suddenly I felt an arm round my shoulder. It was Ben Grauer in masterful form. 'Hi there, Leslie,' he said. 'Don't waste time. Just follow me.' I followed him obediently through the gigantic sheds while he was saluted and hailed by all the Customs officials. 'Just a friend of mine from the BBC – Mr Leslie Mitchell.' They all smiled and bade me welcome.

At last we were on the city sidewalk outside. Ben stopped and turned to me with a grin. 'How's that for service, old timer? Bet you never got off a ship quicker than that!'

'Fantastic, Ben,' I answered. 'But what about my luggage?'

'My god,' he said. 'You brought baggage?' We slowly walked back to the end of the line at Customs. That was the first time I had laughed for a long time.

Dear Ben, he had the heart to warm an iceberg. He and his wife Melanie insisted on my staying with them though I had asked them to book me into a hotel. They had furnished my room with a miniature television set so that I could keep up with the news and American programmes. They took me round to meet their friends inside New York during the week and outside at weekends. Though they did everything imaginable to take my mind off my loss, Phyl was with us all the time. She and Ben had been devoted, and he was thinking of her too.

I also visited other friends of ours – Sam and Ella Slate, Pat and Jim Smith, and Anna Clarke whom we had known in London when she was editor of a women's magazine. Having married an American and produced two charming daughters, she had recently lost her husband. She and the girls were due to fly to London and she prevailed upon me to change my plans and travel back with them.

Back at Cookham I found the house was bare and too evocative. I could not bear to be there alone and invited friends and their children to stay as often as possible. To take my mind off things, I volunteered to drive some young friends to the South of France to visit their family. And on another occasion I answered an SOS from a widowed friend who had only one arm. She was stranded in Spain and wondered if I would fly out and drive her and her Bentley back to England. The chauffeur who had promised to pick her up had failed to materialize.

I worked out that it was just possible to fit in the trip between my Movietone commitments, and we had a very enjoyable trip through Spain and France, though I spent much of the time at our stopping places explaining that I *really* wanted two rooms. As my companion was far from unattractive, I was given a lot of disbelieving looks. But what I needed desperately was companionship, not romance. And my deep feelings in all respects were on the point of exhaustion.

Eventually I decided it was no good remaining in Cookham. The only thing to do was to sell up and return to London. I spent endless days looking for a studio flat or mews cottage, but they were either too big or too expensive. Talking to Joan Gilbert one day, she told me to contact a friend of hers who was in the property business. As luck would have it, he wanted to sell the house in which I am writing this book.

As soon as I stepped through the front door, I knew it was right for me, as indeed it has been ever since. It had a twenty-seven-year lease, which would see me through.

I hated leaving Cookham after all the days of planning for the future there. But even Flute, our cat, was ill and unhappy and died, almost to the day, a year after Phyl.

17. Happy Ending

The move to London was complicated as all moves are. I had to dispose of many souvenirs of the past and most of the larger articles of furniture, as the mews house was considerably smaller than the cottage and I would have only one bedroom to furnish, the second I planned to make a study. Fortunately Mrs Palmer was able to advise me on many problems, as were my friends in London. Once there, by the spring of 1966, I found living on my own equally unattractive and dated everybody I knew for meals at my club or in the restaurants from which I had so long been away.

I had by now become used to a chesty cough, but presumed it was a long-lived cold, which made it easier to retire early to bed. My wife's doctor, Raymond Daley, and his wife had been foremost in asking me to meals both in London and their country house in Kent. He rang me up one night when I was in bed. 'What's the matter with your voice?' he demanded. 'Is that the cold that prevented you coming to see us three weeks ago?' I thought it was. Half an hour later he was at the front door with his wife. He checked my chest. Before I could say anything he had arranged to drive me to hospital, and I found myself in a ward at St Thomas's.

I have to admit I was exhausted and it was pleasant to be looked after, but I had left no explanation of my disappearance, and I still had workmen in the house. Mrs Daley herself took care of everything and my answering service was advised what to say in case of any telephone calls.

A few weeks earlier I had met a charming Danish girl, Inge Vibeke Asboe Jørgensen, and invited her to dinner at the Savoy Grill – if only to find out how to pronounce her names. I had not been to the Savoy for many months, but even my guest seemed surprised by the warm welcome we received from the head waiter and his staff.

It was Easter time and I had arranged to go to the Profumos' for the holiday, while Inge told me she would be spending Easter in Shropshire with great friends of hers, Bill and Zoë Wesson. When we were both back in London again, we would meet, but Inge had to go to

Denmark on business, so I invited her to dine with me on her return.

It was discovered that I had developed severe bronchial asthma as a result of the strain of the last few years, and Dr Daley was worried about it getting worse, particularly since the house was full of dust and paint fumes from being redecorated. They decided to pierce my sinuses while I was in hospital, so I was wheeled down to the appropriate department to have this done on several occasions – an unpleasant, but sensible precaution. Meanwhile I was content to lie back and rest. I had no urge to get in touch with anybody; it would only be a fresh worry for my friends.

While I was being given a blanket-bath one evening a nurse stopped by to tell me I had a lady visitor waiting to see me. I was naturally puzzled. Who on earth could it be? Suddenly I remembered the Danish girl and our dinner date. When – ? Where – ? Oh lord! What an ass I was – I had completely forgotten the outside world. As they moved away the screens from round me, I looked. Yes, it was Inge. She came into the ward looking rather shy, and stood by my bed.

'Inge my dear. How on earth did you discover where I was? I'm terribly sorry about our date! Was it tonight?' She forgave me and explained she had intended to invite two American friends who wanted to meet me, but they would dine together anyway. And she would come and visit me again when she could.

Apparently when she rang my house the answering service took the call and explained that I would be away for a few days. Inge, stung at being let down over her dinner date, said, 'But he can't be, it's important. Mr Mitchell was supposed to dine with me tonight.'

'Well, if it's important,' said the voice, 'you'll find him at St Thomas's Hospital.'

Now, if Inge had not got an overstrung maternal complex and a soft heart into the bargain you wouldn't be reading this. But she has, and you are.

I was conscious of the fact that I was far from well, but was anxious to get into the summer air outside. I was forbidden to return to the house and would be permitted to leave hospital only if I was accompanied by some responsible person who would look after me and feed me at regular intervals with various unpleasant medicines and pills. In my bereft state there was no one left of my own or Phyl's family to take on this responsibility – and that seemed to settle the question.

Inge however is made of sterner stuff. She offered to take time off and go with me to a Sussex hotel which I had regularly visited through the years gone by. As public relations officer for DFDS – one of the principal Danish shipping companies – she had been working hard here and in her own country. She had also lectured about Denmark all over Britain. Altogether, like me, she *needed* a rest.

So I booked rooms at Birers Hotel near Clymping for us both. Mrs Birer very kindly took us in at the height of the season. Fortunately the weather was very kind too. Inge was bossy and saw to it that I regularly swallowed the prescribed medicines, but found time to meet a number of my friends who were also staying there, and relaxed by swimming and riding with them. Clive Brook, my old friend from acting days, and his wife were there. He tried jokingly to warn Inge from associating with that 'terrible man, Leslie Mitchell' whom he had first met during the twenties. Inge appeared to take no notice.

By the time we left, we had grown closer to each other. She had grown attached to me, I think. And I had learned that her fiancé had been killed in an air-crash. She knew little of my background and had little connection with show business, though she certainly knows how to hold an audience. I have seen her do it many times when she is lecturing, as she now does at the Baltic Exchange.

My health improved quickly and the time came to return to London. The house was now in apple-pie order and the builders had left. In her spare time, Inge helped me to manoeuvre the furniture.

What I have not so far divulged is that she is twenty-one years my junior. It hardly seemed right from any point of view to ask her to marry me. I was now sixty, and my medical history was appalling. I could not match up as a man – or even as a companion. The doctors had suggested I had not many more years to live. Possibly three or four. I tried to see less of my new companion.

But Phyl had left a note for me with her will. It read:

I do want to thank you for our life together – I have been so happy . . . I can only say it's been such fun to be with you.

If I die before you, darling . . . don't feel that you are being disloyal to me if you marry someone quickly. I shall feel so grateful to whoever loves you deeply and sincerely and makes you happy.

So don't live alone.

That helped me change my mind. I proposed. Inge went to ask her family's advice, and the advice of her closest friends in England, the Wessons. There was no necessity to ask *my* friends. They all urged me to marry again.

We were married quietly by special licence on 29 October 1966. The Wesson family generously held the wedding for us at their beautiful farmhouse, and we walked in the autumn sunshine to and from the tiny Norman church in the village of Boningale in Shropshire. Inge's mother and her sister Kirsten came over for the wedding, bringing a traditional Danish wedding cake. Another beautiful cake, made specially by Madame Floris in London, who had known me as a small boy, came from Valerie and Jack. I did not meet the rest of Inge's vast Viking family till it was too late for them to object.

We were both of us working and had commitments we could not break, so it was obvious our honeymoon must be confined to an extra-long weekend. The Profumos, hearing this, came up with a charming and generous offer. Their son David's birthday was the day after our wedding; he was at boarding school and they planned to take him out as a treat. Would we, Valerie asked, like to have their house for a few days after our wedding? It would give them so much pleasure and the staff would be pleased too.

We accepted, of course. After the wedding reception we drove to their home in Hertfordshire in time for dinner. It was a beautiful Georgian manor house with extensive flower gardens and its own swimming pool. Brisco, the butler, was at the door to meet us. As my bride stepped out, he bowed. 'May I be amongst the first to congratulate the new Mrs Mitchell,' he said. 'Who?' asked my wife, still very much a Jørgensen. As we entered the house, Brisco produced a bottle of champagne and two glasses on a silver tray. 'Welcome,' he said, 'on behalf of Mr and Mrs Profumo.'

This was just the beginning of a dream-like weekend. All my favourite dishes for our meals and in our bedroom a scented yellow peony which I had presented to Valerie and Jack when I left Cookham. Their gardener, on hearing of our engagement, had forced it so that it would be in full bloom on the day. There was also a large pot of white heather from the staff with their good wishes. In the morning, accident-prone to the last, I fell between our linked twin beds attempting an early morning embrace, and had to be salvaged by my bride.

Brisco brought all the Sunday papers with our early morning tea, and we found a nicely captioned picture of us in the *News of the World*. That did make Inge sit up.

After a splendid breakfast we received a phone call from Valerie. Was everything all right? We tried to express our gratitude. 'Well,' said she, 'I have a surprise for you. We just asked David what he would most like to do today for his birthday, and he says he *wants* to meet the new Mrs Mitchell. Do you mind?'

So that afternoon, after we had all had a swim in the pool, we assembled in the library for a birthday tea. David, aged eleven, made us a speech which, had been older, might well have made him Home Secretary on the spot. Not long ago we had the pleasure of congratulating David and *his* bride.

Brief though it had to be, it was a wonderful weekend. And a happy, well-kept secret until now.

We spent our first Christmas together with my new in-laws in Aarhus where Inge was born. It was a nerve-racking experience even for a veteran performer like myself. I shall never forget meeting Inge's father who had insisted on coming home from hospital to be in his own house to greet me.

He was desperately ill, but there he was, sitting in an armchair in a smoking-jacket, when I was ushered into his room with Inge. We took sherry together, and he suddenly said, 'Skaal, Leslie and welcome. I like you.' Then he smiled and raised his glass. The remarkable part of this occasion was that he had not been able to speak at all for some weeks, let alone in English.

I had learned that there were four young children in the Jørgensen family, so I determined to concentrate on them for our first Christmas together. After intensive research in the leading London toyshops I bought the presents for them that appealed to me, and which I could perhaps play with myself. They included electrical gadgets, of course. I discovered that clockwork was long out of date with the young. So on Christmas Day I presented the children with their bulky presents and sat on the floor of the playroom with them.

We all spent a happy time together opening the parcels and putting the contents together. Then they took me by the hands and steered me back to the grown-ups. 'Leslie is nice,' they said, 'he speaks very good Danish!' And on Boxing Day we all went to a pantomime, which they took terribly seriously. When the bad wolf suddenly ran through the theatre, they left their seats and chased after him over the stage and out of sight. They had to be retrieved by their parents. I stayed glued to my seat, enjoying the stage antics of a big brown bear. Shades of my own childhood.

All that was some fifteen years ago – and my dear wife (with the help of dedicated medical men) has miraculously kept me alive in spite of all the gloomy predictions. Again I experience the contentment of a happily married man.

I am all too conscious of the debt I owe to Phyl, and to Inge. As some sage once remarked: Love is for all seasons. I do realize what a *very lucky* man I am.

PS: I had intended to call this book *More By Accident Than Design*. Now you know why!

Index